Rhymes & Reason

By Éliphas Lévi

Translated by
Stewart Clelland

With an Introduction by
Mathieu Ravignat

January 2023

Library of Congress Control Number 2022923688

© Steward Clelland 2023

All rights reserved. No part of this publication may be reproduced, distributed, or transmitted in any form or by any means, including photocopying, recording, or other electronic or mechanical methods, without the prior written permission of the publisher, except in the case of brief quotations embodied in critical reviews and certain other noncommercial uses permitted by copyright law. For permission requests, write to the publisher at the address below.

ISBN 978-1-947907-23-2

Rose Circle Publications
P.O. Box 854
Bayonne, NJ 07002, U.S.A.
www.rosecirclebooks.com

INDEX

INDEX 3
INDEX OF FIGURES 7
PREFACE 11
FOREWORD 13
INTRODUCTION 19
    The Origins and Nature of the Rosicrucian 19
    Thought of Éliphas Lévi 19
    Pre-Rosicrucian Influences 21
    Éliphas Lévi and the "Quietist" Mystic Madame Guyon 28
    Levi's Divine Feminine and the Coming Age of the Mother and the Holy Spirit 30
    Lévi's Reading of Swedenborg 31
    Levi on His own Spiritual Experiences 32
    Rosicrucian Influences 42
    Polish Rosicrucian Influences 45
    Lévi and the French Theosophist Guillaume de Postel 50
    The Rosicrucian Reformation of Society and Lévi's Socialism .. 54
    Lévi's Freemasonry 60
    Conclusion 68
    Bibliography 70
HISTORICAL AND MYTHOLOGICAL PERSONS 72
THE POEMS OF ÉLIPHAS LÉVI 81
    Liberty 83
    The Death of Galileo 87
    To Monseigneur Dupanloup 89
    Paris 90
    The Fall of the Column 93
    The Painting of Chenavard 97
    Hormuz and Ahriman 100
    Believe in God 101
    Eternal Loves 103

The Poet and the Realist	106
The Wisdom of Love	109
Anacreon	112
Guillet the Freemason	115
The Hell of Lovers	117
Cypriot Wine	125
To Victor Hugo	127
Seriously	130
The King of Israel	132
The Fox and the Crow	134
The Two Stars	135
The Chastisements of Victor Hugo	136
The Song of the Captives	138
Jacob's Ladder	140
Anacreon to his Dove	143
The Love of an Old Man	145
The Dialogue of Jacob and of Adonai	148
The Poet	153
Christian Humility	158
The Dispute Between Jesus Christ and the Devil	162
Before the Council of Rome	169
A Painting by Zurbaran	174
The Genesis of Love	175
Death	183
An Engraving by Albrecht Dürer	185
Concerning Man	188
Marginalia: *Risqué* Things – School of Victor Hugo	191
The Retraction of Galileo	193
Great Good Sense	198
Theological Reason	203
A Prophetic Vision	208
The Poet	209
The Spirit	210
Epilogue	213
Dedication	216

LES POÈMES D'ÉLIPHAS LÉVI 217

    La liberté 219
    La mort de Galilée 223
    A Monseigneur Dupanloup 225
    Paris 226
    La chute de la colonne 229
    Le tableau de Chenavard 233
    Ormuz et Ariman 236
    Croire en dieu 237
    Eternelles amours 239
    Le poète et le réaliste 242
    Sagesse d'amour 245
    Anacréon 248
    Guillot le franc-maçon 251
    L'enfer des amoureux 253
    Le vin de Chypre 261
    A Victor Hugo 263
    Sérieusement 266
    Le roi d'Israël 268
    Le renard et le corbeau 270
    Les deux étoiles 271
    Les châtiments de Victor Hugo 272
    Le chant des captifs 274
    L'échelle de Jacob 276
    Anacréon à sa colombe 279
    L'amour du vieillard 281
    Dialogue d'Jakoub et d'Adonaï 284
    Le poète 289
    L'humilité chrétienne 294
    La dispute de Jésus Christ avec le diable 298
    Devant le concile de Rome 305
    Un tableau de Zurbaran 310
    La génèse d'amour 311
    La mort 319
    Une gravure d'Albrecht Dürer 321
    Sur l'homme 324
    Marge : choses risquées - école de Victor Hugo 327
    La rétractation de Galilée 329

Gros bon sens 333
Raison théologique 338
Vision prophétique 343
Le poète 344
L'esprit 345
Epilogue 348
Dédicace 351

INDEX OF FIGURES

Figure 1 - Image of Éliphas Lévi on his deathbed 17
Figure 2 - Pantacle of John as transmitted to Lévi 40
Figure 3 – Guillaume de Postel's Key 52
Figure 4 - The Philosophical Cross 59
Figure 5 - Cover Page of Lévi's Notebook 77
Figure 6 - First page of 'To Monseigneur Dupanloup' 78
Figure 7 - Second page of 'To Monseigneur Dupanloup' 79

Rhymes & Reason

By Éliphas Lévi

PREFACE

French occultists of the *belle époque* often began their careers by pursuing literary endeavours, and Alphonse Louis Constant (1810–1875), better known as Éliphas Lévi, was no exception. Born under Napoleon, Lévi's poetic work embraces an *ennui* more typical, perhaps, of the *fin de siècle*. Dead a decade or so before the Decadence, he was, in many ways, a man before his time. His visions of the symbolic and the decadent, whilst rooted in a Romanticism that exalted emotion, nature, and the sublime over the rational and the classical, are tempered by a socialism no doubt gleaned from a life led amid the violence of class struggle and civil unrest. Exploring themes of decay and disgust, theology, sickness, skepticism, perversion, humour, revolt, creativity and the natural world, this little book of Lévi's is his account of what he saw of the long nineteenth-century.

Translated from scans of an original document found by the author in the archives of the Sorbonne, the manuscript's provenance rests with the famed Dr Gérard Encausse (Papus). Dated 1871, the poems, in Lévi's own hand, give us an insight into the poetic mind of the great Parisian Mage in the last years of his life. Reflective and playful, the poems feature an array of names synonymous with mid-nineteenth-century French intellectual life. It is a collection that will hold as much interest to the literary scholar as it does to the occultist, Martinist or the Mason. A contemporary of Charles Baudelaire's, we see Lévi here embody the practical magician *par excellence* of French letters. Engaged as equally with Socialism as he is esotericism, Lévi's satirical critiques are as scathing in their range as they are elegant in composition. These lost poems have now been recovered, translated and published for the first time. We shall, of course, never know what the poet's own definitive edition might have looked like. The present edition is an attempt, albeit imperfect, to imagine how that might have been achieved.

Stewart Clelland
2022

FOREWORD

I am delighted to be able to write a Preface to this intriguing book. Stewart Clelland approached me towards the end of 2021 with the idea of publishing this extraordinary find, but prior commitments put off realizing the project until now. But it was certainly worth the wait!

As he explains in his Introduction, he found the poems of Éliphas Lévi while perusing the catalogs of a number of French Libraries, and discovered this manuscript, which had once been in the possession of Dr. Gérard Encausse, or Papus.

Now, I must admit I had never known that Lévi wrote poetry. While a relatively common practice among the wealthier classes, the working class rarely had time for such frippery, so it was exciting to hear that he had used this medium to set down what is a reflection of his inner thoughts. The fact that he wrote them towards the end of his life is also significant: instead of reading the hyperbolic declaration of a frenetic youth, we are instead privileged to see the considered writings which bring together a lifetime of experience. And what a lifetime that was! Raised in poverty, Lévi received the best of educations for his time in two seminaries, and this exposed him both to a deep understanding of religious life and a detailed analysis of the scriptures. Yet he was also married, admittedly unhappily, and fathered several children, not always in wedlock. He was a sometime Socialist, writing inflammatory pamphlets which saw him sentenced to prison, yet he was a great empath, feeling the sufferings of his class, even though he perceived the resolution to their suffering through the lens of a benign clerical dictatorship. He was a Mason for a time, though unfortunately his experience was less than stellar, even though he never lost sight of the good that a well-ordered Masonic society might do. He was fierce in his condemnation of those who sought power, and particularly against the atheists; while moved to eulogizing those philosophy accorded with his own. Of course, we all know the most visible part of his story, that as an occultist of such erudition and standing that many of his ideas and practices have been since carried into almost all of the esoteric Orders which saw light towards the end of the nineteenth century. All this he poured into his poems.

The Foreword by Mathieu Ravignat is a very welcome summary of Lévi's life and helps us to put these poems into context. Indeed, Mr. Ravignat is shortly publishing a book of his own about the Rosicrucian influences on Éliphas Lévi, in which he reconstructs some of his magical practices; and the Introduction by Stewart Clelland puts the discovery of the poems into context.

The poems themselves were in manuscript form, gathered together into 116 folios or sheets of semi-glossy cloth paper, each 180mm by 140mm, or 7 inches by 5.5 inches in size. This initially confused me since the overall length of the original book was 232 pages. However, it was clear he was referring to a 'sheet' as two sides or pages. The title, *Rhymes and Reason*, is interesting in itself, since it implies that the contents are both truly poems but also that they adhere to a certain logic, and therefore contain important messages to be unearthed, instead of being what is often referred to as 'light' poetry. That they are indeed poems is evidenced by the fact that, with some freeform exceptions, the lines rhyme. There is no consistency to the style he uses. In some cases every two lines end with a word which rhymes (AABBCC); in others, they take the form AABCCB to give two examples. For example:

*Et pourtant qui pourrait s'irriter contre **vous** ?*	(A)
*Vous mêlez au fumier d'adorables **bijoux***	(A)
*Vous semez sous nos pieds les trésors de l'**Asie***	(B)
*Avec la feuille morte et la paille **moisie***	(B)
*Racine près de vous n'est plus que de l'**orgeat***	(C)
*Et racine pourtant n'était point un **goujat***	(C)

One can detect the syllable-times stress traditional in Romantic languages in the lines in many places. For example, each line of the following excerpt has 12 stresses (though it is sometimes hard to distinguish them, since poetry has a unique rhythm, not unlike singing French where endings which are silent when spoken are now fully enunciated. Perhaps a famous example is the round Frère Jacques, where one would say '*Frer Djak*' but sing '*Frer-ē Djak-ē*):

Ton trésor dévorant c'est la folie humaine
L'abîme est tout entier dans le cœur des pervers
Et ma miséricorde opprime les enfers.
Torturant de mon jour leur nuit qui se lamente
Je fais paisiblement le bien qui les tourmente

The poems are usually of a traditional form, but in some cases they are presented as dialogs, particular in the discourse between Jacob and Adonaï, and that between Jesus and Mephisto. A number are also dedicated to various contemporaries, such as Auguste Barbier, Victor Hugo and Paul-Marc-Joseph Chenavard, sometimes to praise and sometimes to scold!

While a Preface is not the place to go into deep analysis, I do want to look at one character who merits two dedications in the eyes of Lévi: Auguste Barbier, who also warrant the very first dedication on the first page of the poems. The dedication reads: "Liberty: Iambe: To August Barbier." Barbier (1805–1882) was a contemporary of Lévi. He was a supporter of the July Revolution of 1830, which overthrew the restored monarchy under King Charles X, an arrogant ruler who dissolved anybody which stood in opposition to him, ending with the unsupportable declaration that the freedom of the press was suspended, and that the business class were no longer allowed to vote. Since they couldn't run for office, these businessmen closed their factories and the financiers refused to lend money, and the workers were turned out on the streets. As a result the King abdicated and a distant cousin, Louis Philippe, was placed on the throne in his stead.

Now Barbier's support of the July Revolution led him to produce a number of lively poems in 1831, denouncing the monarchy and the turbulent times. These are spoken of collectively as the *Ïambes*, named for André Chénier who had opposed the first revolution and who had been guillotined in its early days. He had written a series of scathing satirical poems in alternate lines of 8 and 12 syllables, denouncing the revolutionaries. And 'iamb' is a poetic foot of two syllables in which the second syllable is emphasized, such as in the word 'be-stow'. It is hardly surprising, then, that looking at the first few lines of the first poem (in French) we find the lines in iambic meter, alternating between 12 and 8 syllables:

La bouche aux vils jurons peut se noircir de poudre
Et se crisper en rugissant,
Les mains aux sales doigts peuvent lancer la poudre
Puis se laver avec du sang

The detailed analysis of this poem is an attempt to show just how much lies beneath the surface if you are prepared to investigate. In a similar vein I would recommend any Freemason to read the poem entitled: *Guillet the Freemason*. It will not take much effort to recognize most of the allusions in this poem!

Overall, there are two ways you can approach the poems: the æsthetic way and the scholarly way. Sadly, the English version will always suffer from the fact that they cannot rhyme or produce the same meters of the original French verses. It is of course impossible to recreate those nuances in another language. However, in reading the poems with no preconceptions, one can still admire the word-crafting and the skills with which Lévi attempts to bring some of his deepest-held idea to light through the medium of the artistic muse. This is the æsthetic way. The scholarly way is to sit with the poems before a computer or smartphone and be prepared to look up the names mentioned in the text – be they his contemporaries in nineteenth century France, or perhaps to refresh your memory on earlier history or ever the names of the great Romans and Greek who are mentioned. This is easy enough to do in *Wikipedia* or *Google*.

Whichever way you choose, I can assure you that you will find many interesting, exciting, and unexpected ideas buried within the inner mind of Éliphas Lévi!

Piers A. Vaughan
2022

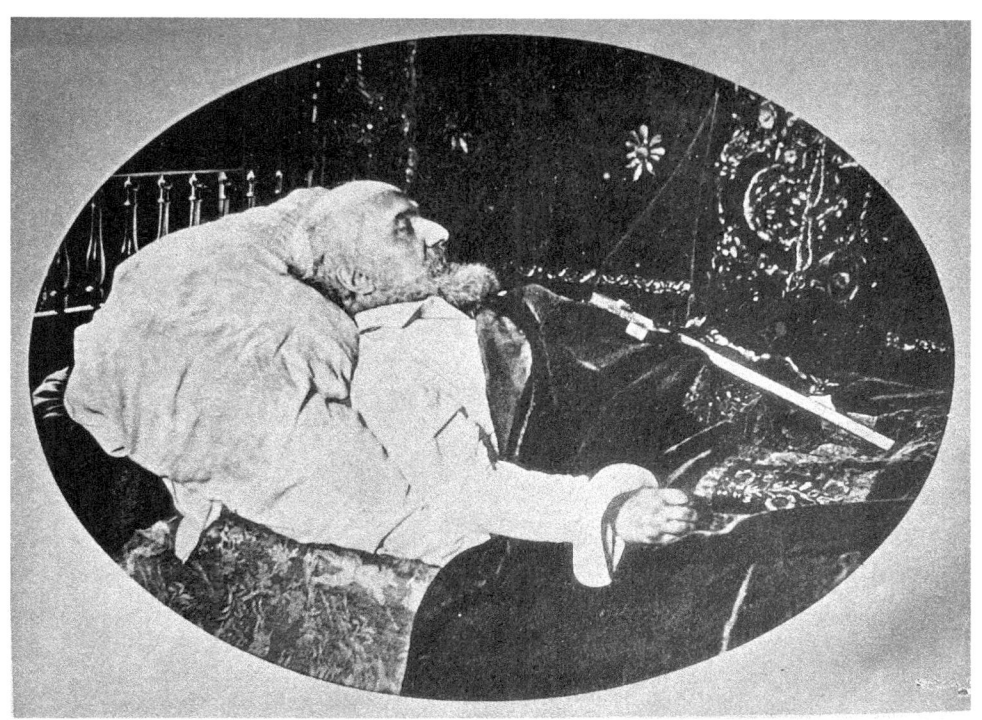

Figure 1 - Image of Éliphas Lévi on his deathbed
from Traité Méthologique de Science Occulte by Papus (pub. 1891)

INTRODUCTION
by MATHIEU G. RAVIGNAT

The Origins and Nature of the Rosicrucian Thought of Éliphas Lévi

Éliphas Lévi's legacy is truly impressive. His influence on modern occultism is in many ways fundamental and only now being truly understood. But explorations of this influence have been, in our opinion, rather one-sided. A deeper interest in Lévi has mainly come from Golden Dawn and Thelemic scholars and they have focused almost exclusively on his Kabbalistic-Magical (Theurgical) thought and practices. This has of course been invaluable, but it has meant that many other sides of Lévi have been ignored, particularly in the English-speaking world, including his mysticism, rationalism, and reformism.

We therefore thank Stewart Clelland for this privileged space to allow us to present the origins and nature of the Rosicrucian Thought of Éliphas Lévi in a more complete way than has been done before, and to address some misconceptions that have persisted concerning his ideas. While doing so, this article will explore parts of Lévi's intellectual life and thought which have hitherto been ignored.[1]

But first let us turn to the poems found in this book. In our opinion, Stewart Clelland has done English language Éliphas Lévi enthusiasts a great service by translating his *Rhymes and Reason*, which contains some of his less well-known poems. Lévi wrote a surprising amount of poetry throughout his life, a habit which was widespread amongst the learned of the nineteenth-century. It could be called one of his hobbies, another way

---

[1] One of these hitherto unknown influences is the extent that women had an important and secret impact on the development of his thought and at key moments during his life. The influence of less well-known women is that hidden part of intellectual history that we wish, among others, to shed light upon with regards to Lévi's thought in this article.

to communicate his thoughts and his affections to his friends. His biography shows that he used it as a means of correspondence and later in his life, as he sought to simplify his message, he turned to poetry as a means of expressing his ideas "in a nutshell" so to speak.

The manuscript was owned by Papus, and dates from 1871 which is during the latter, though no less prolific part of his intellectual life. It was a period of consolidation and synthesis in which he was struggling to express the complexity of his thought in different and more accessible ways; as shown by the fact that between 1871-1875 he not only wrote these poems, but also three books of aphorisms and dialogues; all shorter and simpler works.[2]

However, one should be cautious about calling Lévi a poet. It is true that, like most learned of his time, he wrote and published poetry; but he does not appear to have had much of a talent for it, unlike his drawing and prose work.[3] Take for example the following opinion of Emile Victor Michelet; a respected dramaturge, poet and President of *La société de poètes français*:

> "His numerous prose which is crowned with beautiful images attests to a poet. I cannot say as much for his verses – sadly he wrote many – and all are lamentable." [4]

Sadly, this is also the case for the poetry Stewart Clelland has painstakingly translated here. They are of variable quality, and many seem to be simply thumbnails of poetic ideas. In addition, our reading of them doesn't reveal anything intellectually new in them, and they don't add anything to our overall knowledge of his thought. However, they are nonetheless truly worthy of publication, as they do allow us to discover with what ideas and

---

[2] Examples include: *The Paradoxes of the Highest Sciences* and *Le Livre des Sages*.
[3] As for his drawing and painting, Lévi was at times able to make a living out of it, for example he illustrated editions of Alexandre Dumas' *Louis XIV et son siècle and Le Comte de Monte-Cristo* and he was even commissioned by the Ministry of the Interior to paint two religious themed paintings; one of the Holy Family and the other of Christ in the Garden of Olives.
[4] Michelet, Victor Emile, Préface, p.xvii, in Chacornac, P. Éliphas Lévi (1810-1875), *Éditions Traditionelles*, 1926, 1989.

themes Lévi's mind was preoccupied in 1871, near the end of his life, and perhaps more importantly, to what extent Lévi remained a very consistent thinker even in his older age.

The poems contain many long held and cherished themes which are common to his other works, for example: nature and the universe as a reflection of the divine mind (poems: *Believe in God* and *Seriously*); criticism of the Roman Church as representing modern Pharisees (*To Monseigneur Dupanloup);* criticism of atheistic revolutionary Freemasonry (*Guillet the Freemason*); the special role that "rational Jewish religion" has to play today (*The King of Israel*); sympathy for the Jewish people (*The Song of the Captives*); doubt on the actual existence of the Devil and skepticism towards Persian dualism (*Hormuz and Ahriman*); Hugo's role as a sort of "failed prophet" of modern times (*To Victor Hugo* and the *School of Victor Hugo*); and the need for a universal religion (*Theological Reason or Reasonable Theology*).

Having briefly stated our purpose and discussed the poems found in this volume; let us turn now to our exposé of the origins and nature of Lévi's Rosicrucian Thought.

Pre-Rosicrucian Influences

Lévi is considered a kabbalistic and an occult writer, and for good reason; however, many aspects of his thought have their roots in the period of his life before he became aware of occultism. As early as his first seminary, Lévi butted heads with the orthodoxy of the Roman Catholic Church and its dogma. Born in 1810 from working-class parents, one of the only avenues for education open to him was the Church, and his mother, a very devout Roman Catholic, placed much hope in her son becoming a priest. Lévi entered his first seminary (an entry-level seminary called *Le Petit Séminaire*, lit. Small Seminary) in 1825, when he was only 15 years of age.

As fate would have it, Lévi had the luck of being admitted into a school headed by a Teacher-Priest who flirted with unorthodox theological ideas; a certain Abbé Antoine-Philippe Frère-Colonna (1786-1858). Lévi says of him, while referencing his own later theological troubles:

"He was the most intelligent and the most sincerely pious Priest whom I have ever known: he is also the one who did me the most good and the most harm. He did me a great good by breaking the short strings of my Catholic religious education up until that time in order to open me up to a vast career in the progress of the future. He taught a dogma which was convincing and energetic and professed a blind obedience to the men and things of the past. At first I didn't see that he was wrong (in his dualistic asceticism) and, on the basis of his faith, I walked for a long time along a false road." [5]

Though it is true that Lévi would abandon the austere and ascetic nature of Frère-Colonna's teachings it is equally true that he carried many of his ideas forward for the rest of his life; particularly those surrounding the doctrine of the coming time of the Holy Spirit:

"The history of religion was divided in the following way for l'Abbé Frère into four great epochs: the epoch of penitence, or the age of the Great Flood and the malediction of Cain; the time of faith, with the vocation of Abraham, the faithful father; and this time lasted from the time of Moses' passing through the desert to the coming of Christ, who having died on the cross, gave to his well-beloved disciple his Mother and hope; and under the auspices of the Holy Ghost, the third person of God not yet completely revealed, will open a future century of happiness for the entirety of humanity, which will sit in the shadow of the apple trees of a new Eden, and feel a breath of love cool upon its forehead beneath the beating of the wings of the mysterious dove, the last symbol of the Divinity." [6]

Later in 1844, no doubt still under the influences of the ideas of Frère-Colonna, Lévi would revisit and develop similar eschatological ideas after his reading of Mme. Guyon.

---

[5] *L'assomption de la Femme*, p.IV-VII.
[6] *L'assomption de la Femme*, p.IV-VII.

It is also interesting to note that Frère-Colonna wrote a book on Animal Magnetism, theorizing that it came from the Devil, and that years later Lévi would refer to this magnetism as the Astral Light and devise his famous Baphomet image to represent it. However, for Lévi, the Astral Light (and his Baphomet image) was not of the Devil, but rather it consisted of a neutral universal and a natural force which could be manipulated by the human will.

Also worthy of mention is the fact that it was at this time, and under L'Abbé Frère-Colonna, that Lévi learned Hebrew well enough, as Charconac relates, that by the age of eighteen he could easily explain the Hebrew exegesis of most passages in the scriptures.

Therefore, it is likely that the very beginning of Lévi's unorthodox positions can be traced all the way back to his teenage years and at his first seminary.

L'Abbé Frère-Collonna would later get into trouble with the Church hierarchy and would be forced to change his progressive ways of teaching with moderate success. Eventually a legate was sent to replace him and to "put the school back in order," and anyone who spoke well of him was also severally reprimanded.

After graduating from the Small Seminary, Lévi was sent to Issy to join a much more orthodox and stricter seminary under the direction of the Sulpicians. It is there that his natural mysticism grew even stronger, seemingly out of a reaction to what Lévi described as "the cold, monotonous, dogmatic nature of the teachers." These Sulpicians were clearly different from the good Abbé Frère-Colonna. However, Lévi contented himself while he was there with staying "under the radar" with regards to his innermost thoughts, and after this seminary concluded he was ordained a Deacon on the 19th of December, 1835 in order to then receive the Priesthood on May 1835. This, however, would never happen.

During this time he was appointed a teacher of girls at a small Sulpician Catechism school, and it is there that he met a young woman and fell platonically in love with her.[7] Clearly, she was old enough for Lévi to

---

[7] This was a certain Adèle Allenbach, and after being estranged due to Lévi's intense mourning of his mother, their relationship would last his lifetime. She became a decent

realize that he would prefer to have the love of a woman in his future life, and so he decided to leave Seminary without having received Major Orders.

Of this love he would later write:

"I cannot repent for having loved her; because love is a reward in and of itself, and if she returned to me now, I would wash her tainted dress with my tears and wipe her eyes with my caresses (kisses). And I would rejoice in her return as though she had never abandoned me: for I love her as God has loved me." [8]

It would appear by this statement, and many made afterwards, that Lévi had difficulty reconciling his spiritual love for the "Ideal of Woman" with the real thing. Despite trying love again and even having a son, he would never successfully marry, and would end up knowing many women but never consummating his relationship with them.[9] As one of his correspondents put it to him in reference to his book, *La Mère de Dieu*:

"My dear, your work is deplorable in its idealism, it is celibacy gone to your head, your excessive purity has made you a libertine, my dear: if you knew them more closely, you would not adore women so much." [10]

Lévi does indeed seem to have been temperate in all things, as he admits of himself:

---

actress and he often served as her confidant and mentor. She would even accompany his coffin to his grave.

[8] *Bible de la Liberté*, 1841, p.35.

[9] He was once compelled to marry his lover Noémie Cadiot out of the shame of her parents. They were ill-suited to one another, but despite that they tried to make the best of it. They even had children, all of whom died at a young age; including Marie at 7 years old which broke Lévi's heart, as witnessed in a letter to his student the Baron Spedalieri. Noémie seems to have had several affairs behind his back and left him for a lover not too long after the death of their child. Lévi also had an illegitimate son (Xavier Henri Alphonse Chenevier, 1848-1916) with another one-time lover called Eugénie Chenevier, but the child never bore his name, as Lévi also had a falling-out with her over money. However, he did insist that he get to know his son and even funded his education. A sort of friendship grew between them despite their distance, since he moved to England with his mother, and the son even attended Lévi's funeral.

[10] Mgr Olivier in *La Vérité*, November, 1845, p.102, in Charconac.

"As to the joys of life, I don't know what I would do with them, so I do without. I have abused at times of wine and of good meat, without however becoming a gourmand of a heavy drinker. Abuse seems for me to be necessarily followed by disgust, so that all sensual excess is a lesson in temperance." [11]

Paul Charconac says of his relations with the many women in his life:

"Certainly, Constant enjoyed the society (company) of women, and if he did seek to please them it was not in order of acquire from them the vulgar gifts of sensual love, but their grace, their vivacity and all their intellectual gifts."[12]

It is perhaps this spiritual idealization of women which led Lévi to a total breakdown after the suicide of his mother. His mother's mental health had been fragile for many years, but it appears to be Lévi's abandonment of the Priesthood which was the direct cause of her taking her own life. The guilt must have been unbearable, as he spent a year in a convalescent-home provided by the Church, after which he was abandoned to his own devices.

It is at this low period during his life that he became a kind of proto-socialist journalist drawing and writing for a number of working-class newspapers. But he always struggled with identifying with the early socialist movements, since their supporters were mainly anti-clerical and atheist.

Charconac theorizes that Lévi, apart from wanting to live a more concrete form of Christian charity, became an active socialist under the influence of another woman: a certain French-Peruvian proto-feminist named Flora Tristan.[13] Charconac describes her as:

---

[11] *Le Livre des Larmes*, p.217.
[12] Charconac, p.78.
[13] Born Flore Celestine Thérèse Henriette Tristán y Moscoso (1803 - 1844) Flora was a writer and activist who made important contributions to early feminist theory, and argued that the progress of women's rights was directly related to the progress of the working class. She famously wrote in *The Emancipation of Woman and the Testament of the Pariah*: 'The most oppressed man finds a being to oppress, his wife: she is the proletarian of the proletarian.' (*From the English Wikipedia Article*).

> "Gifted with an ardent imagination, a rigorous reason, a remarkable beauty and in particular a courage quite rare for her sex. All her life was her work, and all her work was love for her brothers." [14]

As a Cleric, Lévi became a sort of confidant of hers and provided her with advice on several issues, including her love life! He was chosen by her to edit her manuscript *l'Emancipation de la Femme ou Le Testament de la Paria*, but it had to be published posthumously because she died during its preparation.

These were Lévi's "young-militant years," and he found financial support through another childhood friend who had become a socialist: a certain Alphonse Esquiros, who wrote a controversial biography of Jesus as a social reformer.[15] Esquiros seems to have introduced him to various contacts which hired him to observe, draw and write about the "popular classes."

However, as an observer of the early socialist movement, Lévi was also terribly shocked by its social norms. The seedy Paris underground in which real *bona fide* socialists rubbed shoulders with pretenders and libertines, seemed to him to be evidence of the moral collapse of society. This is how he put it:

> "I was staying in a great hotel haunted by students and grisettes (young working women). This race of men and women made me pity them and they disgusted me. I entered in the confidence of what they called their "loves." What I observed, rather, was their orgies, and I saw them return from their masked balls, drunk, pale,

---

[14] Charconac, p.31.
[15] His full name was Henri-François-Alphonse Esquiros (1812 – 1876), a French writer born in Paris. After some minor publications he produced *L'évangile du peuple* (1840), an exposition on the life and character of Jesus as a social reformer. This work was considered an offense against religion and decency, and Esquiros was fined and imprisoned. He was elected in 1850 as a socialist to the Legislative Assembly, but was exiled in 1851 for his opposition to the Second French Empire. Returning to France in 1869, he was again elected a member of the Legislative Assembly, and in 1876 elected to the senate. (*From the English Wikipedia Article*). [16]

disheveled, sick, covered in blood. My heart was heavy…I would have wanted to cover my eyes and block my ears, shut down my thoughts in order to throw myself imprudently into a servitude of love, and to sacrifice myself to the magic of a memory (the Priesthood). Oh, how many times my eyes filled with tears when I thought of a purer life, hidden and buried in God in the simple and confident practice of religious practices…" [16]

And that is exactly what he did, for he decided to enter Seminary a second time, this time at the Abbey of Solesme, to prepare to receive Major Orders.

This is a very fortunate event for us, as it is at this Abbey that Lévi would deepen his study of mysticism. According to Charconac, their library possessed more than 20,000 volumes. Ever curious about new ideas, Lévi took full advantage of it, and this is how he describes the year he spent there:

"I had the necessary leisure to study the doctrines of the ancient Gnostics, that of the Fathers of the primitive Church, the books of Cassian and other ascetics, and finally the pious writings of the mystics, especially the admirable books which are sadly still ignored, of the saintly Mme. Guyon." [17]

It is through the influence of the books in that great library, though we don't know exactly by what authors, that by his own admission Lévi became a pantheist:

"It is in such a state, with my soul abandoned to itself that I aspired, by the sole force of His love, to Divine unity, to this great religion of the future which reunites all beings into a single being, all sciences into a single idea, all hearts into a single love. It is this pantheism which men of false motives want us to flee from, as if it were a monstrous error, which is the final word of the sublime doctrine of Christ and of his Apostles.

"Despite this, I was still a docile and fervent Catholic; I felt that God was all love, and I admitted the dogma of hell with a blind

---

[16] *Le Livre de Larmes*, p.208.
[17] *L'assomption de la Femme*, p.XVIII.

submission; even when my reason submitted itself to this monstrous fiction of Manichean dualism, my heart protested against it by a sublime cry, and I wanted to be able to be God, not in order to die on the cross, and save only men, but in order to damn myself in order to fill all of hell and by doing so snuff it out."[18]

Éliphas Lévi and the "Quietist" Mystic Madame Guyon

As indicated above, it was also at Solesme that Lévi would discover the most important pre-Rosicrucian influence on his thought: Mme. Guyon (1648-1717) the "quietist-like" mystic.

Let us briefly consider her biography before discussing the fundamental impact she had on Lévi.

Jeanne Marie Bouvier de la Motte Guyon had mystical tendencies at an early age, but as a noble woman was forced into marriage with a wealthy suitor. After 12 unhappy years she became a widow and sought mystical instruction from François La Combe, a Barnabite.

After a third mystical experience in 1680, Madame Guyon felt herself drawn to Geneva, where she unsuccessfully attempted to create a religious community: her religious thought brought condemnation from the Bishop of Geneva and she was forced to flee. She ended up in Grenoble, where she spread her religious convictions more widely with the publication of her *Moyen court et facile de faire oraison* in January 1685. After this publication she was again chased out of the city by the local Bishop and returned to Paris, only to be imprisoned in the Bastille.

For the rest of her life, she had to defend her ideas against the Church hierarchy, and was eventually released after which she lived in Blois. There she passed some fifteen years surrounded by a stream of pilgrims, many coming from the Netherlands, England and Scotland. She also continued

---

[18] *L'assomption de la Femme*, p.VII-XIII. Later Lévi would abandon pantheism for what may be characterized as panentheism, the theological position that God is both within and without His Creation.

writing and in 1717, the year of her death, she published *Âme Amante de son Dieu, representée dans les emblems de Hermannus Hugo sur ses pieux désirs*, which features her poetry written in response to popular emblematic images of Herman Hugo and the Flemish master Otto von Veen.

Her writings emphasized the importance of being in a constant state of prayer and love for God and advocated against the Roman Catholic Church that grace was more important than good works. She was very much a bridge figure uniting mystically inclined believers both from Roman Catholic and Protestant churches.

Here is how Lévi describes her important influence on him:

"The life and the writings of that sublime women opened many doors to the mysteries for me which I had been unable to penetrate until then. Her doctrine of pure love and total passivity towards God turned me off completely from (the ideas of) hell and free will. I saw God as the only Being in which must be absorbed all human personality. I saw (with her ideas) the phantom of evil disappear...I was stunned to find in Mme. Guyon predictions of the future reign of the Holy Spirit, that consummation into unity through love which all Christians have waited for in all centuries, and I understood how the Cult (Worship) of Mary served as a transition from the reign of Christ to that of the Celestial Dove." [19]

It is also due to her that he was shaken from the orthodox belief in an actual Satan and Hell:

"I breathed like a man who, after a long trek, arrived at the summit of a steep mountain and discovered a vast and joyful countryside. I triumphed in having crushed under my feat that ugly figure of Satan; I felt my heart dilate in the thought that all men were to be saved, and I could no longer conceive how, at the same time, I could have believed in an Almighty Good God and eternal damnation." [20]

---

[19] *L'assomption de la Femme*, p.xxi.
[20] *L'assomption de la Femme*, p.xix-xxi.

What is clear is that Lévi left Solesmes more unorthodox than he entered it, and for the second time refused Major Orders (this would be his last time), this time on doctrinal grounds.

This persistent idea of the Reign of the Holy Spirit and Universal Salvation, which he learnt from l'Abbé Frère-Collonna and Mme. Guyon, would lead to his most mystical work entitled: *La Mère de Dieu* (1844).

Levi's Divine Feminine and the Coming Age of the Mother and the Holy Spirit

In *La Mère de Dieu* Lévi explicitly links the coming age of salvation to that of the Reign of the Holy Mother:

> "Now he (Lévi) presents, in turn, his synthesis and his utopia, which subject is the great religious and moral construction of Woman.
>
> "The world up to the present has recognized in God the idea of a Father and of a Son; but it has not yet been initiated to the secrets of the love of the Mother, on which reposes (rests, dwells) the Holy-Spirit.
>
> "This revelation shall be the last, and will consume humanity into God... When man will have rendered freedom (liberty) to women by respecting them like a mother, woman shall return to him love, and the sin of being born will be erased.
>
> "This is therefore the Gospel of the Future, this mystical poetry of the woman. The last social and religious construction which must give love to the world is, in one word: woman. This is what I wished to outline in this book in order to foretell the reign of the Law of Love." [21]

---

[21] *La Mère de Dieu*, p.261.

Another important section from *La Mère de Dieu* reveals that this 'Reign of the Mother' has a universalistic cosmic significance. In it he describes seeing a vision of a women after the great wars of the Apocalypse who tells him that she has:

> "...hid myself in the ruins of the world in order to hide the germ of life which was in my heart, for I know that love can't die. Just as Fire has won over all the rival Elements, all visible forms have entered, by fusion, into the unity of one same substance, and all the invisible forms from now on will have, as a soul, the unity of the same love, for only death died in the cataclysm of the fire: I have absorbed (aspired, lit. breathed-in) into me all the life of humanity; and the convulsions of the earth have aided me in my labour (birthing process)." [22]

Though it is true that in *La Mère de Dieu* Lévi refers to this Divine Mother as Mary the Virgin, it is interesting to note that, according to Paul Charconac, Lévi had a painting of the Sophia prominently placed in his apartment, and that it was created by him from an existing Orthodox version of the Virgin by modifying some details and adding various symbolic ornaments.[23]

Clearly the universalism and eschatological thought of Mme. Guyon opened mystical doors which caused sublime visions and transformative experiences for Lévi throughout his life.

Lévi's Reading of Swedenborg

Our section on pre-Rosicrucian influences would not be complete if we did not discuss Lévi's early reading of Emmanuel Swedenborg. Of this discovery Lévi admitted in his book *Le Livre de Larmes* (1845), that he did not immediately see the value of Swedenborg's system:

---

[22] *La Mère de Dieu*, p.263.
[23] Chaconac, p.228. After Lévi's death this painting wound up in the hands of Baron Spedalieiri. As far as we are concerned the fact that he went to so much trouble to have an icon of the Sophia is significant.

"This reading did not immediately make the impression on me that it did afterwards; I found it obscure, diffuse, singular, not to mention anything worse. It is only after a deeper knowledge of his system, and particularly its philosophical basis, that I could appreciate its immense wisdom." [24]

However, he also admitted that Swedenborg's writings:

"...do not possess the full truth but they infallibly lead towards it." [25]

This is high praise indeed from Lévi, who is generally very conservative in his literary compliments.

Levi on His own Spiritual Experiences

It is important to take a pause here to focus on Lévi's own personal mysticism. There is, in our opinion, a danger when discussing the lives and thought of spiritual people of emphasizing too much what they read and who they knew in abstraction of their own spiritual experiences. Lévi did not learn everything in books, despite his impressive dedication to study, and he had his own inner experiences as the book *La Mère de Dieu* has shown us. These mystical and prayerful experiences resulted in unique ideas which he then promoted, and it could be argued that his own mystical intuitions, particularly expressed in his drawing, are just as important to an understanding of the evolution of his thought than what he may have read.

By mysticism, we mean a direct rapport with God through prayer and contemplation. We admit the distinction between mysticism and theurgy is difficult to make, but generally speaking, mysticism does not rely on the "ritual technology" of Magic.

A careful read of Lévi throughout the entirety of his career reveals that he believed he had such a direct personal mystical contact with God, that he

---

[24] *Le Livre des Larmes*, p.212.
[25] *Le Livre des Larmes*, p. 212.

claimed that he was given a mission through it, and that in some ways he conceived of himself as a modern Prophet. That mission was to help bring forward what he referred to as the Messianic Age. This included reforming the Roman Catholic Church and society in general to unite Science and Faith into a universal religion. This new religion was nothing less than a form of mystical and militant Charity.

However, despite his emphasis on reason and the need for the Church to embrace Science, it is clear through his many writings that Lévi also maintained a direct spiritual contact with God. So Lévi, while being a rationalist, was at the same time a mystic.

Lévi's mystical mission and status as prophet is made possible because he sincerely believed in what today we would call "continuous revelation," and he made that very clear in his letters, particularly when he discussed what beliefs he expected his disciples to adhere to (a kind of Profession of Faith). Here is a relevant passage in a Letter of Baron Spedalieri:

> "We believe in the perpetual and progressive revelation of God in the development of Love and our Intelligence." [26]

This belief is truly one of the landmarks of Messianism. The idea that God is still revealing himself through new Prophets and revelations.

And of course, as with most mystics, he believed in the non-duality between God and Man, take for example:

> "We believe in the principle of universal life, the principle of Being (God) and of beingness always distinct from Being and beingness but which is necessarily present in Being and in beingness...We believe that the Principle is in us and speaks to each of us through the voice of our conscience." [27]

However, as a one-time seminary student, Lévi never lost his humility towards God, and he often engaged in self-deprecating behaviour about his role. Despite this, at several places in his letters to his students, he feels

---

[26] *Livre des Splendeurs*, p.221.
[27] *Livre des Splendeurs*, p.218.

comfortable enough to open up about his direct mystical relationship with God:

> "All the mystic sects have sent their ambassadors to me. The Grand Orient of France has asked me for instructions and the most advanced Masonic Lodges have welcomed me without fees and without trials. Why do you question me about such details? Will they render your confidence greater in me <u>if the voice of God which has been given to me</u> for you doesn't suffice?" [28]

And:

> "May the will of God be done!
>
> "*Infirma mundi elegit Deus et ea quæ non sunt ut confundat fortia* (God choses the weak of the world and those that are not weak in order to confuse those who are mighty.)
>
> "I am amazed and terrified of the great works that he has made me do, and if you just knew how little merit I have – I who am naturally selfish, epicurean and sensual! I am a true corpse for the Holy Spirit. I just want to dream, sleep, sing, and do nothing, and yet there is an unknown force which animates (agitates) me: (and so) I take my pen and I write marvelous things which I did not think of yesterday. I write these things trembling, and sometimes, when rereading them, I learn them for first time, with a kind of delight mixed with awe (terror). Will you now believe me to be a little bit of a lunatic?" [29]

And:

> "But when the spirit grabs me and takes me into space, it is then that I find myself alone and afraid. It is at these times of anxiety that I seek to find some support. My spirit (mind) sees things which leave me in a kind of stupor, and which render me indifferent to all the vicissitudes of existence.

---

[28] *The Kabbalistic and Occult Philosophy of Eliphas Levi…*, Letter of March 3-6, 1861.
[29] *The Kabbalistic and Occult Philosophy of Eliphas Levi…*, Letter of April 9, 1862.

"After I have heard the voice of God, or rather the whispers, men tire and bore me: that is all my melancholic letter was meant to say. Otherwise, believe me, I am the happiest and most beloved of mortals." [30]

Lévi also referred to his spiritual experiences when discussing spiritualism, of which he had a very low opinion. One of the motivations in writing his book *La Science des Esprits*, was to criticize (even debunk) and then give an alternative view of spiritualism; one which was more rational. Lévi had a very "scientific" understanding of spirituality and God; calling him the Supreme Reason or the Sovereign Reason. However, what the following quote from *La Science des Esprits* shows is that he did not come to this approach merely intellectually, but through actual hard spiritual practice:

"The author of this book is not afraid to admit that he himself has had the most astonishing and formidable visions: he saw and touched demons and angels as the followers of Maximus of Ephesus and Schoepfer of Leipzig made their followers see and touch them.[31] Because of this, he was able to make a comparison between the hallucinations of his former days and the illusions of dreams; and from all this he has concluded that reason directing faith, and faith supported by reason, are the only true lights of our souls; that everything else is just vain fatigue of the brain, an aberration of the senses and delusions of thought. So, he does not just write what he supposes; he boldly teaches what he knows. That is why his book is entitled: *The Science of Spirits*, and not the "Conjecture" or "Essays" on spirits."

---

[30] *The Kabbalistic and Occult Philosophy of Eliphas Levi...*, Letter of February 23, 1863.
[31] Maximus of Ephesus (310 – 372 AD) was a Neoplatonist philosopher who exercised a certain influence over the emperor Julian. He supposedly pandered to the emperor's love of magic and theurgy, and by "judicious administration" of omens won a high position at court. Whereas, Johann Georg Schröpfer (1738? - 1774), born in Leipzig, was an independent Freemason and necromancer. He performed ghost-raising seances for which he secretly used special effects, possibly including magic

And:

> "It is after descending through chasm to chasm and from terror to terror, to the bottom of the seventh circle of the abyss, and it is after having crossed the shadowy sleeping city in all its length, , that the Dante, by returning and taking, if I may say so, the Devil by his rough hairs, has risen victorious and consoled towards the light. We have made the same journey, and we present ourselves to the world with confidence in our minds (*lit.* security on our foreheads) and peace in our hearts. We have come quietly to tell men that hell, the Devil, the abysses without hope, the chimeras, the satyrs, the ghouls, the sins personified, the three-headed dragon and all the rest of the dark phantasmagoria are only nightmares of madness, and that God alone is alive, real, present everywhere, fills all things without leaving voids, and fills, I say (with the meaning of "I witness"), the boundless immensity of the splendor and eternal consolations of Sovereign Reason."

To this we should add that Lévi had several dreams and waking visions in his life which produced quite concrete results, leading, for example, to finding needed or lost manuscripts, equipment and artifacts.[32] Our favorite of these is the one related by Charconac and involving Paracelsus:

> "Once, when perusing by candlelight the magical Archidoxes of the great occultist (Paracelsus), very tired, he (Lévi) fell asleep only to awake in the laboratory of a Hermeticist, where a mysterious form appeared….it was of Paracelsus.
>
> "Éliphas Lévi having shared with him the vain results of his research (on the Tarot), Paracelsus handed him a copper coin which he took out of a purse and which hung at his belt. It was a Tarot key. But where could he acquire such a piece? Paracelsus told him to follow him…and not far from Pont-Neuf…while bending towards the pavement… between two cobbles…

---

[32] Lévi also healed a number of people using magnetism, including the wife of a student and his own daughter.

"The next morning Éliphas Lévi went to that spot, while passing by le quai Conti near the Pont-Neuf and in a box of a medal seller, his eyes saw appearing, amongst a diverse number of coins, the piece that he was seeking." [33]

Many have also wondered if Lévi was a practicing alchemist and Lévi did indeed have several contacts who were practicing alchemists; including a certain Louis Lucas and Dr. Ferdinand Rozier. It is in the writings of Rozier, who was actually a student and not just a friend of Lévi's, that we learn that Lévi did in fact teach practical alchemy:

"As far as I can remember, it was in 1859 or 1860, the exact date is not important, let's just say it was a long-time ago. Éliphas Lévi was struck by the similarities of a number of Hermetic figures to the martial pyrite or? Sperkise? This mineral is in fact composed of crystals of ferrous sulphur grouped in such a way as to imitate the word Vitriotum (here follow several lines about its scientific properties: Rozier was a chemist and pharmacologist) ...whatever, its properties were supposed by Éliphas Lévi to indicate that it was a primal matter which could feed the Fire. It is true that all combustion emanates heat, and there was here a slow combustion with a weak heat, this weak heat could be the Slow Fire. After all his arguments and under the directions of Éliphas Lévi; I procured for myself a rather large quantity of this pyrite (here Rozier describes what he did with the Pyrite)... But I repeated this experiment under varying conditions without ever obtaining anything at all, and when all things are considered, that did not surprise whatsoever. However, one day Éliphas Lévi believed that he saw and faint black tint to it; the powder would have taken a darker colour. We had got close to obtaining the Head of the Crow..." [34]

So, we can assume that Lévi was schooled in Alchemy some time before 1859. The source of his Alchemical teachings is hard to figure out since he read a number of works on the subject, but it is interesting that Lévi did have a good alchemist friend who was an aristocratic Pole, named the Count

---

[33] Charconac, p. 230.
[34] *Journal l'Hyperchimie*, No.10, October 1900, in Charconac.

Alexandre Branicki, with whom he would make his second trip to England. According to Charconac, Lévi had supper with this Count about once a week where they conducted alchemical experiments together:

> "Two of the Branicki brothers, Alexander and Constantin were very well versed in the Highest Science, especially Alexandre, a practicing Hermeticist (Alchemist). A laboratory was installed at the Château Beauregard, and Éliphas Lévi and Alexandre Branicki succeeded in producing some of the most conclusive experiments in the Great Work." [35]

Later, in a correspondence dated after these experiments, he would confirm to his student the Baron Spedalieiri that:

> "I possess the most curious of manuscripts on the Hermetic Art, and I profoundly know all the mysteries of the Science of Hermes. I have seen the Secret Fire produced, and I have seen how the two metallic sperma are formed: the white which resembles Mercury, and the red which is a viscous oil in fusion. I also know how we can make gold, but believe me I would never make any. The secret is the chemical production of a binary in the metallic and mineral worlds. From one substance we make two and of these two substances one which does not resemble anything like the first." [36]

We note that Lévi was rarely so confident about his knowledge and skill. Could Alexandre have been his Master, rather than a disciple or friend? It would make sense, if Alexandre was an advanced student of Wronski's, that Lévi would have sought him for instruction, but we admit that this is speculation on our part, though we note that he does say of Alexandre, in a letter to Baron Spedalieiri, that he is: "a savant of the first order in Hermetic philosophy."[37] We are uncertain why such a savant, with whom he also did alchemical experiments, would be a student of Lévi.

---

[35] Charconac, p.193.
[36] *Correspondence*, Vol 1, in Charconac.
[37] *Correspondence* Vol.1, in Charconac. We note that he also referred to his student the Polish Doctor from Berlin Nowakowski as a "great Kabbalist and a high grade Initiate." With all his Polish esoteric contacts, we are never truly certain if they are his disciples or his teachers.

Finally, this section would be incomplete if we did not address what is known as Lévi's Evocation of Apollonius in England and which has spilt a lot of ink over the years. Despite this intense debate there are some important details about this series of evocations which have been overlooked in English language books and which we would like to point out.

In fact, the Evocation of Apollonius was only one of many magical experiments conducted between July 20 - 26 in London, and done with an unknown female adept introduced to Lévi by Sir Edward Buller-Lytton. Actually, most of the evocations were of Christian saints, including John the Evangelist and even Jesus himself.

This over-emphasis on the Evocation of Apollonius in the English language could stem from the fact that Lévi emphasized that part of the experiments in his book *Dogme et Rituel de la Haute Magie* and that this part of the work was translated into English (as *Transcendental Magic*) by the popular author A.E. Waite. However, in his original personal notebook recording the full events, Lévi discusses the importance of the other evocations as well, including the communication of a rather orthodox magical seal:

"The preparations lasted 21 days and the first evocations were of the spirits of Joannès (John) and Jehoshua (Jesus or Yeshua). The second was a vision of Apollonius which told him (Lévi) where to find his Nuctemeron by indicating to him the street and the place.

"In the third vision (during the first evocation), John explained his seals to him (Lévi): Yeshua severely reprimanded him and revealed the future to him. He handed him the book of Rabbi Inaz, taught him celestial magic, gave him the key to miracles, and commanded him to honour the crown, the polar vestments, and the ceremonies of the Gallican Evangelical Church." [38]

Monday morning, the 24 of July, a new evocation:

---

[38] This might indicate that Lévi was no longer a practicing Roman-Catholic but had left the Church for this other one and had received the permission of Jesus to do so.

"John brought him a pantacle (seal) of two sides, one side with a dove carrying an olive branch with the words: *Pax hominibus Bonae Volontatis* (Peace to men of good will) and a crown of twelve flowers and twelve pearls. On the reverse, the character M crowned with seven flames with the words: *Unus spiritus sanctus qui ex Patre fililoque procedit* (One Holy Spirit which proceeds from the Father and the Son). The word filioque is to be found at the top, in the middle of the legend (design), Above the monogram, is written: *Unus Pastor* (One Shepherd), et below: *Unus Fides* (One Faith)." [39]

Figure 2 - Pantacle of John as transmitted to Lévi

However, it should also be noted that Lévi consistently spoke against the practice of evocation, not only in the well-known passage in *Dogme and Rituel de la Haute Magie* but also consistently in his future works; including this rather emphatic passage in *The Paradoxes of the Highest Science*:

"At each round of the ladder the Spirit which rises is equal to the one that descends and can take his hand; but he still must needs follow him who ascends in front of him. This is a law which those who do evocations should seriously meditate on.

---

[39] From Lévi's *Carnet* (Notebook) reproduced in the Appendix of Charconac.

"To ascend eternally is the hope of the blessed; to descend eternally is the threat that weighs upon the reprobate.

"Men invoke superior spirits, but they can only evoke inferior spirits. Superior spirits whom men invoke attract them upwards; inferior spirits whom men evoke draw them downwards.

"Invocation is prayer, evocation is sacrilege, except when it is a very dangerous devotion.

"But the rash mortals who plunge into evocations have no thoughts of making spirits upon whom they call ascend with them; they want to lean on them to rise, but by doing so necessarily lose their balance, since they are leaning on what is descending.

"The spirit which descends is as a load to him who would raise it up, and it necessarily drags him down who abandons himself to it! To renounce reason and follow the inspirations of a phantom, is to plunge into the abyss of madness." [40]

Having said that, it is also clear that these experiences had a long-lasting effect on him, and he later wrote a Kabbalistic commentary on the Book of Revelation including its seven seals and translated and commented the Nuctemeron. [41]

It should also be noted, however, that Lévi gave just as much practical advice on living an ethical and mystically oriented life, including the use of several prayers, than on the practice of theurgy.

In conclusion to this section on pre-Rosicrucian influences, it is important to remember that the major ideas discovered during this period of his life would be carried over into his occultism, including: the coming of the Reign of the Mother of God and the Holy Spirit, the need for a new Society based on the principle of charity, the non-existence of a separate principle of evil and of a Devil; and, just as important, his own capacity to be in touch with his God in a mystical manner.

This is evidenced not only by the many references to all of these ideas in his major works after 1854, but also by the fact that Lévi continued to

---

[40] *Paradoxes of the Highest Science*, p. 107-108. Good advice considering today's supposed 'Jungian' Magic fad of 'integrating the shadow.'
[41] Posthumously published in *Les Mystères de la Kabbale*, and *Le Grand Arcane Dévoilé*.

recommend some of his earlier works to his occult students, particularly *La Mère de Dieu*, which we know he enclosed in a letter to Baron Spedalieri so that he might understand the idea of the Divine Mother in the Kabbalah. It also contains his vision of the future reign of the Holy Spirit to which he also refers in his correspondence with his students. In other words, some of his earlier pre-Rosicrucian ideas made their way into his "Rosicrucian curriculum."

Therefore, it is our contention that the student of Lévi should be careful not to trace an artificial line between his non-occult and occult periods.

Having discovered the major influences and ideas of his pre-occultist phase, let us turn now to the more "Rosicrucian like" influences. The reader should note here, that by "Rosicrucian" we mean those influences which Lévi himself considered as part of the secret Rosicrucian Tradition. We do not mean anything historically or scientifically precise in our use of this term. It is enough for us that Lévi considered them generally "Rosicrucian" and as part of an ancient esoteric genealogy to label them in that way here.

Rosicrucian Influences

The subjects of Éliphas Lévi's Rosicrucian initiation and the origin of his esoteric teachings have confounded scholars for some time, and there have even been doubts expressed on whether he was in fact a "Rosicrucian," or whether he was initiated at all.

However, of the fact that he did receive an initiation there should be no doubt, since the fact is made quite clear several times in his correspondence to his students, where he often refers to himself as an Initiate. With regards to his actual initiation, here is one of the more obvious references:

> "I enclose a copy of a book of which I am the author and which I wrote before my initiation." [42]

---

[42] *The Kabbalistic and Occult Philosophy of Eliphas Levi*...Letter of November 30, 1861.

As for identifying himself and his students as Rosicrucians (Rose+Croix) this is also made obvious in his letters, which he signs several times in the following manner:

> "We can now then, in the name of Emmanuel, embrace each other as Brothers of the Rose-Cross and address each other with the saying of the true Adepts: Peace profound, my Brother. May this peace be always with you and with your worthy Companion." [43]

Let us move onto when he might have been initiated him into a Rosicrucian current and by whom.

Internal evidence in his writings indicate that esoteric themes first appear in an indisputable manner in his 1845 book *Le Livre des Larmes* and that the first time he uses his spiritual name, Éliphas Lévi Zahed publicly, was in 1854. So it is likely that his initiation would have occurred sometime between 1845 and 1854.

The astute reader will have noticed that these dates contradict a theory currently in vogue that Lévi was initiated during his trip to England in 1854 by Edward Bulwer-Lytton. Many problems exist with this English transmission theory, including the following:

- Esoteric themes are evident in his works as early 1845, almost a decade before his trip.
- Lévi already had a disciple, Adolphe Desbarolles as shown by a letter received by him during the same year as Lévi's trip to England.[44]
- To write a book such as *Dogme et Rituel de la Haute Magie* (over 700 pages in length) requires a vast knowledge of esoteric subjects and practices acquired over several years.
- His first truly esoteric and popular work had not yet been published when he left for England and he is already being welcomed as an initiate there and being asked to demonstrate his magical skills, and this by English aristocrats. We may rightly ask, as does one of his Biographers, Arnaud de L'Estoile, why English aristocrats would

---

[43] *The Kabbalistic and Occult Philosophy of Eliphas Levi*...Letter of February 14, 1862.
[44] This was in July, 1854.

- welcome a failed clergyman and radical working-class Socialist convict with little reputation to speak of into their circle, if he was not already an high initiate and had not something precious to teach or give them?[45]
  o The purported reason for going to England (other than to rest from the chaos of his personal life) is not to be a student but to find equals to exchange with. Regarding this, he was quite disappointed about the low level of understanding of the English occultists he met.
  o He already had a list of prominent aristocratic initiates in his possession, which included Sir Edward Bulwer-Lytton and Dr. Ashburner.
  o He was capable of identifying a high-level Adept when he met one (perhaps by the exchange of certain phrases and words). Take the following passage in *Dogme et Rituel de la Haute Magie*, for example: I saw a woman dressed all in black and which I precisely recognized quickly to be an Initiate, not of the first order, but of an elevated high degree. We had a few very long conversations in which she always insisted on the need to engage in practice in order to compliment initiation.[46]

Incidentally, during the exchange with this unidentified woman Adept, Bulwer-Lytton is referred to as a mutual friend and not as Levi's teacher. Interestingly, many years later he would have a similar low opinion of another English Rosicrucian visitor to his Paris home, Kenneth Mackenzie. His bad impression of him was related by him in his correspondence to his student the Baron Spedalieri.[47]

Now, we don't want to deny that some kind of Rosicrucian exchange may have happened between Lévi and English initiates over the years, but

---

[45] De l'Estoile, p.39.
[46] *Dogme et Rituel de la Haute Magie*, p.266.
[47] In a letter to his student Spedalieri dated, Thursday, December 5th, 1861 Lévi announces: I have the honour of receiving today a scientific deputy (delegate) from England, coming expressly from London to see me. He seems quite enthusiastic about the meeting; but then later Spedalieri asks him about it and he reports in a letter dated between the 14 - 18 of January saying: You asked me whether I was happy with my English visitor – I found him intelligent but a little too inclined toward magical and magnetic experiences. It's the character (fault is implied) of his Nation. The English are curious almost to the point of childishness and comprehend only external facts and results.

it seems clear to us that way too much has been made about these contacts by some commentators. In all circumstances it seems that it is the English who are contacting Lévi or visiting him for instruction, and not the other way around.

Polish Rosicrucian Influences

To explain the advanced knowledge displayed by Lévi in 1854, we have to turn (other than to his own impressive studies) to possible Rosicrucian continental contacts, and this is where his Polish-Prussian contacts come into play.

At the time, Poland was in chaos and at war for its independence against the Prussian (German) and Russian Empires. This caused a massive immigration of Polish aristocratic refugees (not all of them ethnically Polish) to Paris and France. In fact, many of their descendants remain in France today.

Lévi almost always has a high opinion of the German tradition; for example:

> "The sage Eckartshausen therefore didn't hallucinate when he saw in Jakob Boehme the symbol of the mysteries of Nature in the dogmas of religion. Our predecessors, the brothers of the Rose-Cross, were not mad when they said that these were the keys of the Great Work. The key to the Universal Medicine of souls and bodies." [48]

In addition, in another letter to his student Spedalieri, Lévi will answer questions on the origins of his "true primitive dogma" and on his concept of an original esoteric Church, which he calls the "Truly Messianic Church." Lévi goes on to say that this dogma and this Church cannot be found in the Rite of Misraïm because it has been profaned by the French materialists, nor in the Palaprat Templar Church now led by the Baron

---

[48] *The Kabbalistic and Occult Philosophy of Eliphas Levi…*, Letter of January, 1862.

Szapari. He claims that the doctrine has been corrupted and "materialized" by these and then goes on to affirm that:

> "...the <u>true messianic circle</u> today is represented by the Poles Towianski, Wronski and Adam Mickiewicz." [49]

He then goes on to discuss the importance of their work to him, as he did in *Dogme et Rituel de la Haute Magie*, and explicitly ties himself to their school:

> "My preliminary discourse to the second edition of *Dogme et Rituel* summarizes and clarifies the principle ideas of the Messianists (Towianski, Wronski and Mickiewicz) who have preceded me." [50]

It becomes abundantly clear when one studies all of Lévi's early esoteric works that, of these Messianist Poles, the most important to him was Josef Hoene-Wronski (1776‑1853).

Wronski was the son of Antoni Hoene, the architect of the last King of Poland who was from a Czech family which settled in western Poland.[51]

From 1791 to 1794, he participated in the war for the independence of his country against Russia and Prussia and distinguished himself during the siege of Warsaw by the Prussians. He was then taken prisoner at the Battle of Maciejowice and subsequently given a commission in the Russian army, which he left in 1797 with the rank of lieutenant-colonel.

After 1797 he moved to Germany where he studied Law, Philosophy and Mathematics. He reportedly spoke many languages, including: Polish, German, French, Latin, Greek, Hebrew, Arabic, and Aramaic. It is in Germany that he began his studies of mysticism, and where he likely had his reported "revelation of the Absolute." The exact date of the revelation

---

[49] *The Kabbalistic and Occult Philosophy of Eliphas Levi...*, Letter of February 27, 1862.
[50] *The Kabbalistic and Occult Philosophy of Eliphas Levi...*, Letter of 3-6 March, 1862.
[51] The family name was in fact German and appears in different forms: Höhne, Hoehne, Heyne, Hoëne or Hoëné, the `de Wronski' was added later when the family was ennobled in Poland.

was never specified in his writings, and it could have occurred while he was in Germany or while he was travelling across France, in 1803.

After this revelation he dedicated most of the rest of life to what he called his general theory of "Messianism", or "Paracletism." He never ceased to expound his ideas, through numerous philosophical works, which all sought a universal theory of God and nature through the rationality of mathematics.

In 1810, he moved to Paris, where he married the Marquise Henriette Victoire Sarrazin de Montferrier, sister of Alexandre Sarrazin de Montferrier, where he would meet other mystically minded Poles and Frenchmen, including a young Alphonse Louis Constant or Éliphas Lévi.

Proof of the direct discipleship of Lévi under Wronski is preserved in a letter Lévi addressed to him and which we give here in the original French with translation:

Copie de la lettre de M. A. Constant à M. Hoëné Wronski:

Monsieur,
J'ai lu avec admiration votre beau livre, et je vous remercierais au nom de l'humanité tout entière, si j'avais comme vous le droit de parler en son nom. Vous avez le premier assigné un but incontestable aux immenses travaux du dix-neuvième siècle, et vous donnez pour bases à la synthèse universelle que nous cherchions tous, les véritables colonnes d'Hercule! Vous pouvez être incompris longtemps encore, et l'on pourra ne pas vous savoir gré des efforts que vous faites pour venir au-devant de l'humanité; mais que vous importe? Ne sera-t-elle pas forcée d'alles à vous?
Si je croyais que le nom d'un homme soit quelque chose, je vous remercierais d'avoir immortalisé le mien en le transcrivant dans votre livre (l'Historiosophie); mais, j'aime mieux vous remercier d'avoir fait faire un grand pas à mon intelligence dans la voie de la véritable immortalité.
Recevez, Monsieur, les hommages qui sont dus au génie encore inapprécié; je voudrais être digne de vous les offrir au nom

de la postérité qui ne manquerait certainement pas d'acquitter le billet quand viendra pour vous le jour de l'échéance.
  Votre sincère admirateur et <u>dévoué disciple</u>.
  Signé Al. Constant.
Paris, 6 Janvier 1853.
(Conforme à l'original. B[athilde] C[onseillant])

Copy of the letter from M. A. Constant to M. Hoëné Wronski:

  Sir,
  I read your beautiful book with admiration, and I thank you for it in the name of the entirety of humanity, if I had, like you, the right to speak in its name. You are the first to have assigned an indisputable goal to the immense works of the Nineteenth Century, and you give the foundations of the universal synthesis that we were all looking for, the true Pillars of Hercules! You will likely be misunderstood for a long time yet, and humanity may not be grateful to you for the efforts you are making to advance it; but what do you care? Won't she be forced to consider (*lit.* go to) you?
  If I thought a man's name was worth anything, I would thank you for having immortalized mine by transcribing it in your book (in *l'Historiosophie*); but I prefer to thank you for causing my intelligence to take a big leap forward in the way of true immortality.
  Receive, sir, the homage that is due to genius yet unappreciated; I would like to be worthy of offering them to you in the name of posterity, which will certainly not miss to pay it (his genius) its due (*lit.* pay the ticket) when the end day (*lit.* deadline) comes for you.
  Your sincere admirer and <u>faithful disciple</u>.
  Signed Al. Constant.
  Paris, January 6, 1853.
  Faithful (lit. conforms) to the original. B[athilde] C[onseillant] [52]

---

[52] We are indebted for this letter to Rafał Prinke who published it in his Polish language article: *Uczeń Wrońskiego – Éliphas Lévi w kręgu polskich mesjanistów* [Wroński's disciple – Éliphas Lévi in Polish Messianic circles], 2013. The English translation is ours.

It is true that one cannot overstate the importance of Lévi's self-study, particularly of Medieval and Renaissance esoteric sources and which he refers to in many of his works and letters, including: Paracelsus, Jakob Boehme, Raymond Lully, the Keys of Solomon, Agrippa, Tritheme, Le Petit Albert, Louis-Claude de Saint-Martin, etc. However, when it comes to determining his first exposure of a "Rosicrucian current" and his first initiation into it, in our opinion, it is Polish-Prussian roots which are most promising.

It should also be noted that Wronski was likely Lévi's first Kabbalistic and theurgical teacher, as he attests in this part of a Letter to Baron Spedalieiri:

> "Wronski was so prodigiously intelligent, intelligent to the point of being intelligible to everyone and even sometimes to himself, and such a fanatic partisan of occultism (secrecy) that no matter what the cost, he did not want to ever let on that <u>he was a kabbalist and that he studied magic</u>..." [53]

There are also indications, though we only have Lévi's word for it, that he was the successor to Wronski. He reveals this after having found his prognostication machine in a local antique shop:

> "I had in my hand the chef-d'oeuvre of this poor savant, who when dying, <u>had designated me to be the inheritor of his religious thought</u>: Messianism, but he had never consented while he was still alive to me touching his famous prognosticator." [54]

Might this little known fact elegantly explain why Lévi had several Polish aristocratic students latter in his life; including the Brother Counts Branicki and a certain Dr. Nowakowski from Berlin? We think if Lévi was indeed considered Wronski's successor, it would naturally follow that Wronski's former Polish students would seek him out for instruction.

---

[53] *Correspondence* Vol.1, in Charconac.
[54] *Correspondence* Vol.1, in Charconac. In this letter, Lévi gives details on the purpose of the machine and how it is related to the Kabbalah and its Hebrew letters.

Lévi and the French Theosophist Guillaume de Postel

Though Lévi studied a truly impressive number of original Kabbalistic sources that had likely been recommended to him by Wronski, among all of the many references he makes to Kabbalist thinkers over the centuries; one in particular stands out as crucially important to his ideas; the French Christian Kabbalist, Theosopher, Philosopher and early scientific thinker: Guillaume de Postel (1510-1581).

Lévi credits Postel for several of his fundamental ideas, including the importance of the Kabbalah as the key to understanding all religions; the idea of the reformation of religion to create a new universal faith; and even the fact that the Tarot or Rota is the key to all Mysteries.

The importance of de Postel to Lévi is also evident by the number of times he cites him in his letters to his students, as well as the amount of space allotted to him in his many books and particularly in *La Clef des Grand Mystères* and *l'Histoire de la Magie*. Here are some examples of Lévi's glowingly opinion of de Postel:

> "We now come to the mild and pleasing figure of that learned and sublime Postel who is known only by his over-mystical love for an elderly but illuminated woman. There is something far different in Postel from the disciple of Mother Jeanne, but vulgar minds prefer to disparage rather than to learn and have no wish to see anything better in him. It is not for the benefit of these that we propose to make known the genius of William Postel." [55]

> "He discovered rare and priceless manuscripts, including the apocryphal gospels and the Sepher Yetzirah; he initiated himself into the mysteries of the transcendental Kabbalah, and in his simple admiration for that absolute truth, for that supreme reason of all philosophies and dogmas, it was his ambition to reveal it to the world. He therefore spoke the language of the mysteries openly

---

[55] *History of Magic*, p. 335.

and wrote a book entitled the *Key of Things kept Secret from the Foundation of the World*." [56]

"Ironically, de Postel was accused of being mad, and the proof of his madness is that he wrote, as already said, to the Fathers of the Council of Trent, entreating them to bless the whole world and to launch anathemas against no one. As another example, he tried to convert the Jesuits and cause them to preach universal concord among men – peace between sovereigns, reason among priests, and goodness among the princes of this world. In fine, as a last and supreme example of his madness, he neglected the benefits of this world and the favour of the great, lived always humbly and in poverty, possessed nothing but his knowledge and his books, and desired nothing but truth and justice. May God give peace to the soul of poor William Postel." [57]

"These four figures, which is a tradition misunderstood by the Church itself, given as attributes to the four evangelists, represent the four elementary forms of the Kabbalah, the four seasons, the four metals, and finally also the four mysterious letters of the TORA of the Jews, of the wheel of Ezekiel, RO-TA, and of the TAROT which, following Postel, is the key to the things that have been hidden (secret) since the origin of the world." [58]

Lévi also praised Postel through a drawing which he said was revealed by him.

It was placed as a frontispiece to his *La Clef des Grand Mystères* and Lévi called it "the absolute key to all occult sciences." True praise indeed!

Postel was at one time a highly respected recognized teacher at the court of the most Hermetic of French Kings, François I, and in 1544 he wrote *De Orbis Terræ Concordia* (Concerning the Harmony of the Earth) in which he advocated a universalist world religion. The thesis of the book was that all Jews, Muslims, and Pagans could be united once it was proven

---

[56] *History of Magic*, p. 336.
[57] *Dogme et Rituel de la Haute Magie*, p. 295.
[58] *History of Magic*, pg.400.

that their faiths could be shown to have common foundations. He believed these foundations to be the love of God, the praising of God, the love of mankind, and the helping of mankind.

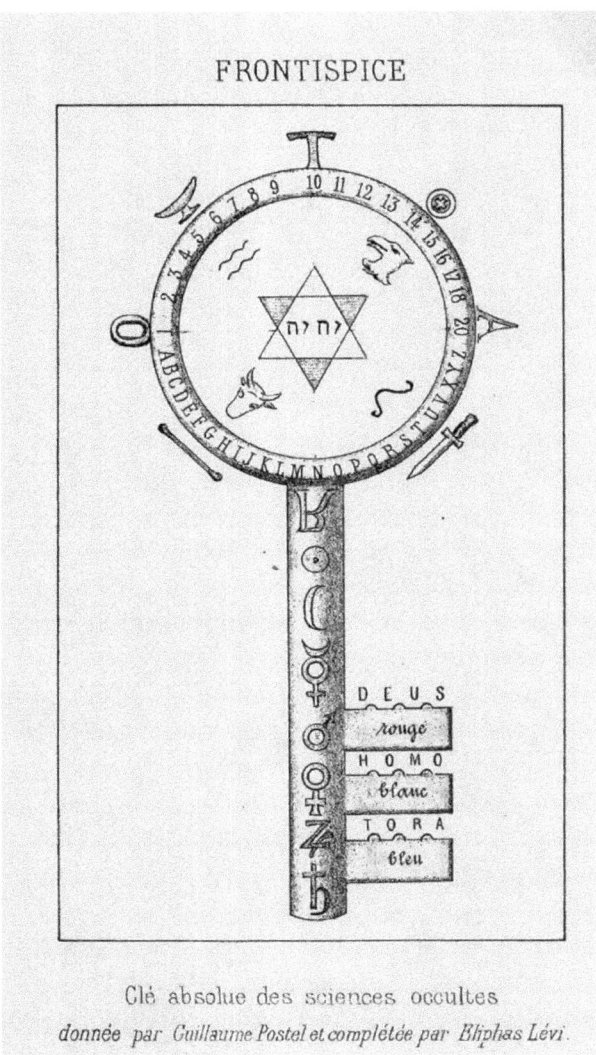

Figure 3 – Guillaume de Postel's Key

Postel was also a relentless advocate for the unification of all Christian churches, a real concern during the period of the Protestant Reformation, and remarkably tolerant of other faiths during a time of intense sectarian fratricide. This tendency led him to try and work with the Jesuits as the most educated of Catholics about other cultures, but the militancy and incompatibility of their doctrine prevented any progress on his part.

While working on his translations of the Zohar and the Bahir in Venice in 1547, Postel became the confessor of Mother Zuana, an elderly woman who was responsible for the kitchen of the hospital of San Giovanni e Paolo. Zuana confessed to experiencing divine visions, which inspired Postel to believe that she was a prophet of the Holy

Mother, that he was her spiritual son, and that he was destined to be the unifier of the world's religions.

Postel also believed that the human soul is composed of intellect and emotion, which he envisaged as male and female, head and heart and used the terms *animus* and *anima* for these indwelling natures in the human being. The soul's triadic unity was only possible through the union of these two halves.[59]

Apart from being a Theosopher, Postel was also a true polyglot and was an early geographer, map maker, linguist, translator, mathematician and diplomat.

Unfortunately, the Inquisition finally got him because of his personal visionary experiences and the works he wrote based on them, and he was tried for heresy, but instead of executing him they simply found him insane, and in 1564 he was detained to the monastery of St. Martin des Champs in Paris. He was released sometime after, but an alleged miracle at Laon in 1566 had a profound effect on him, and that year he published an account of it, *De summopere considerando miraculo*, in which he could not resist returning to his former theses about the interrelatedness of all parts of the Universe and the imminent restoration of new Holy World Order. As a result, he was sentenced again to confinement and spent the last eleven years of his life restricted to the monastery of St. Martin des Champs without the right to publish.

It is truly unfortunate that he is less known today than other Theosophers and Christian-Kabbalists such as Jakob Boehme, Paracelsus, Reuchlin, etc. Lévi made it emphatically clear in his writings and letters that he hoped to renew the study of his works in his lifetime.

---

[59] All of these gender-spiritual ideas can be found in Lévi's works.

The Rosicrucian Reformation of Society and Lévi's Socialism

Let us turn now to Lévi's ideas surrounding the reform of Society which we will argue, despite dating from before his occultism, in fact became Rosicrucian.

It is true that Lévi was a Socialist, and wrote many Socialist tracts and works; the most important being *La Bible de la Vérité*, which earned him a prison sentence for eight months.[60] However, it would be an error to believe that he was a Socialist as we understand the term today. It is particularly important to note that Lévi's Socialism came from his Christian convictions and his observations of the poverty of Paris at the time. It is equally important to note that Lévi was a pre-Marxian Socialist. He would be best described, if we wanted insist on using the label "Socialist," and which was not really accurate in his later life, as a Mystical Christian Socialist.

This is made abundantly in his *Le Livre des Sages*:

"Christian law has been promulgated for the last nineteen centuries now, and the reign of Charity has not yet reigned on earth because this Divine word, which charms hearts, has yet to receive a sufficient explanation; it is by solidarity that Charity is explained, and solidarity is socialism, the last word of Christianity; it is the property of all for everyone and everyone for all." [61]

And again, in *La Clef des Grands Mystères*:

"One sole obvious and Divine thing for all has been manifested in the world: it is Charity. The work of true religion is to produce, conserve and spread the spirit of Charity." [62]

---

[60] He would be imprisoned a second time for six months (sentenced to a year) for publishing his *La voix de la famine* (The Voice of Famine) again defending his pacifism and the Christian nature of his political beliefs, and then again briefly by Napoleon III for having satirized him in a poem.
[61] *Le Livre des Sages*, p.63.
[62] *La Clef des Grands Mystères*, p. 81.

As much as he embraced working within the nascent Socialist movement, he was equally very critical of it and its thinkers. He was also marginalized by Socialists themselves, and many of them did not even come to his defense when he was imprisoned for his book *La Bible de la Liberté*, because he was a believer and a cleric.

We argue that we are better armed in understanding Lévi's political convictions if we consider that Lévi was a Christian Mystic first and a Socialist because of this and not despite it. His commitment in bettering the plight of the working classes comes from his belief that the essence of the Christian Religion (and of every religion) is the principle of charity. It does not come from some atheistic belief in the equality of men or from the values of the French Revolution, and Lévi could just as well be characterized as a Conservative Socialist; as the following quote shows:

> "Emancipation! Thus is the cry of all vices. Emancipation of murder by the abolition of the death penalty; emancipation of prostitution and of infanticide by the abolition of marriage, emancipation of laziness and of rapine by the abolition of property... Thus turns the vortex of perversity, until it reaches the supreme and secret formula: Emancipation of death by the abolition of life!" [63]

He did not believe in revolution nor in levelling the social hierarchies, and he went out of his way to make this very clear, as can be seen by the following quote in which he discusses his intentions in publishing *La Bible de la Liberté*:

> "In order to give it (the people) the right to resist all tyranny, I wanted to constitute (promote) liberty, first in the family, by the emancipation of women and also by the respect for children's rights... The desire to react against the almost generalized egotism of the owners made me embrace the idea of Communism. But I wanted this communism to be founded on spiritual beliefs...In my thoughts I never wished to provoke or justify any forfeits (violence), but given that this is the impression my words have

---

[63] *La Clef des Grand Mystères*, p. 272.

given, I retract them in all horror, entirely, without restriction, of my own volition, and in the presence of God and men..."[64]

Resist did not mean violence and revolution in the mind of Lévi, and he even made this clear during the 1848 revolution in a letter to the Editor of the newspaper Populaire:

"Aggressive and violent communism has never been for me but a dark menace and a terrible paradox...I never want my name to serve as a banner for anarchy and vandalism, and I am the first to declare the infamy of those who would like to trouble and dishonor the nascent Republic."[65]

Socialists knew this about him, and he was denounced because of it in one of the most popular labor periodicals of the time *L'Humanitaire*:

"You have dedication and energy to the cause, but you are wrong to talk to us about God, of the Spirit and of Love: we only recognize matter and nature."[66]

It should also be noted that Lévi criticized all the major schools of Socialism at the time, including Saint-Simonienisme, Fourrierisme, and Blanquisme.

However, the Socialist writer he seemed to have considered the most seriously, was Charles Fourier, the founder of Fourierisme and a fellow proponent for the emancipation of women. Lévi seems to have been originally attracted to some elements of his thought; as many esotericists were.[67] However, this sympathy did not go very far, and he eventually concluded that Fourier's attempt to create an ideal society (le Phalanstère) based on the harmony of individual passions and attractions would lead to a form of chaotic hedonism which would destroy it from the inside:

---

[64] *Journal de L'Évêque d'Evreux*, no.10, Aug., 1843, in Charconac.
[65] In Charconac, p. 112. One should keep in mind that Lévi even published a kind of pacifist manifesto entitled: *La Fête de Dieu ou Le Triomphe de la Paix Religieuse*.
[66] In Charconac, p. 55.
[67] Another example is Léonce Fabre des Essarts the second Patriarch of the French Gnostic Church after Jules Doinel, and who was also a proponent of the emancipation of women.

"It is true (as Fourier says) that the attractions are proportionate to the destinies, but he was wrong to not distinguish between the fatal attractions and the factice attractions. He believed that the evils just aren't understood by our Society, whereas, in fact, it is the opposite, it is the evils that don't understand Society and which don't want to understand it." [68]

Whereas the form of Socialism which he most rejected and which inspired his profound ire was the anarchism of Joseph Proudhon, who was a contemporary:

"He (Proudhon) affirms that God is an evil, that social order is anarchy, that property is theft! What society is possible under such principles?" [69]

It seems obvious to us that in order to understand Lévi's "Socialism" it is not to Socialist thinkers that one must turn to but rather to religious, mystical and occult ones, and particularly those which had a vision of the coming age of the Holy Spirit and its full realization of Christian Charity. To individuals such as l'Abbé Frère-Colonna, Mme. Guyon, Jakob Boehme, Jacob del Fiore, Saint-Vincent de Paul, and of course to the Messianism of the Poles such as Wronski.

The fact is, the will to reform society, is not only a socialist trait but also a Rosicrucian "landmark" and one can hope for a more just, progressive and equal society without being a socialist. This "Rosicrucian will to reform" is most clearly seen in the Fama and Confessio and other tracks which followed close upon it and it was welcomed by Lévi and became one of his constant themes.

After Lévi became a Rosicrucian, he developed a new more specific mystic-political "reform project" which began with the creation of a new religion, an idea much less present in Lévi's writings before 1854. Lévi very much saw the creation of a new Rosicrucian- and Masonic-like spirituality as the necessary condition for the emergence of the new Society, and his societal project became spiritual first and political second.

---

[68] *Le Grand Arcane*, p. 35.
[69] *Le Grand Arcane*, p. 37.

The "reform project" was nothing other than the creation of a universal purified religion reconciling religion and science that would unite humanity together in a great fraternal Brotherhood. Does that sound Rosicrucian or Masonic? It should!

This goal is beautifully and succinctly put in the following excerpt from his article *Les Classiques de la Kabbale*:

"But this purified religion will not be created from nothing, it exists, and it has always existed amongst human beings; but it had to be concealed from the profane by the wise, which were incapable of comprehending it. It is the Tradition of all the Great Sanctuaries of Ancient Times; it is the Philosophy of Nature; it is God dwelling in humanity and in the world; it is what can be demonstrated by being; it is harmony proved by reason; it is the analogy of the contraries; it is belief based on science and science elevated by faith."

This religion for Lévi is the only truly "catholic" or "universal one" and it exists partially in many spiritual traditions in history, and it is from this perspective that Lévi will analyze and criticize all political and religious/spiritual movements of the past and present times. It also explains how he can be simultaneously critical of Roman Catholicism and of Esoteric movements. Both, in their own ways, from his perspective, represented a degenerate version of this original religion.

The key to the reconstruction of this "original religion" is, in Lévi's opinion, the Kabbalah, and idea he took from his reading of Guillaume de Postel. It, above all other Traditions, allows us to find the true essence in the dung heap of human spiritual history and it is based on her that the new universal faith can be built.

The coming of this new universal faith has very concrete ramifications, as can be seen in this very interesting quote from his *Le Livre des Splendeurs:*

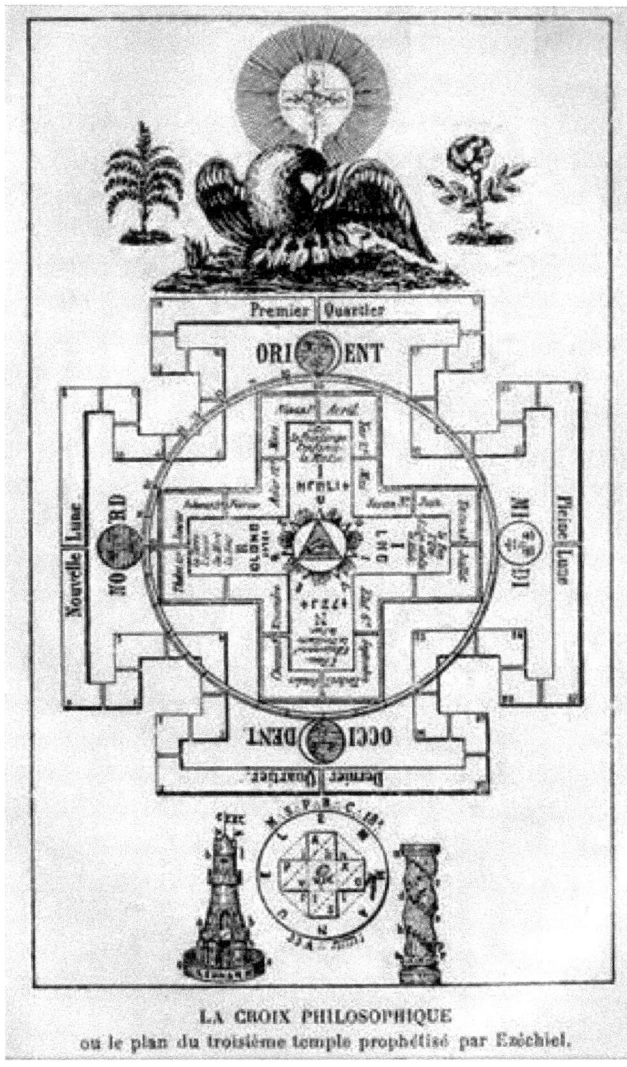

Figure 4 - The Philosophical Cross

"When all particular religions (denominations) are dead, the unique universal religion will come to life. It will consist of the agreement of all men in a belief in a universal solidarity, the unity of aspirations, but the diversity of expressions, belief in one sole God, liberty in symbolism and tolerance of images, orthodox in charity, universal in its depths, and I would not say indifference, but difference in its forms, analogous to the genius of each people, perfectability of its dogmas and possible improvement of its means of worship, but at the base of all of this, the great and immutable faith of Israel in one sole God, immaterial, immutable and non-substantial, of which all conventional and imagined images are but idols, in a one and only reason which is the universal law of beings and in one sole nation; which is the instrument of God for the creation and conservation of insects and universes! And it is under the auspices of the influence of commerce...that we hope to see established on earth: an association of all interests, the federation of all peoples, the alliance of all means of worship, and a universal solidarity."

Having discussed the influences of the Polish Messianists, William de Postel and Rosicrucian reformism let us turn to the influence of Freemasonry; arguably the most influential "esoteric movement" in European history.

Lévi's Freemasonry

Due to Lévi leaving Masonry abruptly, only after two years as a member, there is an assumption in certain circles that Lévi was an anti-Mason. This opinion is usually coupled with the view that he was a Roman Catholic apologist. Both of these opinions are false, and are caused by a too shallow reading of Lévi. Lévi was a complex thinker, and one needs to carefully read all of his works to understand what he understood his true mission to be.

In fact, as shown in all his writings published after being initiated in "*La rose du parfait silence*" (The Perfect Rose of Silence) Lodge: on the 14th of March 1861, including, in *Le Grand Arcane* (1868), *Le Livre de Splendeurs* (1870) and *Le Grimoire Francorum-latomorum* (1871), Lévi maintained a very positive and publicly stated view of Masonry for the remainder of his life.

So, one might rightfully ask, why did he leave Masonry in the first place?

To understand this, one must keep in mind that Lévi was favourable to a mystical and spiritual, and not just moralizing, understanding of Freemasonry. However, Lévi was initiated into a Lodge which was part of the Grand Orient of France, and in a decade in which the reference to the Grand Architect of the Universe and the presence of the Bible in Lodges was intensely debated.

It is in this context that Lévi's outrage to the reactions from a Brother to a speech he gave in his Lodge, must be understood. Here is what transpired:

> "…following his speech, a Brother, Mr. Ganeval, took the floor in order to present some observations on his work (on Lévi's speech). These upset Lévi so much that after the meeting he gave his resignation from Freemasonry, and this despite the supplications of the Worshipful Master Candet." [70]

Lévi would later express that:

> "I ceased being a Freemason, because the Freemasons, having been excommunicated by the Pope, believed that they should be intolerant towards Catholicism; I therefore separated myself from them to keep my freedom of conscience, and to not be associated with their reprisals, which are perhaps understandable, even perhaps legitimate, but certainly not inconsequential, for the essence of Freemasonry is tolerance towards all means of worship (cults)." [71]

Most commentators leave it at that and conclude that Lévi took the side of the Church against Freemasonry or did not want to be excommunicated. If this was the case, then Lévi would have never joined in the first place, since the Papal ban on membership for Roman-Catholics was in place since 1783 and reiterated strongly by Pope Pius IX in 1846, 1849, 1864, 1865, 1869, and 1873. Also, several of Lévi's works had already been placed on the Roman Catholic index and he was openly condemned by Church authorities; including the Bishop of Paris. One must also keep in mind that Lévi was a very well-known and public Socialist; a political movement strongly condemned by the Church hierarchy at that time.

To truly understand his views of Freemasonry, we have to read him in more depth, as in his *Livre des Sages*:

---

[70] Buisset, Christiane, in the Préface to *Livre des Splendeurs*, p. iv.
[71] *Livres des Sages*, p.13.

"What does the word Catholicism mean? Does it not mean Universal? I believe in a Universal dogma, and I keep myself from the aberrations of any specific sect (denomination), and yet I support them all in the hope that progress will accomplish itself and that all men will unite themselves in faith and to fundamental truths, something which has already been accomplished in that society which is now spread across the world and which is named Free-Masonry." [72]

It is reasonable to conclude by this that the Brother who intervened, likely with the support of others, was against Lévi's concept of a universal faith based on a belief in a Divine Being. It is at this moment that Lévi may have realized that the Lodge he was initiated into was actually one in which a majority of members were aligned with the humanist-atheist trends, and clearly anti-Roman Catholic because of this. Quite simply, Lévi was in the wrong Lodge and was preaching to the wrong crowd!

It is also important to note that even near the end of his life Lévi was writing chapters on the importance of Freemasonry, for example in his *Livre des Splendeurs*, and this during the very year when the Grand Orient allowed those not professing a belief in the Divine Being to be initiated; leading eventually to the Grand Orient being declared as irregular by the United Grand Lodge of England (UGLE). His chapters on a spiritual interpretation of Freemasonry may have actually been intended to help save Masonry from this growing atheistic influence.

It is also interesting to note that Lévi may have had a mentor in all this. Lévi maintained a good friendship with his Masonic senior J.M. Ragon who wrote such titles as *Maçonnerie occulte* and *l'Initiation hermétique*. Jean-Marie Ragon (1781-1862) was a Belgian initiated in the loge *Les amis du Nord* (Friends of the North) in Bruges. He eventually moved to Paris, where he became a highly influential member of the Rite of Misraïm and of the Grand Orient of France. He was also the Master of the famous lodge *Les Vrais Amis* and its Aeropagate *Les Trinosophes*, which became highly respected for its knowledge and for possessing many early masonic and occult manuscripts. It is Ragon who was said to have received the original

---

[72] *Livre des Sages*, p. 13.

Misraïm Arcana Arconorum Naple degrees from Italians, and who was an opponent of both the Bédarrides and Marconis de Nègre.

Ragon even praised Lévi's *Dogme et Rituel de la haute Magie*, in his *Maçonnerie Occulte*:

> "In a lengthy and profound work, a learned magist enumerates and elaborates on a truly diverse number of sciences which relate to magism." [73]

It is interesting to wonder what would have happened if Lévi had entered a different Grand Lodge jurisdiction where belief in a Divine Being was celebrated. Of course, many of these jurisdictions had yet to break with the Grand Orient, so this is a truly "What if?" scenario.

In any case, Lévi continued to believe that Freemasonry had an important role to play in his Messianic vision of the future because for him it was the bearer and teacher of reason and science. It was the philosophical and rational flipside of faith and of the Catholic Church. To this end, he believed that Freemasonry could help reform the wider Church:

> "The universality of the Church Fathers and the saints is true. But the Catholicism of a Veuillot is a lie… It is that lie which Freemasonry has the mission of fighting for the profit of truth." [74]

Veuillot was what we would call today an Ultraconservative Catholic (an *Ultramontane*); and a combination of a journalist and modern inquisitor. He wrote for the militant Catholic press and actively fought against Liberal and Socialist ideas (Lévi was both a Liberal and a Socialist). A contemporary, Matthew Arnold said of Veuillot:

> "Louis Veuillot is a polemicist worthy of the golden age of polemics. He is singly devoted to ultramontanism…" [75]

---

[73] Ragon, J.M., *Maçonnerie Occulte*, Dentu, Paris, 1854, p. 84 in Charconac.
[74] *Livre des Splendeurs*, p. 209.
[75] *Livre des Splendeurs*, pp. 211-212.

Therefore, at the same time as supporting Freemasonry Lévi was also a critic of the Roman-Catholic Church, which he believed had to be reformed and had erred in significant ways. He makes this abundantly clear in his *Livre des Splendeurs*:

> "Catholics have erred in three fundamental ways:
> "They have believed that faith must impose itself by force on reason and even on science, which progress they fight.
> "They have attributed to the Pope an infallibility, not only conservative and disciplinary but absolute, like that of God.
> "They have thought that man had to be diminished, annulled, and render himself miserable in this life to merit his future life, whereas, on the contrary, man must cultivate all his abilities, develop them, expand his soul, learn (know), love, beautify his life, in one word become happy; because the present life and the preparation for the future life and eternal joy begins the moment that he has conquered the profound peace which results in perfect balance.
> "The result of these errors was the protestation of nature, of science and reason, which lead to the belief that one can abandon faith and obliterate all religion on earth.
> "But the world cannot live without religion (faith), just as a man cannot live without a heart." [76]

Though it is true that Éliphas Lévi wished to see the Roman Catholic Church reform itself, and hoped it would do so under the influence of science and reason, at several places in his later writings he expressed doubts that it ever could. He was even quite vociferous in his criticisms of it, likening modern Priests to the Pharisees of old. Here is an example:

> "May the occult sciences be studied by the aspirants of the holy ministry (Catholic Seminarians) and particularly the great Jewish Kabbalah which is the key to all symbols. Only then will the true universal religion be revealed and the catholicity (universality) of all ages and all peoples will replace this absurd and hateful Catholicism, enemy of progress and of freedom which continues

---

[76] *Livre des Splendeurs*, p. 209.

to fight in the world against justice, but whose reign has passed forever." [77]

On the coming of a Universal Religion Levi said:

"The Religion of the future will not be Catholicism but catholicity (universality). Universal adoration of God through the marvels of science; Love of the living God in humanity and the synthesis of light which shall explain, by the divergence of its rays, the nuances of all the ways of worship (cults)." [78]

Finally, it seems to have been the declaration of the doctrine of the infallibility of the Pope in 1870 after a Vatican Council, which totally broke the camel's back for Lévi, as he attested in a letter to his student:

"Until the 13th of this month I had been a dissident, a rebel subject of the Church… Now I am the voice of the future and I make it my duty to leave the condemned Babylon to apostasy. Now I am on the side of Jesus Christ and his Apostles! I am absolved! I am rehabilitated! I am free! Hosannah!" [79]

This may explain why, on his death bed, Lévi didn't seek or receive the last rites in the Roman Catholic Church, despite having access to a Priest who was a friend and from whom, after a few long conversation, Lévi consented to receive absolution.[80]

Ultimately, Lévi was critical of both Freemasonry and Catholicism. Freemasonry, as it existed in France, for abandoning spirituality, and Catholicism for fighting against reason and science. The solution was a new synthesis, a new universal religion and harmonious society characterized by mysticism, rationality, charity and solidarity.

Having discussed the major Rosicrucian influences on Lévi, we thought it fitting to conclude this section with what the practice that Lévi

---

[77] *Le Grand Arcane*, p. 178.
[78] *Livre des Sages*, p. 156.
[79] *Correspondance* Vol. VIII, in Charconac.
[80] Charconac, p. 289.

actually taught, which he called the Divine Science of High Magic, was all about. He puts this very clearly in his *Paradoxes of the Highest Sciences*; which is one of his later works and which in our opinion is too often overlooked:

> "The Mage, or if you prefer the Sage, welcomes pleasure, accepts riches, merits honours, but he is never the slave of any of them. He knows how to be poor, to stint himself and to suffer; he endures forgetfulness willingly, because of his happiness, which is his own, expects nothing and dreads nothing from the caprices of Fortune.
>
> "He can love without being loved, he can create imperishable treasures and raise himself above the level of honours and the gifts of Chance. What he wants he possesses, for he possesses profound peace. He regrets nothing of that which comes to an end, but he remembers with joy all that has been good for him. His hope is already a certainty; he knows good is eternal, and that evil is transitory. He can enjoy solitude, but he does not fear the society of man; he is a child with children, joyous with the young, staid with the aged, patient with fools, happy with the wise.
>
> "He smiles with all who smile, he mourns with all who weep. He takes part in all festivities, sympathizes in all mournings, applauds all strength of mind, is indulgent to all weaknesses; never offending anyone, he never has to pardon, for he never thinks himself offended; he pities those who misunderstand him, and awaits the opportunity of doing them good. It is by the force of kindness that he loves to revenge himself on the ungrateful. Ready, himself, to give everything, he receives with pleasure and gratitude all that may be given to him. He leans with affection on all arms stretched towards him in time of difficulty, and does not mistake fretful pride for virtue… He thinks that it is doing a service to others to give them an opportunity to do good, and he meets neither an offer nor a demand with a refusal…
>
> "Arriving at perfect equilibrium, this man may walk or run without fear of falling. One must be someone to deserve to exist, but one must be someone to do something; we exist only to act; we think

to speak. Reason also is the Word, but the Word is not only speech: it is life in action. We are strong in order to work; we are learned in order to teach; we are physicians in order to heal the sick. We do not light a lamp to hide it under a bushel, as Christ said…

"To live is to love, and to love is to do good. We should desire the progress of humanity, the prosperity of our country, the honour of our family, the welfare of all the world. He who interest himself in no-one is a dead man who should be forgotten.

"If any man will come after me," Christ said, "let him deny himself, and take up his cross daily, and follow me." To renounce oneself is to come out of egoism in order to enter into charity. The true life of man is not in himself but in others." [81]

Furthermore, Lévi says that the purpose of magic is:

"…what can be the use of magic? It enables men to understand better Truth, and desire Good in a wholesome and more effective manner. It helps to heal souls and comfort bodies. It does not confer the means of doing evil with impunity, but it raises man above animal lusts. It renders man inaccessible to the agonies of desire and fear. It constitutes a divinely radiating center, chasing away before it phantoms and darkness, for it knows, it wills, it dares, and it holds its peace. This is the True Magic, not that of the Necromancers and Enchanters, but that of the initiated and the Magi.

"True Magic is a scientific force placed at the service of Reason. False magic is a blind force to the blunders and disorders of Folly." [82]

And this is what Levi says a True Magician should really want:

"He wants (wills for) the beauty of nature, which he enjoys in its fullness, because he never abuses it.

---

[81] *Paradoxes of the Highest Science*, p. 90-93.
[82] *Paradoxes of the Highest Science*, p. 73-74.

"He wants springs to come flower laden, the roses to bloom in their beauty, the children to be happy and the women beloved.

"He wants men mutually to assist each other, to encourage the young and help the old.

"He wants Eternal Good to triumph over transitory evil, and he takes part patiently and peacefully in the work of Society and Nature.

"He wants order, he wants reason, he wants goodness, he wants love, and for that which he wants he works with all his strength, for thus he wins immortality and happiness.

"Desiring nothing, he is rich; fearing nothing he is free; wanting only what he ought to want, he is happy." [83]

Magic therefore is nothing else but the practice of Equilibrium and Temperance. The ancient Philosophers and Biblical Prophets would no doubt be nodding their heads in agreement.

Conclusion

The above is what we like to call the base of the iceberg of Lévi's Rosicrucian thought. We could have discussed so much more, including the influence of the various grimoires and alchemical manuscripts he studied at the Arsenal Library on his magical practice, but this ground, as we said, has been largely covered by Golden Dawn and Thelemic authors. Also, another entire area which we have not addressed is Lévi's magnetism and theory of the Astral Light, as well as his indebtedness to but also criticism of Mesmer and his school.

To his mind the Astral Light truly served as the scientific basis for understanding miraculous religious phenomenon. It is literally the bridge

---

[83] *Paradoxes of the Highest Sciences*, p.88-89.

which links faith and reason in a practical way in his system; but again, that has been discussed elsewhere.

The Astral Light and his magical practices are, to our mind, just the tip of the iceberg and not its base, as they are but expressions of his more profound mystical and spiritual ideas; and what we have tried to do here is discuss the major influences of those individuals and ideas that have been largely ignored in English language publications.

In conclusion, let us attempt to summarize, in point form, the major themes which form the basis of Lévi's Rosicrucian Thought:

- The coming New Age of the Holy Spirit where the Feminine Divine Principle is foremost.
- The need to emancipate women spiritually and socially.
- The creation of a Universal Religion combining the rationality of Judaism with the compassion of Christianity.
- The reconciliation of science and faith, reason and emotion.
- The study of the Kabbalah as the knowledge revealing the universality and rationality of all religious beliefs .
- The Devil does not exist but rather human choice is at the origin of transitory evil.
- The creation of a new political and mercantile order based on charity.
- The goal of men and of every Mage should be to become equilibrated and in harmony with his fellow men and nature,
- God has a shadow side which is not evil but rather just a reflection of him in the microcosm: it is a part of God, the secret to equilibrium is to see in this shadow the work of God.
- The source of miracles and spiritual phenomenon and their bridge to scientific thought is an invisible plastic medium or magnetic force called the Astral Light.
- The harnessing of this magnetic force through the rituals of Divine or High Magic in order to realize man's domination of the natural forces (the shadow of God) is what will lead to a more equilibrated and harmonious human being, life and society.

Mathieu G. Ravignat, M.A.
December 2002

Bibliography

**Books Consulted by Éliphas Lévi
as Alphonse-Louis Constant**
1841: *La Bible de la liberté*
1841: *l'Assomption de la femme ou le Livre de l'amour*
1844: *la Mère de Dieu, épopée religieuse et humanitaire*
1845: *la Fête-Dieu ou le Triomphe de la paix religieuse*

As Éliphas Lévi
1854: *Dogme et rituel de la haute magie (tome 1 de 2)*
1859: *Histoire de la magie*
1859: *la Clef des grands mystères suivant Hénoch, Abraham, Hermès Trismégiste et Salomon Lire en ligne*
1865: *Philosophie occulte. Seconde série : la Science des esprits*
1854: *la Clavicule universelle des clavicules de Salomon ou le Grimoire des Grimoires*
1856: *Carnet de notes d'Éliphas Lévi*
1868: *Cours de philosophie occulte. Lettres au baron Spedalieri*
1868-1869: *Le Grand Arcane ou l'Occultisme dévoilé, Chamuel*
1869-1870: *le Livre des splendeurs*
1869-1870: *le Livre des sages*
1870: *les Éléments de la Kabbale*
1873: *les Paradoxes de la haute science*
1874: *la Sagesse des Anciens*

Other Sources Consulted
Buisset, Christiane, *Éliphas Lévi: sa vie, son oeuvre, ses* pensées, Guy Trénadiel, 1984.
Charconac, Paul, Éliphas Lévi (1810-1875), *Édiitons Traditionelles*, Paris, 1989.
De Estoille, Arnaud, Lévi, Pardés, Grez-sur-Loing, 2008.
Trans. Lévi, Éliphas, *Paradoxes of the Highest Science*, Berwick, Ibis Press, 2004
Trans. Lévi, Éliphas, *The History of Magic*, trans. By A.E. Waite, York Beech, Weiser, 2001.

Prinke, Rafał *Uczeń Wrońskiego – Éliphas Lévi w kręgu polskich mesjanistów* [Wroński's disciple – Éliphas Lévi in Polish Messianic circles, 2013.
Downloaded June, 2022:
https://www.academia.edu/5779977/Ucze%C5%84Wro%C5%84skiego%C3%89liphasL%C3%A9viwkr%C4%99gupolskichmesjanist%C3%B3wWro%C5%84skisdisciple%C3%89liphasL%C3%A9vi inPolishMessianiccircles

The Kabbalistic and Occult Philosophy of Eliphas Lévi Volume 1: Letter to Students, Daath Gnostic Publishing, 2017.1

HISTORICAL AND MYTHOLOGICAL PERSONS

Lévi collected these poems together nine months after the end of the disastrous Franco-Prussian War. Taking place from 1870 to 1871 between the Second French Empire and the Kingdom of Prussia, the war had a number of significant impacts on France, Prussia, and Europe as a whole. One of the most significant impacts of the Franco-Prussian War was the loss of Alsace and Lorraine, two regions located in eastern France, to Prussia. This loss was a major blow to France, as these regions were important industrial and economic centres. The loss of Alsace and Lorraine also had a lasting impact on French national identity. It contributed to a sense of resentment and bitterness towards Germany that persisted for many years. Such *ennui* permeates throughout the entirety of Lévi's poems. The war also significantly impacted the balance of power in Europe and had significant social and political impacts within France. The war and its aftermath were marked by political instability as various factions within France struggled for power and influence. The war also contributed to the rise of the socialist movement in France and Europe, as many people were disillusioned by the defeat and the economic hardships that followed. The poems make several allusions to actual historical and mythological figures that convey the overall mood of the age: national disillusionment and discontent, which is often characterised by a sense of hedonism, excess, and a preoccupation with aesthetics and pleasure. Lévi's poetry represents then the vanguard of a coming fascination with the exotic, the occult, and the forbidden, reflected in the period's literature, art, and architecture. What follows is a short collection of biographical details to help the reader better appreciate the literary and historical allusions made throughout the collection:

Henri Auguste Barbier (1805-1882) was a French playwright and librettist who lived in the nineteenth century. He is best known for his collaborations with the composer Jacques Offenbach (1819-1880), for which he wrote the *libretti* (texts) for many of Offenbach's operettas. Some of his most famous works include "*Orpheus in the Underworld*," "*The Tales of Hoffmann*," and

"*La Belle Hélène*." In addition to his theatre work, Barbier was a journalist and critic, and he wrote several plays and poems on his own.

Félix Antoine Philibert Dupanloup (1802-1878) was a French bishop and prominent figure in the Catholic Church during the nineteenth century. He served as the Bishop of Orléans from 1849 until his death in 1878 and was known for his liberal views and efforts to modernise the Church. Dupanloup was a vocal opponent of the French government's policies towards the Church, and he played a key role in the fight to protect the rights of Catholics in France. He was also a prominent figure in the field of education and worked to improve the quality of schools and universities in France.

Paul Chenavard (1808-1895) was a French painter and draftsman who was active in the nineteenth-century. He was born in Lyon in 1808 and studied art at the *École des Beaux-Arts* in Paris. He became a member of the French Academy of Fine Arts in 1854 and was known for his portrait paintings and landscapes. Chenavard was a respected artist in his time and his work can be found in museums and private collections around the world.

Hormuz and Ahriman are figures in ancient Iranian mythology and Zoroastrianism, a monotheistic religion founded in ancient Persia (present-day Iran). Hormuz is the God of fire, light, and goodness in Zoroastrianism and is often depicted as a benevolent deity who represents purity and righteousness. Ahriman, on the other hand, is the God of darkness, evil, and wickedness and is seen as the embodiment of all that is wrong and wicked in the world. According to Zoroastrian belief, Hormuz and Ahriman are engaged in an ongoing struggle, with Hormuz representing the forces of good and Ahriman representing the forces of evil. This struggle is believed to reflect the ongoing battle between good and evil in the world and is seen as an important aspect of Zoroastrian teachings.

Anacreon was an ancient Greek poet who lived in the 6th century BC. He was born on the island of Teos, located off the coast of present-day Turkey, and is known for his poetry, which celebrated love, wine, and pleasure. Anacreon's poetry was written in the Ionic dialect of ancient Greek, and he is considered one of the foremost poets of the Ionic school. His poetry was known for its light-hearted and playful tone, and he often wrote about the joys of love and wine. Anacreon's poetry was widely read and admired in ancient Greece, and his works continue to be studied and appreciated by readers today. Some of his most famous works include *"Ode to Wine," "To a Fair Youth,"* and *"To a Lovely Girl."*

Monsieur and Madame Prud'homme were a pair of fictional characters created by the French writer and artist Honoré Daumier (1808-1879). They were featured in a series of satirical prints and caricatures published in the French magazine *"Le Charivari."* Monsieur Prud'homme was a portly, middle-aged man with a stern expression and a penchant for pontificating about trivial matters. He was often portrayed as a self-important and pompous figure, and his character was meant to be a humorous commentary on the societal norms and values of the time. Madame Prud'homme was the wife of Monsieur Prud'homme and was depicted as a dutiful and submissive spouse. She was often shown standing in the background, quietly observing her husband's antics. The characters of Monsieur and Madame Prud'homme were popular with readers and were frequently featured in *"Le Charivari."* They became well-known figures in French popular culture and remains remembered as enduring symbols of French satire.

Victor Hugo (1802-1885) was a French writer, poet, and statesman who was active in the nineteenth century. He is considered one of the greatest French writers of all time and is best known for his novels, plays, and poems. Hugo was born in 1802 in Besançon, France, and began writing at a young age. He published his first book of poems, *"Odes et Ballades,"* in 1826, and went on to produce a wide range of literary works, including the novel *"Notre-Dame de Paris"* (The Hunchback of Notre-Dame), the play *"Cromwell,"* and the poem *"La Légende des Siècles."* Hugo was also active in politics and was a member of the National Assembly and the Senate in France. He was a vocal advocate for social justice and reform and was known for his progressive views on education, democracy, and human rights. Hugo's work has had a lasting impact on literature and has been widely translated and adapted for stage and screen. Some of his other famous works include the novels *"Les Misérables"* and *"The Man Who Laughs,"* and the play *"Ruy Blas."*

Francisco de Zurbarán (1598-1664) was a Spanish painter active in the 17th century. He was born in Fuente de Cantos, a small town in the province of Badajoz, Spain, in 1598, and is known for his religious paintings and still lives. Its realism and attention to detail characterize Zurbarán's work, and he is considered one of the greatest Spanish painters of the Baroque period. Zurbarán is best known for his paintings of religious subjects, particularly his depictions of the life of St. Francis of Assisi and the lives of the saints. He also painted still lifes, works of art depicting inanimate objects, such as fruit, flowers, or household items. Some of Zurbarán's most famous works include *"St. Serapion," "St. Francis in Ecstasy,"* and *"Still Life with Lemons, Oranges and a Rose."*

Albrecht Dürer (1471–1528) was a German painter, printmaker, and theorist active in the 15th and 16th centuries. He is considered one of the greatest artists of the Northern Renaissance, and his work has had a lasting impact on the history of art. Dürer was born in Nuremberg, Germany, in 1471 and began his career as an apprentice to a goldsmith. He later studied painting and printmaking and became known for his detailed and realistic depictions of animals, landscapes, and religious figures. Dürer was also a skilled draftsman and printmaker known for his woodcuts, engravings, and etchings considered some of the finest examples of these art forms. In addition to his art, Dürer was also a theorist and wrote extensively about the principles of art and the artist's role in society. Some of his most famous works include *"The Apocalypse," "The Four Horsemen of the Apocalypse,"* and *"The Great Passion."*

Théophile Gautier (1811-1872) was a French poet, novelist, and critic active in the 19th century. He was born in 1811 in Tarbes, France, and is considered one of the leading figures of the Romantic movement in France. Gautier was known for his love of beauty, and his fascination with the exotic and the bizarre, and his work often explored themes of love, passion, and the supernatural. Gautier began his career as a poet. His early works, such as *"Mademoiselle de Maupin"* and *"Emaux et Camées,"* are considered some of the finest examples of French Romantic poetry. He later turned to prose and wrote several novels and plays, including *"Arria Marcella," "La Comédie de la Mort,"* and *"Le Capitaine Fracasse."* Gautier was also a critic and wrote extensively about literature, art, and theatre.

Galileo Galilei (1564-1642) was an Italian astronomer, physicist, and mathematician considered one of modern science's pioneers. He was born in Pisa, Italy, in 1564 and is best known for his contributions to physics and astronomy. Galileo made important observations and discoveries using the newly invented telescope and is credited with discovering the four largest moons of Jupiter, now known as the Galilean moons. Galileo's work helped revolutionize our understanding of the universe and our place in it, and he is the father of modern observational astronomy. He is also known for his contributions to the field of physics, particularly his formulation of the laws of motion, which were an important precursor to the work of Sir Isaac Newton. Galileo's work has had a lasting impact on the scientific community and continues to be studied and admired by scientists and researchers worldwide.

HISTORICAL AND MYTHOLOGICAL PERSONS 77

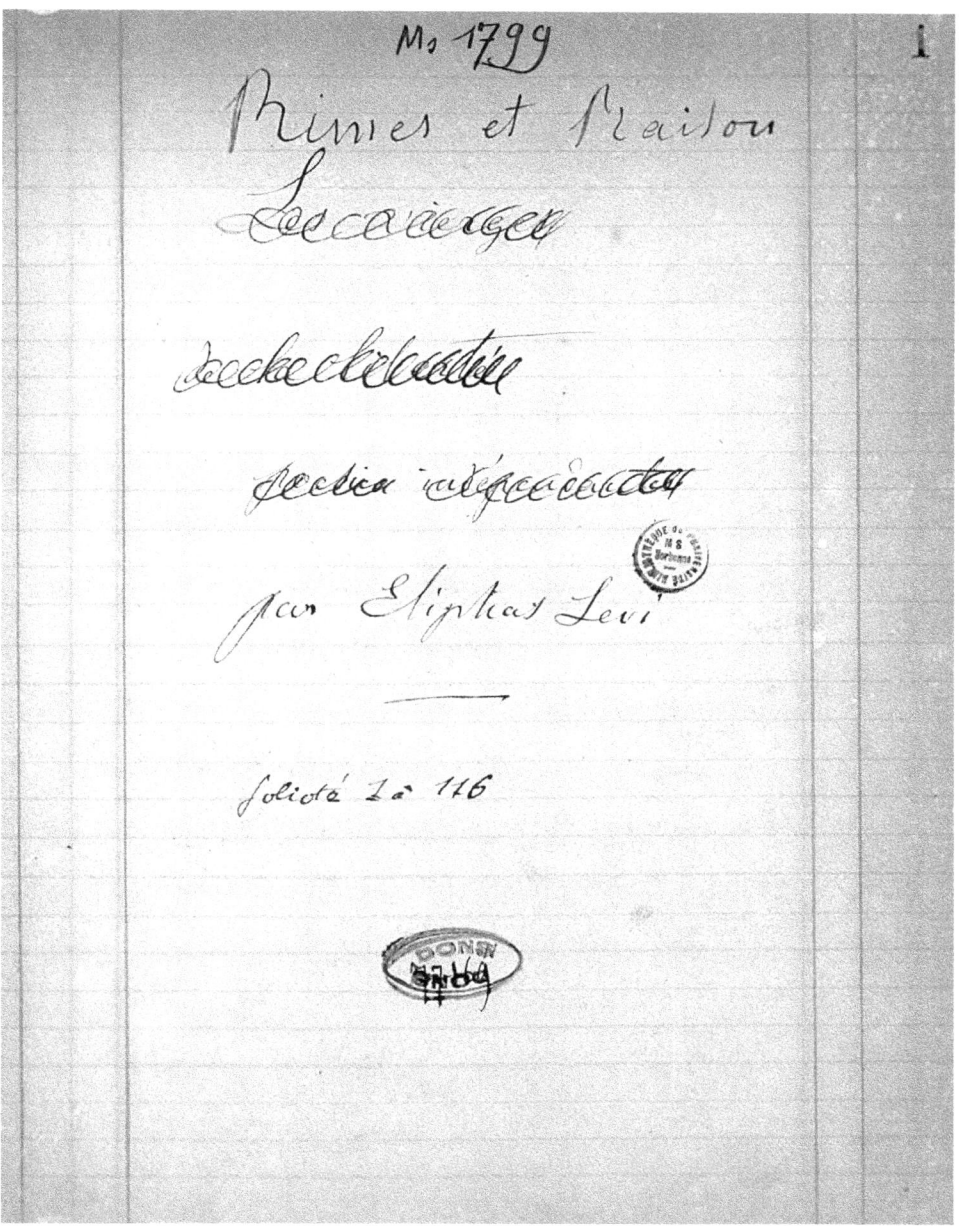

Figure 5 - Cover Page of Lévi's Notebook

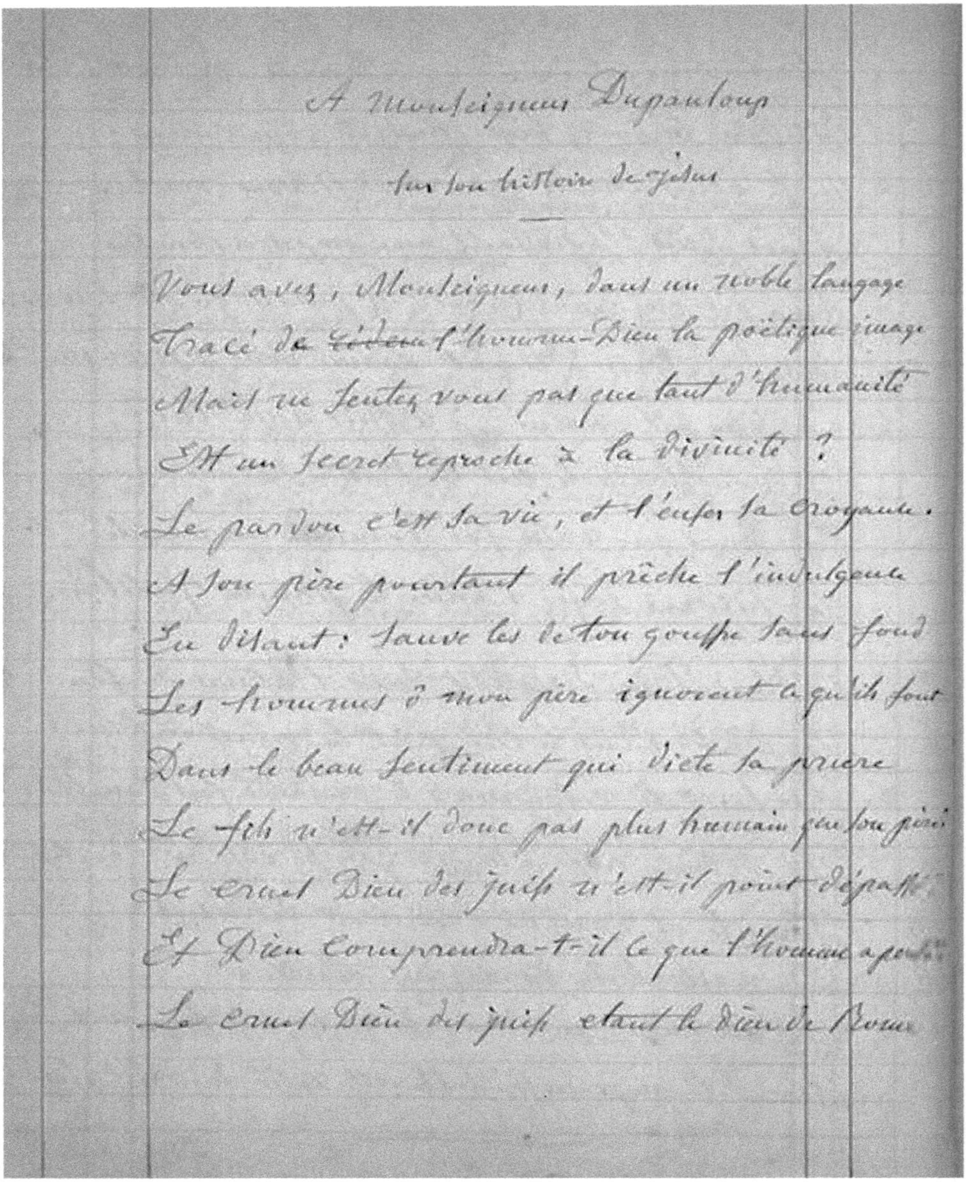

A Monseigneur Dupanloup

sur son histoire de Jésus

Vous avez, Monseigneur, dans un noble langage
Tracé de ~~l'idéal~~ l'homme-Dieu la poétique image
Mais ne sentez vous pas que tant d'humanité
Est un secret reproche à la divinité ?
Le pardon c'est sa vie, et l'enfer sa croyance.
A son père pourtant il prêche l'indulgence
En disant : sauve les de ton gouffre sans fond
Les hommes ô mon père ignorent ce qu'ils font
Dans le beau sentiment qui dicte la prière
Le fils n'est-il donc pas plus humain que son père
Le cruel Dieu des juifs n'est-il point dépassé
Et Dieu comprendra-t-il ce que l'homme a pensé
Le cruel Dieu des juifs était le dieu de Rome

Figure 6 - First page of 'To Monseigneur Dupanloup'

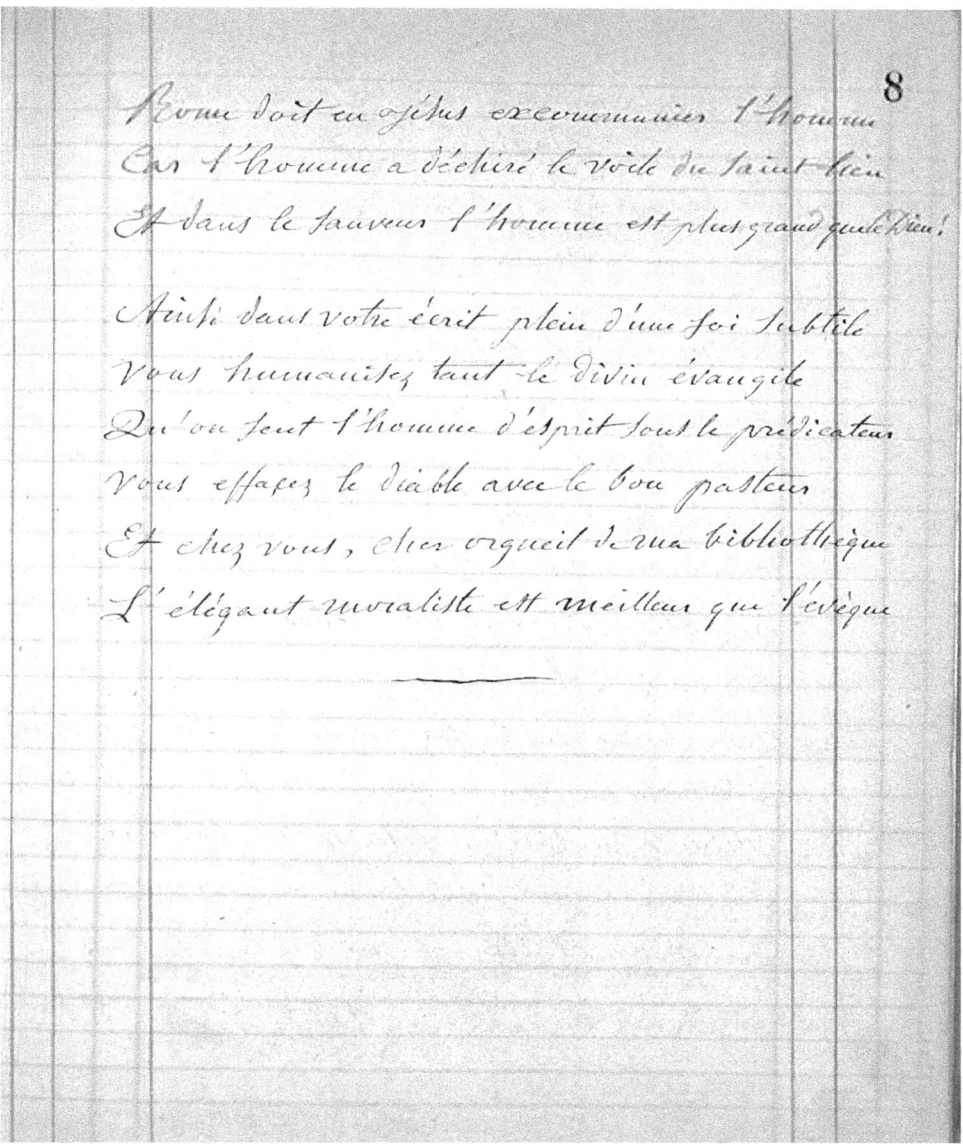

Figure 7 - Second page of 'To Monseigneur Dupanloup'

THE POEMS OF ÉLIPHAS LÉVI

English Translations

1 Ms 1799

"Rhymes and Reason"

by Éliphas Lévi

Folios 1 to 116

[2]

Liberty

Iambe

To Auguste Barbier

Lips with base oaths may be blackened by powder
And redden upon tightening,
Hands with filthy fingers can throw powder then be washed by blood
The blind multitude has its day of victory;
But when the people are roused
They take to the streets against disaster and never for glory
The tocsin has never rung
to announce peace as a source of abundance
The People blinded by fury
Seek and always find a head that thinks
of evil thus, three times evil
for all, as if by chance, the head that replaces
disorder by attack
And makes its body of the populace
Is the head of a villain!
It is thus that the empire belongs to the brave
Thus that the furious Titans
One by one, fought to climb in place
As if to reach the heavens
Dreadful politics is a competition in crime
Tiberius instructed Caligula
Claudius enhardened Nero, their victims have faded away
Marius resembled Sulla
Tallien with a dagger threatened Robespierre
The rostrums are bloodied
The swinging double-edged sword of the People's executioner

---

[1] The numbers on the left refer to the original page numbers.

Strikes and cuts on both sides.

[3]

The Supreme reason is the final agony
The true right is impunity
And all equally ignoring Justice
Disregarding Liberty
Liberty is not a street girl
With her hair and breasts in the wind
Who takes from the gutters her hideous recruits
of the revolt from the moving flow!
It is not a flabby and sordid gossip
who, in an unnameable frenzy
Belted in the red flag and hoisting up her frock
Mounts as a horse a cannon
Oh, Auguste Barbier particularly demented
who, stealing our love
for our liberty, for the Angel of France
chose Théroigne de Méricourt!

For certain, Liberty is not a countess
of the noble Faubourg St. Germain,
But it is even less this infamous girl
brandishing a sword in her hand! ...
She has the divine calling of Saint Joan of Arc
And the strict chastity
She always avenges the rights that we destroy
She is strong in truth
She protects the body of each member
And her golden scales
Reject equally the pikes of September
and the Knife of Thermidor.
She never wished for the blood of Louis the Sixteenth
Nor that of the dreadful Marat
Before her court all must be calm

[4]

She will sign no contract
Other than one between proud dignity and sovereign law,
If she strikes, it is to save.
But she is without weakness and no Captain
may ever remove her.
When the most base instincts as a pack of devouring hounds
Thought themselves beneath the arrows of evil
And in the dark net of demented hatreds
See the social body fall
When the deaf grumblings the Kennels sense
And when the hunter's horn
has sounded to quarry the bloodhounds who leap
baying with hunger, scenting horror
the howlers pressed together and thus they tear at each other,
push each other, bite each other
without every attaining the flesh to which they aspire

Because the Virgin with fearsome eyes
The austere almost dead Liberty that lies dormant
Pale but with a crown on its head
And in its hand a whip, on inexorable watch
to guard against a cowardly assault
Then when the crowd with baying voices
Chokes itself in a final effort
She draws herself upright, wrathful and immense
And touching the almost dead
She galvanizes him, awakens the living flesh
Commands him in the name of the law
Wipes away the suffering from his brown so he revives
And says: Lazarus, arise!
And the true People finally, the People who work
The People of humanity

[5]

Of downtrodden power shall rebuild the wall

and reconstruct authority.
The nation will be amazed and leave behind its drunkenness
All ranks shall join hands
We shall curse anarchy, search for wisdom
Progress shall follow its path
And the soldier displaying the laurels that flower
upon his controlled rifle
The farmer repairing his barns that are filling
The mother offering her new-born
The labourer putting his hand to his cart
The herdsman counting his cattle
And the People walking peacefully in the streets
With their arms of work
The rich without pride, the poor without envy
All, and each to his own.

Shall say whilst demonstrating their rights in life:
"Here is my part in royalty!"

[6]

The Death of Galileo

The god who formulated vulgar belief
read upon the background of science books
Because the eternal may well free himself a little
Even though Rome has decided what God shall do
God, therefore, this God half-blinded by ignorant priests
Found himself placed within their barbaric dogmas
And feeling joined by inquisitors
By decency, saying: these books hold lies
It is the sun that turns and the earth stays still
Uphold my ancient Rome, infallible Sybil
Rome didn't feel the ground move
And when Rome has spoken God must stay mute!
Mute also stay the angels of the stars
But of the immense space having pierced the veil
Copernicus wrote: "You are wrong, Lord."

Upon these insolent words the electorate were afraid
But God always serene in the starry night
Said: to know more of this, let us ask Galileo
Who with confused disavow and repenting
Said whilst striking the earth: It is turning though!
That the angel of death shall come down and take him
But Galileo despite his Roman faith
Trained his telescope upon the depths of the firmament
And the angel dared not take him at that moment
But to an inquisitor trailing the black robes
He appeared, at the doorway of his observatory
The wise one trembled, made the sign of the Cross,
The heavenly instrument fell from his fingers
And Death triumphed; he was no more than a man.
Galileo arrived before the God of Rome
And he cried: Lord I consent myself to Hell
Yes, despite even Satan and his claws of iron

[7]

It turns, Lord, it turns, the Earth!
And you know it full well despite your rage;
I shall even demonstrate it if you wish.
Then God addressed the assembled Fathers
asking them "What do you want? It seems that it turns.
For a long time I have regrettably stayed amongst you
Galileo is damned, I shall be also with him.
I shall leave you the heavens full of your boredom
And so that your faith shall remain immaculate
I shall follow into Hell poor Galileo
Thus God descended into the fires of Hell
The Devil in Heaven took the place of God
And everything was reversed; Paradise darkened
Science with God lit the shadows of the Abyss
Socrates and Vanini became the elected ones
The truth spoke in definitive dogma
Conscience had the right to worth and sincerity...
But the infallible Pope stayed in church!

To Monseigneur Dupanloup

On his History of Jesus

You have, Monseigneur, in noble language
Outlined the man-God of poetic imagery
But don't you feel that such an amount of humanity,
Is a hidden reproach against Divinity?
Forgiveness is his life, and Hell his belief.
To His Father meanwhile he preaches indulgence
Saying: Save them from Your bottomless abyss
Oh, My Father, Men know not what they do
In the beautiful sentiment that dictates his prayer
Is the Son not therefore more human than His Father?
Is the cruel God of the Jews overthrown?
And does God understand what Man thinks
The cruel God of the Jews being the God of Rome.

[8]

Rome should through Jesus excommunicate Man
Because Man tore down the curtain in the Holy of Holies
And in the Saviour Man is greater than God!
Thus in your writing full of subtle faith
You humanize the divine Evangelist so much
that one feels the spirit of Man beneath the preacher
You erase the Devil with the good Pastor
And for you, dear pride of my library
The elegant moralist is better than the bishop.

Paris

To Auguste Barbier

There is beneath the sun a superb city
with green squares full of flowers and lawns
A golden Babel of splendid contours
Alive with bells and carts and drums
Where of past worlds the living renaissance
seems to have mixed together Thebes, Rome and Nineveh
And in which, the Universe holds congress
upon the rows of spearheads far from progress
It is the mind of the world and the soul of the earth
Rival of the Sun, godson of Thunder
It is the gigantic heart where all vessels come to
Which devours ideas and reproduces them.
It is Paris, it is Heaven, it is Hell, it is Earth.

[9]

It is a temple built upon an immense cesspit
There, shamelessness reigns upon a throne of silver,
Works there and plots an intelligent People
There, hides and keeps silent terrible misery
Ancient Sphynx still standing beside horrible vice
And the pale lout, mocking and half naked
Is the human face of this unknown monster.
Paris splendid in vice and innocent in cynicism
Stupid in knowledge, farce of heroism
Spartacus in a false collar, Homer in a lightshade
Comedy or often the sublime as such
Where the sobs together form a peal of laughter
Where gaiety reigns when the scene is over
Hospital de Gilbert, forum of Mirabeau
Where the carriage clinks glasses with the cart
Parthenon, the Pantheon brothel, Gemonian stairs
Shameful success, trading sublime agonies!

The old man who never tires of running
And who without catching him pursues the stray Jew
The great sower of forgetfulness of things gone
Time becomes a dawdler strolling in the streets
Because he has never seen it as resisting the law
Nothing is so abundant or as beautiful as you!
The race of Paris is a living race
Intuitive instinct, knowledgeable idleness
It is Plato defending the basket on your back
It is Voltaire incarnate in the faith of passers-by
It is Chauvin without fear, Prudhomme without reproach
The Devil and Figaro summarized as an urchin
It is the cold whore with an exaggerated hairstyle
In a monstrous frock puffed out on hoops
Who lolls in the sun pulled by two ponies
And made up with a pince-nez her cheek floured
It is the small broken well taught doll
That judges horses and women by their price.

[10]

And who knows how to trill in flowery language
The purest terms ... of a stable boy
It is the fat-bellied trader gloved in fresh butter
Who from disastrous accounts has made profit by charges
And rubs his hands since the market rises
when honour lessens and when shame grows
But it is also, higher than this cowardly beast
Intelligent study that illuminates work
It is the thinker stating laws to the tribunal
It is merit finally correcting fortune
Does the poet Barbier take, by chance,
as the heart of Paris the Mouffetard suburb?
Where, therefore, will he look for his infernal study
and his foraging for work boiling away in a flask?
Has he, to inspire his sickening foibles
Booted himself to the thighs to explore the sewers?
Full of black water that hardly stirs

Does he in his fury take the Biévre for the Seine?

Let us leave rottenness in old Montfaucon
The morgue is far from the Louvre and distanced from Apollo
With abject realism let us avoid foolishness
In a delicious wine let us not put lees
If Paris is the vat in which trodden grapes
pour new wine, the flow still disturbed
within its stormy flanks the abundant nectar
And glory shall overflow from it upon the world.

[11]

The Fall of the Column

Iambe

Whilst Vitellius like a pig upon straw
Lay agonized and bloodied
And meanwhile around him the Roman rabble
salivated with cowardly cruelty
Butchered by knives blunted upon stones
Swollen, ghastly, purple
He wiped away, it is said, neither tears nor prayers;
Snorting like a bull he raged
Then at the final moment he became a man once more
And taken by the pain
He murmured the words that stigmatized Rome
"But I was still your Emperor!"

It was Sejanus' man that was dragged to the Gemanian stairs
Here is the senile man, the cretin
Who sold our France to such ignominy
Here is the excrement of fate
See, such a nose! such eyes! such a sinister brow
See his moustache like fangs
It was the King of the Greeks the Prince of the galleys
The Napoleon of crooks
He was taken prisoner; the troop was sold out
He fought to deliver them
Our honour is withered, the homeland is lost
Prussia is going to devour us
He reigned by theft, murder and adultery
He has made us rotten to the core!...
It is well, noble French, I like your anger
He was still your Emperor!

[12]

You have acclaimed him the bloodstain of December
You have raised him as a hero
The Franks recognized as their chief this proud Sicambri
With seven million voices!
You have forgotten the wild escapades
And Boulogne and Strasbourg
Paris will cost him his palaces, his swords
And the bare-armed of his suburbs;
Because it was the nephew of the Legendary Hat
So dreaded abroad
Of the Great Man of Bronze forever popular
In the songs of Béranger;
The column was there to tell of the glory
Of which he became heir!
The universe was preparing its pencils, his memory
and the Pope his font.

Misery! This man took Olivier as his minster!
Seven million times misery
This man was mad, this man was an oaf
He was still your Emperor!
Ah cursed column the populace said
It was you then that betrayed us
Trochu deceived us, the enemy surrounds us
And our homes are invaded
Courbet told us clearly that your bugle
was nothing but a giant reed pipe
Go to Hell with Imperial glory
Henceforth doomed to nothing
That from the exiled nephew, the wave shall be united
Down with brazen lies
Of glory, throw it down to the ground
And make way for supreme contempt!

[13]

Let us go engineers, from manure make ropes
Scaffolds, capstans
Unbolt the bronze and smash the faces
Of our fathers, old combatants
Cut away with your heckles the base of the column
Then stand ready for the signal
And you, come to repeat the great shadow of Cambronne
Your word heroic and brutal!
That's right, turn, heave; the ropes are taut
Here are the Lilliputians
Who upon great Gulliver, comfortable at the centre of the streets
Torment their dreadful ties
The colossus did not seem to wish to come down
But still after a cracking noise
Within the attentive crowd a cry was heard
We saw a slight movement

It was in fact the Caesar who moved ... he leaned
The column snapped in the air
Under the bronze in pieces we saw the white stone
Like bones piercing flesh
Then with a dull sound an immense dust cloud
All movement ceased
Broke into a hundred pieces and made the earth tremble
Even the sewers shook:
From the Emperor's hands slipped victory
Adieu Napoleon the first!
Never has been seen so much bronze and glory
Falling into so much shit!
And you were not the soldier of the pyramids
In the defence of an old soldier!
You have never mourned the wounded then
After the stupid attack
The children spat upon the crosses of their fathers

[14]

[*In the margin*]
Go! may the tatters of the column pursue you!
May it bite at your heels
May its relief be engraved deeply in living flesh
May she bloody her minions

And foreigners are watching them!
Ah this day follows the downfall of ignoble miseries
May fortune keep us
Remove the dead leaders, unburn the ashes
Is there nothing more monstrous?
And you who until now have brought us down
Speak of hideous anarchists
That made of you a ghost insulted in the grave?
Nothing, they say with fury
But his name disgusts us and we wanted him to fall
It is the uncle of your Emperor!
Ah well your Emperor in his demented cowardice
Was dignified by your failures
It is said he sold the martyrs of France
And you blew them out
May this bronze avenger in all places follow
Your unpaid crimes
May we melt him into bullets and make you a shackle
to drag the column at your feet!

The Painting of Chenavard

Great Sphynx of painting, oracle of the grave
Your enigma is to date; here is your painting:
In the mysterious night where Christ agonized
Over our illusions the clouds broke
Forgotten religions gave themselves to combat
The earth went up to the heavens, Heaven fell down below
A darkened dusk with livid tint
spread its pallor across the immense emptiness.
From Hormuz and Ahriman unnamed spirits fought over the body of Jupiter Ammon.
The ancient fable under the traces of a muse
Wanted to quickly fix time by showing Medusa,
Time held under a false Venus and her lovers
And at her violated face he still strikes away.

[15]

Mercury took to Heaven from where the reaper strikes
Pregnant Pandora dead in bed from lack of Hope!
Prometheus is the captive of another Jupiter
And looks at Christ without hoping for Luther.
Justice is overturned, blind with magnanimity
Has dented her scales by striking at crime
Marsyas flayed ruled the sacred valley
And insolently warmed himself under the feet of Apollo
On the right hand of God is power and redress.
The Fates in Heaven peacefully spin their thread
To crown a god hidden as under a spell
The spirits fly at the head of Death
Drunken on divine bile, but dreaming of ambrosia
In a fatal circle turns poetry
That the Chimera holds around ideals
and invasion giving the terrible signal
France, drunken without a doubt, with a strange horn
Seems to call odious the god of a barbaric world

And we see lit from afar burning without brightening
The eyes of the Ferris wolf ready to devour all.
You were, Chenavard, only a sinister poet
And events to you were a sacred prophet
It seems that Jesus, Jupiter, Jehovah
Nature, love, all is dead all is gone
The savages from the north share France amongst them
Life has no attraction, Death without hope
From his ancient, prestigious altar has been stripped
And the incense of mortals by death has been sullied!
Paris fills with undignified funerals
And with its own hand has ripped out its entrails
The Ferris wolf away from its other siblings
Has fattened itself upon blood and human remains
Alas, all is lost, all up to honour itself
The dogs through the gutters drag the diadem

[16]

Bloody Liberty has dirtied her flag
Death no longer counts its horrible troops
Because from a foul and revolted multitude
We wash away with blood the bloody stain
True right is now nothing, strength makes the law
Power is masterless and the temple without faith!
Oh, Master, I understand the profound sadness
of your great painting that makes the world afraid!
Kings pushed it away, Paris didn't want it;
The critic whistled whilst admiring him quietly;
The doors to our palaces were firmly shut to it;
And in Luxembourg for it to be able to enter,
It took the cannon of our invaders,
The dissidence of the great guns of our vile oppressors
And the ruthless order crushing their audacity!
In the collapse the giants made a place for themselves
For you, O Chenavard, the thunder has spoken
Your painting fills the ruined palace
And the prediction that we shall tax madness

shall be for our nephews our immense epitaph!

Hormuz and Ahriman

Directing the seasons the solemn convoy
Hormuz was sat in its eternal calm
At its feet nature breastfed in silence
The worlds suspended from its enormous breast
When suddenly drawing himself up to his full height
Ahriman said: I am like you creator
It is me that makes evil! and God who encourages me
Admiring my audacity and proud of my bravery
To occupy the boredom of his eternity
Creating from chastisement his terrible majesty.
I said: no more justice! And she: no more hope
Thus God smiling replied: My vengeance
Is to allow you even to cause insult in My name
I shall crush your rage with an eternal forgiveness
Your torture is yourself, your torment is your hatred.

[17]

Your devouring treasure is human folly
Destruction is all completely in the heart of perverts
And my absolution oppresses hells.
Torturing with my day their night which it laments
I peacefully do good which torments them
External order imposes itself upon their mocking pride
My renewing good deeds tear at their heart
My reign spreading forth overturns their empire
And to strike them down I need only smile!

Believe in God

Believing in God is to think that He is good, just and wise
That work honours him and fear outrages him
That he wishes that by doing right he shall let us adore him
Without questioning him and without destroying right.
It is beings recognising him as the Father
Who moderates the strong, in Whom the feeble hope
Who reigns without caprice and in whose future
He shall keep eternity to cease punishment.[2]
To know and to love him thus is therefore His true religion
Through all cruel dogma obscurity insults Him
His symbol is written in the immense universe
Read by humans through various sign
But for pure truth unchanging till the end
Humanity uses it for hate, for blasphemy
And despite the hells invented in His name
For to never absolve him He pardoned Nero

[18]

As He must even forgive a homicidal priest
Even a true believer, a perfidious Pharisee
But as He is without hate He is without pity
And in His bounty He does not punish by half
The penalty is the evil provoked by our crimes
It is disorder that in the end we are victims of
And by which the Redeemer is never saddened
Because to redress all he has eternity
Oh, God, Whom in my heart I feel You think and live
I never look for Your commands without a book
Books are lions, all wordless powerless
Time still changes the ageing Doges
Your name does not resonate on the human side
All voices to say it are unheard and in vain

---

[2] * God was on His Throne, Osiris was on his throne

Your Name is not a noise and Your Religion, Lord,
Is not an instrument, it is the breath of life!
Your Houses of stone imprison my soul
Which to overturn them strikes alight its flame

What am I saying? My heart itself filling with hope
Feels Heaven tighten upon it like a press
The deaf droning of hymns on Earth
Are lost upon rising on the voice of thunder
And the thunder dies away, the solemn song of organs
In the temple muted by eternal silence
shapes and voices, the heavens and images
My soul has seen the boundary and touched the shores
And in the dark azure of your expanse
My distraught desire falls quickly
Ah human religions of no matter which edifice
Where tongues often confuse artifice
Do You deign to see, My God, the errors of Babel
When Your face brightens with gaiety at the smile of Abel?
A flower upon which a sunray searches its lips
Drinks lovingly the sun which touches
And with its soft sighs embalms the sky

[19]

Our soul is a flower in which Your grace is the nectar
Our tears are the dew where Your sunshine soaks itself
And Your love is the air that our sap rises to!
In You we let our errors be forgotten.
To love You, Lord, is to live and living is praying.
We live to love, we love to live
The universe is a temple and Heaven is a book
Wherein we read Your name a thousand times adored
Whilst at the doorway of Your Holy courtyard
A hundred diverse religions with strange symbolism
Resembling the hundred colours of an Archangel's wings
Nuancing the dark golden or vermillion reflections
Of the same light and the same sun!

Eternal Loves

Eternity! Always! These words, supreme error
Or truth for a day mean to say: I love you!
To love is absolute. Time is not love
One moment of happiness an make a day eternal.
Eternity is God, it is beauty, it is the soul
It is the creative fire of which time is the flame
It appears to us then hides from our sight
Happily for us or we should be as gods
And the gods too often in love with mortals
Deserted Olympus or Hell for them.
Eternity all-great that divides a moment
Wife of this god that shows himself inconstant
To create for once, of yourself, fecund
You are not the nursemaid and the mother of the world
In the midst of the Empyrean and floating suns

[20]

Your infinite duration is the space of time
As the immensity of space unveiled
Is an eternity of stars upon stars…
Time pursues Love, Love overcomes Time
And when two overwhelmed hearts touched by Spring
Caress with joy ephemeral Hope
It is eternal love that makes its immense work
Thus we say: Always! Forever! and often
This infinite Hope escapes upon the wind
But it is never lost: upon new banks
It likes to explore like swallows do
When one love ends a Winter comes
Then another love grows and the heart remembers
Love, divine secret that a kiss reveals to us
Vague premonition of a life eternal
An already certain measure of a splendid future
Or of a day that is no longer bright souvenir

To feel Your warmth is to live! to know you
Is to be a man and to love You is to be a god perhaps

Yes, loving You forever, understanding Your beauty
Is heaven; in enjoying here is eternity
Because you are merely a passenger in our bad dreams
And even their paintbrush coloured by lies
That quickly sketches You haphazardly upon the canvas of days
Names still eternal the phantoms of love
Ah the poet André, this proud and gentle genius
This new Arion of ancient Hellas
Who destroyed without mercy despite his golden lyre
Against a bloody pitfall the stormy Thermidor
The chants of Neera and of Fanny, my master
Would have avoided death if he had been able to know
His heart with desperation and rage armed
Too altered by love would never be loved
The melodious songs of which his exile cradles us
Are the tears of Tibullus wiped away by Propertius
His lascivious Camille, lover without beauty
Soon discourages ardent voluptuousness

[21]

She has not even running from vein to vein
The fever of Délie and her Roman passion
She is a courtesan of bored kisses
With a plaster tint, eyes in vapours drowned
I would give Lesbian and Camille and Délie
For a single golden hair from pale Ophelia
Who alive with love and maddened by pain
Sleeps in death caressing flowers
I love Romeo her sublime companion
Oh from celestial love magnanimous passion
If Chénier had you as he did not have the universe
To console his heart to inspire his verses
Beloved following only you! His virile rages
Could not affront civil tempests

Miserly with his days and flying higher
He would not have decorated the scaffold with his blood.
And it matters not to love if thrones falter

Of which the debris of old prejudices mounts up
From the wayward people the ebb and flow
Are thrown to the echo of names and superfluous cries?
Love is a summit which fears not lightning
Love is a high-flying eagle that shakes powder
From its superb wing, drops for an instant
Climbs back up to its eyrie where happiness awaits him
Above clouds and in the peaceful sky
This eyrie is suspended inaccessible to the Roc
And there, the bird of the gods, even equal to the gods
Takes his ease eyes fixed upon the sun.

[22]

The Poet and the Realist

The poet

O Vale of Tempe, profound solitudes
Banks that the Spercheios wakened with its waves
Musical waters and melodious woods
That live and make sing the memory of the gods,
Great monuments flowering under the Italian sky
O Venice the red, Oh Nice the beautiful
Exalted places, beloved places, inspirational exiles
No, I do not dream of your enchanted sites.
I like better my obscure and solitary retreat
Full of memory and tender mystery
I love more the dried bouquet that forgot
When she left me yesterday my white Ophelia

The realist

Dried bouquets mean nothing to me
I wanted a beautiful and good housewife.
The worms are bored … but that is only when we study them
I wanted something I could feel in my bed
But I want a love who shall be a resource
And who will put something to feel in my purse

The poet

I do not know which look fascinated my heart
A gentle dream of the child of my soul is victor
O virgin are you not the blonde Aphrodite?
Is it you that the mother-of-pearl was to rock upon the waves
When the sky from the rose borrowed its colours
Enflaming its azure and making it rain flowers?
Would you have been Galatea to young Acis so dear

Or simply the sister of the pale Neaira
And the gods having stopped to contemplate your eyes
Did they leave the heavens to roll in abandon

[23]

As such that Winter shall prolong his empire
To only leave of Spring that which from your mouth respire?

The realist

What nonsense? My pretty listen to me
I am neither banker nor poet nor king
But as soon as I see you, by faith an honest liar
My head spins and I feel stupid
If you also had I know not what desire
By mixing all this we would have such pleasure.

The poet

The flowers in the meadow being all closed
The nightingale sang the song of the roses
The leaves trembled drunken upon new greenery
Beneath the sighing of the breeze and the wings of a bird,
The light wave where floated dying petals
Murmured to the lawns amorous words.
The crickets prolonged their whispering, gentle cry
The drops of water hanging from the prickles of holly
The banks of watercress were all covered
The midges danced, and the green frogs
Shaved themselves to listen to the distant sound of the horn
Their emerald corset and their golden spectacles
Me, I asked of you in the quiet breeze
To the nightingale in the woods I said Ophelia
To the overcome leaves I repeated quietly:
Is she close to you? Don't hide her from me.
I followed in the water the reflection of my dream
In the holly leaf, for you beautiful child of Eve

I said harden the rain as diamonds
I said: mutter little charming crickets
For not being here when my heart reclaims her
Silver little flies that the sun makes shine
Whistle, fly, dance, tell her to return.
The sound of horns in the woods make her remember
That a familiar bird desires to be her prey
Marsh frogs jump so that I may believe

[24]

That you feel her here, that you take care
To announce her presence and with voices here:
That it is in her honour that you make yourselves beautiful
That the white dragonflies are your cool umbrellas
And that you are wearing to see my gentle treasure
Your emerald corsets and your golden spectacles.

The realist

That may be pretty, but the young girl is wise
I have just asked your beauty's hand in marriage
And I shall take her, Oh God, I am telling you quietly
To have children and pull her socks up
She is most reasonable and understands that you should live
That a household at ease is better than a good book
She knows that a good worm is not worth a penny
Adieu poet

The poet

Adieu whore… adieu cuckold
Give me a rude word in favour of a rhyme
Adieu Mistress, adieu, you are either sublime
Or stupid and love laughs into his neckerchief
To find Ophelia in the bed of a suitor.

The Wisdom of Love

We may in passion abandon the reins
When the soul is resplendent with sovereign clarity
When we know how to forget ourselves and suffer as a god
When you have hands of gold you can touch fire.
The vulgar one ignorant of my loves might laugh
And whistle Jupiter who changes into a satyr
But the lightning, dormant and covering its brightness
Knows well that the satyr is still Jupiter!
The raging bull who digs deeply into the ground
With his bellowing makes the world tremble
The swan that is Leda may to an eagle be equal
Her eye fixed and shining climbing towards the sun
Alcides is much greater when his triumphant hand
Quelled his vigour upon the spindle of Omphale
Heavily armed with knots of iron

[25]

Dragging the hound by the maw to the gates of Hell.
I like to see the giant led by a small child
Being lowered by love is human greatness
The love that puts itself above is merely no longer conquered
And we are never base at the foot of beauty
It is to please love that we search for glory
War for love argues victory
Love holds back night to bring back the day
We are noble, we are proud, we are great by love.
Krishna, the pastoral god, the conqueror of souls
Drew to the desert virgins and women
And the sound of his flute held such gentleness
That by charming the ear he ravished their heart
Thus he said to them: Oh virgins too weak
Why have you left behind your mothers' houses?
Women, why have you left your husband's roof
The mothers shall weep, and the men be jealous.

And the virgins said, and the charmed women
Replied: by a mortal yes we were loved
And yes to listen we left forgotten
Our mothers, our husbands, our tarnished heart
Deserves blame and severe punishment
But your song is gentler than the voice of a mother
Your love is more beautiful than a husband's
This is why, son of Heaven, love us and take us
The magical chords of your divine flute
With an eternal breath swell our breast
They penetrate the spirit with light and with fire
And we wish to die under the kisses of a god!
Ah no matter what of happiness the world thinks
When it is shared, love is innocence
For all those forever held under its charm
Love is forever the flute of Krishna

[26]

But of a dishonest love let us fear the impure voice
Let us quieten pride and listen to nature
Let us not throw away the hope of our eternity
Into an insolent gulf of stupid beauty
Let us dread Scylla with her howling belt
And that our madness shall at least be foreseeing
Of passing pleasure let us always extend a hand
Without ever deserting for it the right path!
Tied like Ulysses by word to my fast
I listen, I look and I love the Siren.
My mermaid is pretty, she has blond hair
Her blue eyes are fringed by long, golden lashes
All completely she comes out of the blue waves
And I know that she does not have the tail of a seal
Then she disappeared and seemed to have forgotten me entirely
I am thus happy to be bound to her

Because otherwise, thrown into the gulf, swimming
I wanted to search for her from shore to shore…
But she reappeared when I no longer dreamt of this
Laughing at my transports at my superfluous tears
She approaches and holds the cup of ambrosia
She sharpens again my bitter jealousy
I make ready for her games, I enjoy to suffer
I am saddened sometimes to the point of wishing to die
And I smell a perfume of which her kiss makes me drunk
That suffering and death as well as love… is to live
I find my verse again, my twenty year-old dreams
My Winter reblooms, my snow is a Spring
I am happy to see this blonde Aphrodite
Rise suddenly upon the foam of the waves
Whilst my vessel gently carried
Tends towards science and immortality!

[27]

Anacreon

Old Anacreon said to young girls
Come to me, come my gentle doves
With tenderness and flowers I want to perfume you
I look like winter but my hearth glows
And all seasons have the right to love you
You of whom for me sight is a renaissance
O do not smile at my second childhood
And fear to take part in its happiness for a day
This joyous poet too old for hope
And yet so young, so young for love
At the hour where the gentleness of sleep is so strong
I received Cupid who knocked at my door
The child shivering laughed with a victorious air
I reheated his fingers, prepared for him his arms
And in mistaken hope that brought me to tears
With a cruel arrow he injured my heart

To his triumphant beloved I harnessed myself without fear
And he beat me with a sprig of Hyacinth
God angered once more seemed to arm himself again
Then seeing me weary, sweating in large drops
Walking with heavy steps and my way confused
He said to me: Old man you no longer know how to love
I drank bitter tears upon his vermillion lips
When he went, crying, stung by a bee
In the breast of Venus hid his despair
I said to him: child this bee takes revenge for me
The child amongst tears laughed with a strange air
I said adieu to him; he said to me: till we meet again!
Upon that night I locked my window and my door
I armed myself heavily
In saying Cupid will no longer be victor
But he in great mockery of this invincible old man

Took the form of an invisible arrow
And the plumed monster glided into my heart

[28]

Ah well I want to love I sang with victory
The Atreides, Cadmus, the heroes and their glory
I tried the strings of my lute one by one
One said love the other said I love you
Adieu then, heroes adieu even to glory
My lyre wishes to reply only to love
That love raising her light tunic
Shall pour me happy wine upon a bed of ferns
Of our passing years the way is uncertain
Bring perfumes, give flowers in bloom
I wish today to be all consumed by roses
Who knows if I shall be able to perfume myself tomorrow?
You laugh Lycaris Oh see, young maiden
All these little loves are of my family
They drink from my cup and nibble my bread
Come and see the sun in my flagon that shines
Who knows if we could get drunk tomorrow?

If my hair is white and you are blonde
Blonde Venus blossomed in the foam of the wave
Who from her father formed white hair
White lilies by contrast embellish roses
And the redness of dawn appears enclosed
In the white clouds of a radiant morning
As volcanoes in snow have their heads covered
As flowers with a white brow have a green stem
The dove with a pink beak loves the white pigeon
The hymen gives the virgin a white crown
And of the amorous weeping willow who over the waves bends
A gentle reflection whitens the trembling foliage
Aphrodite amidst her subjects waves
Appears like a lily amongst violets
The white moon to the flowers shows itself every evening

Upon your charming breast where youth spends itself
Let my foolish head forget its agedness
And close to your breast my hair is again black

[29]

And during this time the old sages of Greece
Cultivate boredom in you to celebrate wisdom
And you put death in your Pantheon
Oh sages, believe me your melancholy
Your forgotten books, your crazed doctrine
Are not worth one verse of mad Anacreon

Guillet the Freemason

Guillet the Freemason is not a vulgar drunkard
He walks with his back straight and his feet square;
He wears his false collar straight to look well
He is incorruptible in the place of silence
Show him the scaffold, show him the gallows
It is always the scaffold that we see him choose
In freemason slang the scaffold is the bench
There the dreadful brother and his jovial friend
Skilfully wield the axe and the dagger.
The dagger is a Eustache for chopping meat
The axe is a knife of longer length
And the assassin Hiram is often a rumour

[30]

With red powder, with white powder
He knows how to hold out when Sunday comes around
He keeps secrets known for a hundred years
He has foresworn to never tell us
That in Winter the hoarfrosts hold court
And that the weather is nice when Spring returns
He has splendidly accomplished his task;
He knows to cry: Come to me, O Children of the Widow
When a blasphemer strikes against him
He makes movements wherein mystery pierces
And his name upon the bench where his spirit works
Is preceded by an F with a triple point.
He takes from Solomon the sacred words
And keeps in his pocket something golden
Where the square is opposite to the compass angle
He has Hebrew words that he knows not how to write;
Ask him quietly what it means

I can assure you that he won't reply
At the back of his drawers he keeps hidden

A wide blue ribbon adorned with a trinket
Where we see Mac Bénac written in shorthand
Who is Mac Bénac? an Irishman perhaps
Miserable silence? it is the secret of the master
It is for this many years ago that Hiram's throat was cut.
Are these people mad? are they making mockery of the world?
No, of a deep and meaningful allegory
Their head was once the discreet confidante.
His naïve successors are happy to believe
And no longer even know at the bottom of which cupboard
He has hidden the key to the secret cabinet.
(X) *place here the forgotten verse*
Guillot the freemason is not a vulgar drunkard;

[31]

He walks with his back straight and his feet square
He wears his false collar straight to look well
He is incorruptible in the place of silence
Show him the scaffold, show him the gallows
It is always the scaffold that we see him choose!
(X) *verse forgotten by the copyist*

But they have no less neither companion nor master
Than the actions of a puppet to know each other better
Before their apprenticeship they were Moabon;
Then they had despite the fall of Rome
Their Scottish Grandmaster named Joseph Prud'homme
And Guillot who aspires to be called Gabaon.

The Hell of Lovers

I

Ah long verses! Frankly I am surprised
That we'd be able to read a page at a time
When their cadence is sad and monotone!
Of Despréaux the rigorous laws
The chosen words, the number, the measure
And the repose that we name a pause,
And the pathos, finally what he lends
Causes us to yawn and even he swears
That long verses have a tragic success
And that we are bored in magnificent terms.
Have you seen the Olympian brow
And the pallor of Leconte de l'Isle
The cold disdain of his unmoving lips
And his regard that no longer believes in anything?
He has the spleen of the English the poor man
Meditating upon his marmoreal verses

[32]

His despairs are hyperborean
He is frozen like a false god of Rome.
Victor Hugo at least is amusing
He knows how to draw from haunting ideals
Nightmares for the universal atom
We laugh, we tremble, we cry upon reading it
It is sublime by force of madness
And seizes us with its absurd expanse
And then with verse he overturns the laws
He is grotesque and terrible without choice
With his errors, with his naked truth
He knows how to mix crazy things
That in the night die like a squib.
Hello to you, you big kid!

Quasimodo was created as an urchin
And your thinking to the comets is fastened
Me who am unable to grasp them by the hair
I shall sing of the hell of lovers

II

Whilst all the first seeds
Sleep still under muddy silt
When from chaos the shadowy cloak
Floated upon the water of the cold frog ponds
Survived love which is intoxicated by chaos
And with nectar smeared its face
The old sleeper then became intoxicated
And from the earth he separated the waters
To keep them longer without drinking them
He salted them if we believe in the story
Thus how came to be tarnished the seas
That lived on later was born Venus more fair
Than her azure and sometimes more cruel
Than torment and bitter chasms

III

Finally, the earth ingenious lover
Allowed his author to see him completely naked

[33]

And affectionate nature at the heart of the fire
Shows itself ready for the caresses of God.
Now of the old man when the eternal widow
Of nature has extended her breast
He was surprised by a rebellious angel
Who meditated upon an amorous crime
During six days with the enflamed bride

God lavished celestial dew
But on the seventh day he finally slept
As he was exhausted by tenderness and effort
The Devil then more available and more slender
To nature offered his black bait
The poor mother with the red-hot flanks
Bit into the deadly apple
And the good God was treated as a man
Despite his lightning bolts and his burning furnaces

IV

Of his scandalous and uproarious awakening!
By His wrath paradise trembled;
From a kick received in the fight
For nine days Satan plummeted.
But from the old man the woman was pregnant
First by her husband, then by her lover.
She gave birth first to the Holy City
Where spirits perch with soaring heart
This first fruit was the pure seed
Of Jehovah, our world in its twin
Came at the wrong time…and it is slander
That attributes this to diabolic love.
But in her belly filled with lust
And the conflict between the Devil and the good God
After her childbirth it is said that nature
Felt the heaving of those aborted by fire
Of handsome Satan was the pure seed

V

From her husband she hid her evil

[34]

But one lovely evening, as if to young stars
To amuse herself Heaven gave a ball
To the firmament she lent her veils
Then glided without light and without noise
Having for a guide her negress the night
Outside the manor of the divine Sganarelle.
It was tim; the maternal pain
Came to seize her at the gates to the garden
That our elders had named Eden
But she had had fears so dreadful
When her husband stormed about in the heavens
That she mingled some horrible monsters
With the tender fruits of the amorous Archangel
Because, all at once, twisting her mouth
Like a child who spits out a bitter fruit
She delivered in her last labour
Love, Death, Pleasure and Hell

VI

This is why the dreary solitude
Of Sinai on one solemn day
Saw Moses emulating the eternity
Of the Holy mountain descend with horns.
This is why the dark Jehovah
Against nature is so deep in anger
That he allows to be found the soft bitter apple
By the heirs of the great sin of Eve
Against his woman alas too bedevilled
It is said he made a plea for separation
And the Senate of Holy Zion
(that is the council of the Church Assembly)
Back-to-back send the couple away
And submits us to the laws of a jealous God
In deciding that Mother Nature

Apart from her regard is nothing but an impure beauty
That she must be finished and opposed

[35]

That otherwise we must console our father
By sharing in love his misery And for this we must marry.

VII

The hell of love is therefore marriage
Ah if Pyramus had married Thisbe
Upon his sword maybe he would have fallen
To free himself from the annoyances of the home
Or if rather of his wife at heel
He had found her veil in the forest
He would have replaced his dagger in its sheath
And would not have taken the trouble to die
He would have said: my poor wife! Finally!
She is no longer, it is a sad ending
If I could have I would have delivered her
But all is said and done because she is destroyed.
Then Thisbe hastening to chase him
Would have said rascal you do not want to die!
I have for a husband a hero of whom I am proud!
To punish you I am still alive
Let us go arm in arm
And we shall manage it is the right of spouses

VIII

Ah if Saint Preux had married Julie
He would have been stupider than Wohmar
And more betrayed the poor devil, because
By being jealous he would have done something mad
Julie though would have given sermons

Enough to tire the wives of Mormons;
(but Mormons didn't exist yet)
Hear this pecorate teacher
Reproach her for what she has done for him
And exalt her with rage and annoyance
This Saint Preux or Rousseau (it's the same thing)
Say: What! Here is the prude that I love!
She is in agreement with my enemies

[36]

Adieu happiness that I promised to myself
I leave this knowing woman here
To go and live with some servant

IX

With the same wire are tied two lovers
And each to the other they are tormentors
One wants to fly the other wants to stay put
One wants to go to the woods the other to town
Or to tug or to pull out neck feathers
Or to dislocate a foot, or is crazy.
Yes to make well two lovers it seems to me
That it is sufficient to tie them together.
It is so that love is not a melting pot
Ove is not the act of a notary
Ratified under the paunch of the Mayor...
Love is all: it is the Devil or it is God
It is happy when it breaks its chains
When it confronts and overcomes hatreds
He is happy as victor and detested
But he sleeps once he is accepted

X

Am I going to conclude in the hatred of a notary
For crimes of infamous adultery?
No, adultery is cowardice
It is an ignoble and base impurity.
He who takes the yoke uncaring about her
Must punish himself by staying faithful.
Do you hold in esteem this scrubber of sewers
Who by awful snaring of the disgusting mess
Of an old pig has just cleaned up the place
And that often with kicks we chase away?
Happy lovers know in truth
That joy loves liberty
Hide for a long time your happiness from the world
Free yourselves of the knots of expansive interest
But if ever a maternal hope
Becomes for you both together a duty

[37]

If you need to overcome the love that brings you together
Submit yourselves to buy peace
Marry for the sake of your children… yes… but
To be happy do not live together
Close your eyes and never plead!
Of what use is verse?
And you ask me of what use is verse!
Ask the bird under green foliage
Of what use is the song he always repeats
Ask him why nature is a poet
Ask the Zephyr ask the branches
Why their sounds are in accord with the murmuring of the waters
Ask of the sun covered in gold and in flames
Of what use is his clarity that makes arms sing
And the bird will reply I sing without knowing
Of what use my song is from dawn till dusk
And the tree will reply in its vast branches

I tremble without knowing of what serves the greenery!
And the sun will say I love the enjoyment of flowers
Without knowing of what use is my fertile heat
And the rose will say showing her blossoming flowers
I flower without knowing of what use are roses.

[38]

Cypriot Wine

A Song

One night Bacchus in the arms of Cythera
Having during the day surprised the red god
He chained in their drunken laziness
And by their fires he stole from the sun.
Then fertilising the immortal loveliness
Of the goddess with an enchanting smile
He refilled her with double the heat
And with pure wine he swelled her breasts
Cypriot wine is the son of the golden sun
My cup is empty, friends pour again
Yes of Venus it is the fact he overflows
She has pressed the roses of her breast
Of Anacreon the pale messenger
Has drunk from this divine stream
Then to dream of his innocent madness
She sleeps upon the enchanted lute

And his plumage drunken upon voluptuousness
By kneading makes the lyre breathe.
Cypriot wine is the son of the golden sun
My cup is empty friends pour again
The eagle who drinks of the eternal harvest
Far from nectar turns his forgetting beak
From Cyprus he sees a new desire
And to drink of it he leaves the skies
At worst he prefers an arbour
And let's go the thirst of thunder
That coils like a sacred serpent
To draw himself in the bottom of the bottle!
Cypriot wine is the son of the golden sun
My cup is empty friends pour again

[39]

With Cypriot wine still all embalmed
Of Anacreon drunkenness whispered
He slept offering up his beloved mouth
To a thousand lovers that his breath kindled
Then around his reddened lips
The flowers of the world brought the harvests
Upon grapes the swarms of songs
Suspended there with the bees
Cypriot wine is the son of the golden sun
My cup is empty friends pour again
Cypriot wine embellishes my thoughts
That which I seek it says without effort
It makes my rhythmic heart burst forth
To my gentle dream he lends his accord
He makes youth blossom again in me
From roots god quashes anger

And his madness has such gentle charms
It makes wisdom jealous
Cypriot wine is the son of the golden sun
My cup is empty friends pour again
In our blood the light circulates
Let us climb radiant Olympus
Between our feet the earth accumulates
The table lifts and we are gods
Each embraces the other saying I love you
And we are unaware in this divine conflict
If the kiss is not yet wine
Wine is only a kiss from god himself!
Cypriot wine is the son of the golden sun
My cup is empty, friends pour again!

[40]

To Victor Hugo

After a first reading of his songs
Of the streets and of the woods
Of suns unleashing their chains
Putting to grass the winged horse
That curves the brow of great oaks
Underneath its blue foot the veiled shadows
Then invent Virgil
In celebrating Jarnicoton
And knead the agile calf
Of Lisbeth or of Jeanneton
In the basin of washerwomen
Upturn spilled love
And make foamy stains
Upon its channelled smile
Is not the way to reap harmony

From nature to the heart of the fire
Is to joke with the genie
It is to be naughty with god
Hugo, this book where your agedness
Unkempt in cheeky laughter
Of a titan it is drunken folly
It is an enormous nakedness
And I would like to take the veils
Of a virgin with longer habits
To cover you in our retreat
The muse is not a girl
And it is woeful, by heaven,
Drink a toast in La Courtille
To see the great prophet Ezekiel

[41]

Your smile has an air of sarcasm
Your sighs are puns
Your joyousness coughs like an asthma
Your burning dreams are ovens
Your feet eviscerate your prodigies
And your joy has the air of a lion
Who makes great swipes with his paws
To catch a butterfly
You are not at all Gallic my dear great man
Your leaps break the way :
When you wish to pick an apple
The tree stays in your hand
And I find better the folly
And the good sense of the grey man
In the great pont-neufs of Colmance
Than in your proud amphigouries

After a second reading
I put water into my wine
From the author of *Les Misérables*
This new work is full
Of adorable silliness
It is trivial and divine
It is a full glass of genius
And reason must search in vain
To wrinkle its severe brow
A baroque word is thrown
And Prud'homme all morose
Believes it to be a great sin
But he takes from it a rose
Sometimes flowering kisses

[42]

From this delirious fairy
Seem to spawn a mouse

And it is always a smile
It is risqué, but it is pretty
It is shocking but full of verve
On each page we bend a corner
And the horns of Minerva!

Seriously

Never disdain eternal nature
Always young always dazzling and beautiful
It is our illusion that causes ugliness
There is nothing of Satan in the work of the lord
God makes truth and man tells falsehoods
And the error that sleeps is interpreted by a dream
A spider is beauteous in its proportions
Heaven in creating it had its intentions
But you offend indignant nature
By lending to the bee the stomach of a spider
Each thing besides in its place should stay
And nothing out of season should present itself
Hair is golden around a beautiful face
But filth if found in the middle of a dairy
We can never rhyme Sylvie with Goton

[43]

Nor the soul of Virgil with Jarnicoton
We can see our servant with a greedy eye
But we cannot make a dishcloth splendid
Turlette has two eyes like Callirrhoé
Ninie has white breasts as well as Chloë
That's good: combine then and Ninie has operatic airs
For a joyous refrain keep Turlurette
But do not pretend that the cats in the granary
Miaow a more lovely verse than that of Andé Chénier
All music is gentle in its own harmony
And the art of choosing well is the gift of a genius
The street has its new bridges full of great gaiety
The forests are eloquent in their simplicity
But the birds perched under the green branch
Do not make songs of grotesque structure
Apollo no matter what we say is more handsome than an ape
What does the nightingale say? He never says Margot

If in some dark and badly kept boutique
We happen to see a beautiful spider's web
Provoking the feather duster to stretch out in flight
On the profile of Minerva a skull of Saint Paul
The web in my opinion adorns the images very little
If I found flowers amongst old cheeses
I would not find their perfume more exquisite
A peasant is after all less clean than a marquis
I shall permit you to love them in their simple nature
Satin women under robes of baize
But never stitch together licentious poet
A rhyme of baize with verses of satin
Sometimes in a rugged marvel of a quatrain
In enchanting the spirit you scorch your ear
In a flower that we see gently opening
You throw in snuff that makes you sneeze
I fear when you mix them and the laughter and jokes
That you will not change the graces for bitches

[44]

And yet who could be irritated by you?
You mix into manure adorable jewels
You sow beneath our feet the treasures of Asia
With the dead leaf and mouldy straw
Racine beside you is no more than orgeat
And Racine though was never a cad
As he was conserving harmony and rhyme
You are simple and gentle when you are sublime
Ah you have verses that please Heaven
You lend to love honeyed words
We no longer criticise, we cry and we love you
And embellish you unto even ugliness!

The King of Israel

A Hebraic Hymn (x)

The God of the universe said to the King of Israel
Come and be seated on my right and put down your sword
Your enemies fallen into a dreamless sleep
Keep beneath your feet eternal silence
Your sceptre is in Zion your reign is over the world
Your empire has overthrown terrifying kings
Look around you at your defeated enemies
And reign triumphant in a deep peace
The laws of your power govern destiny
The brows of your nobles at the clap of thunder
And I brought you from the belly of your mother
Before I awakened the morning star
(x) who believed that this grandiose and wild song
Is a psalm that we sing at vespers and
That Catholic teachers pretend was made For Jesus Christ?

[45]

The Lord swore it by the honour of glory
And the sermons of God are never erased
You shall be before Him preacher of victory
As Melchizedek was the King of peace
The eternal at your right has brought back His power
 Israel must reign by the hand of its King
He will break the chiefs on the day of His vengeance
And their vanquished sceptres will fall before you
He Himself shall judge those who wage war upon you
To finish their disaster He will go and find them
Then He will come to take you and will make you walk
Upon the smashed brows of the masters of the earth
Who therefore walk so proudly under a devouring Heaven?
It is the King of Israel who shall never cease
He shall stop with his hand the cold waters of the torrent

And always more superb he shall raise his head!

The Fox and the Crow

Ah what intractable reader
You want more again!
Ah well here it is: here is the fable
Of the fox and the crow
It is new as fables go
New like the pont neuf
The frog with the bull
Are veritable witnesses of this
But we have criticised so
The fable of La Fontaine
Rousseau finds it so full
Of risqué teachings
That for this severe judge
Of which I understand the argument
I shall task myself to do it
No not better, but otherwise

[46]

A crow upon a windowsill
Took a cheese, a fox noticed him
And scraped him against the wall
Saying: Oh hello my master!
You are magnificent in this black habit!
As it is such a pleasure to see you
What must it be to hear you?
You must have a voice
Strong and gracious at the same time
A formidable and tender voice!...
Caw! said the crow, the cheese fell
And master fox swallowed it.
From our flatterers this is what to expect

The Two Stars

A Fable

Two stars shone in the cloudless sky,
An invincible magnetism made them seek each other
We saw them get closer
And their gentle rays blur their mirages
One said: I love you! and the other replied :
I love you! a sole desire guided them both
It seemed at least: but of the two, the most beautiful
On seeing the rays from her sister invade her
Stopped all at once, started to tremble
And said whilst moving back towards the eternal night :
I seek happiness, but I fear betrayal ;
In your confusing light
If I unite myself with you I shall be lost!...
The other replied to her: go you do not love me

[47]

In friendship when we think to ourselves
We should not say we love each other
Exchange in friendship has nothing to do with chance
The interests of the other are ours
We are all alone, we are two
We find ourselves one in the other
What we give we do not lose
It is in the depths that we economise
Even so we do not aspire
To the promised fruits of the earth
Love is the reduction of Heaven
It never makes anyone poorer
Its essential character
Is to enrich when it gives

The Chastisements of Victor Hugo

It is for the gods above all that it is necessary to be severe
The gods owe the laws and example to the earth
The halo of a brow brightly lit
Shows double the blemishes if it is an idiot's brow
The muse with a golden sistrum must have pure hands
And must never put bile into wounds
This is why the poet of vile outbursts
Must suffer forever his punishing words
When Juvenal embittered by the cries at school
Carried to excess his biting hyperbole
His satires kept in their obscurity
Of a vengeful Jupiter his sombre majesty
To punish Crispin for his accrued fortune
He never picked up the injured in the street
He looked with disgust upon ignoble Romans

[48]

Mutilate this Sejanus who perfumed their hands
And did not go sullied by grandeurs too punished
In disputes the rest of the dogs of the Gemanian stairs
I understand that a pig searches in the mire
I do not know if ever an infamous barber
Master Olivier Le Dain in water cloudy and dirty
Searched for residues of royal filth
But I cannot understand that an inspired genius
A radiant thinker, a sacred pact
Plunged into the sewers his patriarchal hands
Dragged his golden wings across faecal things
Too much hatred destroys the rights of reason
We don't execute Mandrin by poison
Whomsoever is in fury is not a victim
They are a jealous brute, an illegal judge.

We do not slap the men we kill
I understand that in your exile your soul must have suffered
Victor Hugo, I admit that far from the fatherland
Bitterness exalts itself and becomes fury
Whilst Napoleon made a gloomy Caesar
I understand your rage tied to his chariot
But when the chastisements have finished their task
When Caesar had fallen the insults became cowardly
We do not trample upon an agonised Claudius
Hugo, this is why I suffer upon reading you
By ceasing to reign Claudius ceased to live
And more dignified than him you shall erase your book
But if for a bit of gold your muse made profit
From the fall of the masters and by impunity
If hatred survives when power is dead
Your anger demeans and is no longer the strongest
Your muse is a ghoul outraging the graves

[49]

Who with a corpse-like power exhumes the scraps
And sells greedily her works of a vampire
It is the last, final shame of the empire!

The Song of the Captives

A Hebraic Melody

On the rivers of Babylon
In the land of exile where God had abandoned us
In our barges at night we went to cry
Upon the willows in the midst of the river
We hung our widowed harps
Which seemed for Zion to tremble and sigh
We hid ourselves far from the banks
To no longer be able to hear the voices
Of the cowardly and savage oppressor
Who said: sing to us your hymns of yore.
Oh Jerusalem Oh my mother!
How can we sing upon this foreign land
The hymns of the God of Israel?

[50]

Jerusalem if I forget you
To my palate may my tongue stick
May my dried hand feel a deathly chill!
That I shall never see you again
If you are not the hope of my heart
And the principle of my joy
And the dream of my happiness!
Remind yourself, God of vengeance
Of the fury of the children of Edom
On the day when blaspheming Your name
They overturned Your power!
They cried: Destroy it!
Burn the whole of Jerusalem!
Destroy, overturn,
Tear down the last stone!
Courtesan of nations

Misfortune! Misfortune upon you impure Babylon!
Happy is he who one day shall repay with interest
Your cowardly profanities!
Good fortune for the warrior hand
Of the just and triumphant avenger
Who shall with your last stone
Crush your last child!
Upon the willows amidst the river
We hung our widowed harps
That seemed for Zion to tremble and sigh
On the rivers of Babylon
In the land of exile where God abandoned us
In our barges of night we went to cry

[51]

Jacob's Ladder

At great heights the spirit must always hold on
But the infinite exhausts it and forces it to climb down.
It will fall straight to Hell if God wills it
Two circles drawn together by light and by fire
From the great divine axis are the extreme poles
In their attraction the forces are the same
Hell attracts the angel and Heaven demons
The heights are in turn deep chasms
Because the whole world turns as the Earth
For eternity the spirits are at war
To change abode and seem to conquer
The central passage that we call dying.
Hell makes Heaven bigger, Heaven digs out the abyss
We are by turn triumphant and victim.
All strive in Cain all die in Abel.

The world of spirits is the Tower of Babel
Which plunged its reflection into the black and sleeping water
When I rise joyously my shadow laments
And descends vaguely into my lost reflection
Nothing has ever risen without having descended
Souls have their night their sleep their dreams
Their black and white sun rises morning and evening
The reprobates of white are the nobles of black
And hope in growing makes despair grow:
But it is the same God that our eye light or dark
Clothes in light or covers with its shadow
He extends both his arms one in the shadow where his fingers
Trace with fire formidable laws
The other in the light where his fingers soaked in shadow
Write upon the day a dark dogmatism
And the expansive pendulum of the universal soul

[52]

With the Creator's work wishes to associate itself
Changes from black to white its course half rounded
And becomes the motor of the clock of the world
Never shall the vanquishing angel rise to the heavens
Without carrying along as captive a furious demon
And always outcast in the dark abode
Will not fall without damning a beautiful angel that weeps
All damned in Hell suffering for a victor
That shall replace him, his cycle revolved;
And each victor shall celebrate in absolving the crime
Of one damned in turn redeemer and victim
God wishes to be offended to become Saviour,
And the Devil in his place upon the Lord's advice
And of Job upon his manure his condensed tears
In stars in the heavens shall be one day placed.
An insolent joy is the crime of the gods,
(x) And it is in being innocent rather than misfortunate
(x) verse of Lafontaine

As such the shadow and the light trick our foolish eye
And God does not permit useless suffering
He who suffers is enriched, to suffer is to gain
He who rests loses, enjoyment is expenditure
When we are ruined we return to our work
He who suffers most may freely spend
Then after each day of work accomplished
The soul before sleeping bathes in forgetfulness
This is the great law, the law of balance
That we cease to submit when the spirit becomes free
This it transforms, it changes place
It is under the infinite creator with God
This final Prometheus that Jupiter adores
And Lucifer victor becomes an egregore
He is the soul and the king of a radiant star
Because God makes suns to house the gods

[53]

Ours is abode where Jesus has rallied
The immortal spirits of Moses and Eli
Enoch preceded them in this brilliant visitation
Upon this earth which suffers he shall return one day
When by the elements one by one exhausted
The earth by fire shall be transfigured
Then God in Heaven shall have only the chosen ones
Sufferance, death Hell shall be no more
The city transparent and pure as glass
Already built in Heaven shall descend on Earth
Then we shall taste fortune and peace
All the streets shall be swept forever
A new Heaven shall luminate a new earth
And we shall remember eternal life
This is the vision of which with his plume of gold
Saint John the Evangelist wrote to Tabor

And he continued to the sound of seven thunders
Upon the Isle of Patmos between seven lights
Our age believes no longer in the visions of the saints
Heaven from science has veiled its intentions
The altar is weakened faith has been obscured
In exhausted mortals the soul has hardened
Something though must soon transpire
Through the curtain ready to be torn.
Let us not renounce, let us pray, faith is hope
Man must before all believe in his ignorance
Admit what he knows, search for the truth
And say he is ignorant without disbelief
Then without deepening unfathomable mystery
Shall sleep like an infant in the arms of his mother.

[54]

Anacreon to his Dove

Pelias, my little dove
You are loving and beautiful
Your pink beak gleams
Your plumage is delicate
You coo with an air so tender
That it is a pleasure to hear you
When with slight tremblings
You fall asleep to my songs
I sing with a gentler voice
The bough beneath the bed shaking
Does no more discretely
Has a baby's gurglings no more charm
Because it seems to me, little white bird
That for you we see Venus bend over
And in coming to admire you
She hears my sighs.
When gently my hand touches you
When I press you upon my mouth

I breath voluptuously
All the perfume of your beauty.
But what! you seek the window!
Do you desire a new master?
Would you like some youth
Curly-haired, shaven, flighty and handsome,
Who will take you, my little dove,
To give as a present to his love?
Alas my sweetheart in times past
You took bread from my fingers
In times past you were faithful to me
Are you like the swallow
Who flees at the decline of fair weather?
Are you hunting for love

Do you thirst for travel
As do all flighty birds?
Go, you shall repent
One day, too late you shall return
Powdered and maybe injured
To my abandoned abode

[55]

Anacreon will no longer be there
Your regrets will be superfluous
Your poet without his dove
Will be lying in his tomb
He shall be on the dark banks
Crying for his loves in the place of the dead
And be consigned to Asphodel
Far from his unfaithful dove.

The Love of an Old Man

Love in an old man is paternal love
His most tender desire holds nothing criminal
And never forgets or shocks
He has all he wants wanting only good
His heart is never jealous and expects nothing
He accepts that which he is given
His late wisdom finally appeases his heart
A pure attachment overtakes the fury
Of his unbridled passions
His soul is filled with calm and sunshine
And the hours for him with the same smile
Pass linked one to the other.
Thus when the eternal created the elements
Of loving chaos with long upheavals

[56]

Tearing the expansive space;
All the rival worlds leapt disunited
And their explosive sounds in infinite chasms
Destroyed the silence
Fire in hand the stars ran
The furious heavenly bodies devoured each other
The days and the nights were jealous
The rocks tumbled to rape the sea
The volcanoes fired themselves up and took from the ether
The comets as their wives
But the vanquished earth finally rested
Under the kiss of the sky the world settled
The universe had love for its beginning.
The waters gave birth to the land and took back the fire
And creation was able to contemplate its God
In an imperturbable ecstasy

Do we know why our hearts beat agitatedly
And why our Springs towards burning Summers
In shaking off their flowers throw themselves
Why worry constrains our loveliest days
And why we walk upon feeble loves
That our desires always outpace?
It is because our soul thirsts for harmony and peace
It thirsts for undying happiness
Love! Love without injustice.
Love that by pride has never been beaten
Pure love, true love, love by virtue
Raised up as far as sacrifice!
It is love that shines and that does not absorb
This love of which hope challenges trespass
Because it holds the key to life

[57]

Its abnegation is enriched by giving:
It does not busy itself by pleasing or surprising
Loving is all it desires.
Jealousy is vain in wanting to keep it
It is handsome without seeing it and without looking at itself
Is the sun absorbed in itself?
It is ever rich with its own treasure
It is that which digs, it is the gold mine
It is the monarch and the empire
That which we love so can distance itself from us
Far from it we might suffer but we are not at all jealous
We love it even unfaithful
We always save for it our forgotten benefits
All ready to return, to die at its feet
If ever its heart reminds us.

But let us not be darkened by superfluous dreams ;
Hearts thus united no longer separate.
No, you are not a chimera
Love of which the ideal renders the gods more gentle

Love of which grandeur lends even to the spouse
The sublimities of the mother!

[58]

The Dialogue of Jacob and of Adonai

Or the battle of Jacob with the Angel

Adonai
I am God I command Heaven as Hell

Jacob
I am not man and I wish to know why I serve

Adonai
You serve to obey the law of your master

Jacob
He who wishes to command me must make himself known

Adonai
You shall know me well enough when I make you tremble

Jacob
It is fever then that you wish to resemble

Adonai
I am stronger than you fall to your knees rebel

Jacob
True righteousness is never the nicest

Adonai
Hear the thunder it speaks for me.

Jacob
Thunder is a noise that grumbles as you do

Adonai
I created the sun, recognise my power

Jacob
My eyes did not see the birth of your sun

[59]

Adonai
I could destroy you

Jacob
I would be nothing
And your existence for me would then be as mine

Adonai
I am adored by all of nature

Jacob
I do not understand it, explain your prayer for me

Adonai
It says that my hand plucked it from nothingness

Jacob
When nothingness might know of this it will laugh

Adonai
Look at the infinite, you shall see my domain

Jacob
The infinite is the end of human science

Adonai
You know well that Heaven was not created by you.

Jacob
Why was it by someone other than me?

Adonai
Because the universe did not make itself

Jacob
And you, who created you? is it the same problem?

Adonai
I exist because of myself

Jacob
And the universe as well

Adonai
No, it is I who made it

[60]

Jacob
It is badly done
Ignorance and evil fight over the earth
Plague, catastrophes, injustice, war
Walk there always with their devouring swords

Adonai
Men are perverse

Jacob
It is because they are ignorant
To escape evil they commit evil themselves

Adonai
Your vain reasonings are nothing but blasphemies
You must believe in silence and bow down before me

Jacob
So you make yourself judge and yet you hide the law

Adonai
You know the law

Jacob
Each people has its own
Do you lack the means to promulgate your own?

Adonai
The means, insolent! Here is my decree :
I shall by my touch bend the back of your knee.

Jacob
Ouch! I limp, Lord, the fact is true
And you are either the Eternal or the Devil

Adonai
Go then and preach my name

Jacob
Lord I am ashamed
To have a limp argument to go by

Adonai
It is perfect people that you need to struggle against
A person with a limp walks straight in the eyes of one with no legs

[61]

Head-to-head we have discussed this here
Without finding between us a word of truth
I bless you Jacob we are partners
You were born very clever to supersede your forefathers
You knew by your art as a rural pirate
How to swindle sheep from your father-in-law Laban
Be the father of the Jews, trade and make your fortune
Pare away the sun, falsify the moon
Write words of me that I shall protest
And name your book as Holy
Adieu Jacob adieu my son and my prophet
Only you understand how much the human race is stupid
And you shall place it entirely under the law

Of a God more menacing but less cunning than you!

The Poet

Dreaming of the memory of eternal music
The poet is a fool for whom foolishness is beautiful
He has in his ears a faint ringing
He possesses a great magical blindfold
That transforms for him toads into geniuses
And the discordant cries into gentle harmonies
He only sees beauty he does not believe in evil
Love this enraged animal desire
Is for him only a trait that brings friends together
When cinders die he sees flames burn
New-born babies these awful little dwarves
Leaving the womb all red all slimy
Their fists clenched and their eyelids closed
Are to him beloveds born amongst roses

[62]

Women these mirrors of capricious change
Who long only pride cloth and money
These cherished vampires of foolish youth
Egos excited by frivolous infatuation
Beings that logic has always irritated
Nurses of untruth and of absurdities
Are for him merely dead elves and fairies
He sees them as periwinkles and coiffed myrtles
In a faint ray of dancing light beside the water
Their importune babblings area s birdsong
A sigh from their lips embalms even the flowers
The rays of the sun make upon them a crown
The gentle Zephyr waits for their life-giving kisses
The grass becomes green again beneath their enchanted feet
When they pass by the air vibrates and is purified
And their grace is the love of all nature

Thus by so many errors charmed poets
Love with a fury and are not loved
Le Tasse became crazy for his Eléonore
Dante no longer pleased his Beatrix
Petrarch became due to Laura illustrious and disdained
Chénier brought Camille to indignant sarcasm
To have her in the arms of an oaf perhaps
Surprised this beauty of whom he believed himself master
We know of Rousseau enchanting paintings
Their burning lies intoxicate their viewers
Louise de Warens preferred a prig
And of isolation the sinister ravings
Made him choose Thérèse a filthy slut
Who for a groom betrayed him it is said
Myself I adored with an insane love
The young Noëmie my beautiful fiancée
Who in my poverty reproached me
And one day abandoned me for a bedridden old man

[63]

When Faust from his prison wished to free Marguerite
Whom he had never forsaken after having seduced her
Because it was Valentin the brutal aggressor
Arriving out of breath from having dishonoured his sister
Faust was prevented from escaping but at the last moment
He came and saved her by losing himself
The madwoman turned upon him in fury
And said to him: leave me, you horrify me
And to beg, happy to have found her
The voices of hypocrites sang: she is saved.
Ah it is because the poet is a great pariah
On the day of his birth an Angel cried to him
Walk under the contempt of a maddened crowd
Be always exiled going from town to town
And may all doors to you be inhospitable
Plato shall banish you crowned with laurels
Of smiles for you fortune shall be miserly

And the hospital for lunatics shall await you in Ferrara
If as Camoëns without asylum and feverish
You do not die lost amongst malingerers
Women might love you after your death perhaps
When from amongst jewels a boor an old reciter
Offers then your richly illustrated verses
Under a cover with golden clasps
If only a library having been able to understand you
Had found some silver to pluck from your ashes!
Sing for nature and like the birds
Lose your chirping amongst the branches
Do as Lafontaine; love solitudes
Long noiseless sleeps, facile studies,
But don't be easily lavish with your verse
Know that the poet is alone in the universe
We love to insult them when we admire them
We want to poison their innocent delusions
And the world plays with vile passions
Wants to strip him of his illusions
If he suffers then it is well deserved superb rhymer

[64]

Will he still cultivate the role of Malherbe
When the blasé century upon sarcasms fed
Returns to old thistles of the soul of Scudéry?
That he should become amusing if he wants us to applaud him
Whether he is a mountebank or an acrobat of vice
And that with a strange colossal barbarism
He sometimes glazes his paradoxical verse
The golden rule, the chosen expression
Wisdom in one word is no longer poetry
You must make them feel in a warming manner
The dew has verses that drink coffee
You must suspend from the nose of an indignant Minerva
Poems woven from spiders' webs
Make from his genius a fountain like no other
With diamonds stone the sun

To play bowls make the stars round
Prefer dishcloths of the most heavenly tissue
Deck yourself in a modest cotton hat
Loosen the belt of Artemis ennoble Margotton

And all this to please who? My God what do I know?
To the little exhausted ones coming out of school
And who in vengeance for forgotten Virgil
And in their own often shrivelled versions
Have need of a moustachioed heroic muse
Capable of hardening their love for schoolboys
Thanks! I like even more poets from the olden days
Search like Gilbert the exile laughing at the woods
Or contemplate the dreamer close to the good Lafontaine
The sun cut by shadows on the plain
See the birds nest upon blessed bells
Follow into the deep blue your infinite dreams
And even to girls lend decency
In not saying that you don't believe in their innocence
Go about like a bee around fresh bushes
For little children compose songs
And neglected, by forgetfulness my hymns shall be consumed
Just as the tree abandons to the wind its dead leaves
I hope to forget those who in turn forget me

[65]

To open my whole soul to wonders of the heavens
Without seeking to know if for other marvels
Midas King Midas had long ears
Ah despite the contempts of the common impostor
The poet is divine whilst he is creator
Homer a beggar in his old age
From Olympus in his turn gave alms to Greece
Poets errant insane radiant
Were immortals then they were made gods
Because this is of the ancient Sphynx the magical riddle
Man had to create God to be a god himself

The sombre Ezekiel, the priest Isiah
Who put the day back on the clock of Achas
The lyric Baruch and the two prophet kings
Were in Israel admirable poets
David cowardly tyrant but inspired psalmist
Was by poetry absolved and consecrated

Solomon all lost in infamous debaucheries
Left behind songs more beautiful than women
As such poor errant poet without hearth or place
Be proud of your rags that disguise a god
You have never committed the adulteries of Daoud
Nor like Solomon slit the throats of your brothers
Be proud to be a poet and a king
The prophets were unfortunate like you
Their songs overturned the ancient priesthood
With others enlightened biblical mystery
Sing, Heaven hears you, you have no rival
The saviours of the world have walked an equal path
You have no servants but you have no master
And of old Béranger who did not wish to be anything
The mocking refrains the malignant songs
Made the muddied ones on their thrones shiver
Be rich in ingenuity and great in independence
And you'll find yourself more glorious I think

[66]

Instead of being a valet to Napoleon the Third
To be a child of Adam nobler than kings
And amongst all the sons of this apple-eater
The gentlest, the simplest and the best of men

Christian Humility

Ever when the titans in revolt piled up
To reach the heavens Pelion upon Ossa
Or when Laomedon patron of manoeuvring gods
Forced them by his theft to submerge their works
Ever when from Tantalus an odious bouquet
Delivers infanticide to the appetite of the gods
Or when of Capaneus struck by lightning
In the noses of the immortals laughed still the powder
We do not live with a pride so measured
So laughable, so drunkenly assured
So paradoxical in its presumptuousness
So victorious in his expansive stupidity
That this hypocrisy with false eyes and kisses
Pressing its yellow brow against the cold marbles

[67]

That this vanity weeping upon the ashes
That flatten themselves continuously and believes to be able to descend
That this abasement of divinity
Of which Christian teachers have made humility.
As such this man, insect trapped in the dust
Believes he has to get down to crawl upon the earth!
Of his immensity holily forgetful
He bends his head to clean the heavens!
From fear of being splendid he throws himself into mud!
He cedes to the eternal his angel's halo!
But you do not know giant equal to the gods
That the earth horses' excrement the sun
Resembles a parasite with grey and black skin
That a child makes fall with his ivory comb
That you yourself are lost upon this insanity
You are not even as a flea to the divinity
That you have no reason no measure no place
And that to humiliate yourself you must have some audacity!

We carry with us, we crush under our footsteps
The infinitely small that we cannot see
What would we say if we know that the volvox
The mobile germ or the ferocious mite
To be saved by our jealous pride
In bending in two curves itself before us
But to observe us do they have a telescope?
Ah well if the sun was a microscope
And if I am an attentive angel looking down below
Searched for us upon the earth he would not see us
The least escapes us and we lose the expanse
Ignorance ends, doubt returns
We know not to which God or which Devil we should pray
And still our pride wishes to humiliate!
Get up on your feet climb onto stilts
Find to make yourself grow some mountains too low

[68]

Climb like Nadar in a giant balloon
Inflated like a desire that dies of nothing
But if your balloon bursts jump astride a hippogriff
See it escape like a white dot the peak of Tenerife
Climb up to the zone where lungs gasp for air
Turn higher upon the wings of demons
And you shall still be as a speck of dust
Snatched by the wind from a clod of earth
And the angel of the sun looking down
Had he the eyes of a lynx he wouldn't notice you.
And you think that your God jealously wanting to be man
Will die in pain for the theft of an apple
He to whom belong great vergers full of trees ever green
Letting in the infinite universes fall!
You think the sun will stop in its track
For Hebrew priests braying before the ark

And that, with the trumpet eternally echoing
Shall fall before you the walls of Jericho!

You believe that by inflating yourself like a frog
You shall fill from yourself the chasm that God dug
Or that by flattening yourself like a popped balloon
You can sigh: Lord I am saved!
Imbecile and cretin! go, infinite glory
Shall never warm itself upon your ignominy
Your greatness before God is noted as zero
But do not be disheartened: that is your number
Saint Cucufin at a royal table
Decorated with egg yolk his already filthy beard
That to be thought of as an imbecile was happy;
But poor Cucufin the turn is already played!
You are no more than a triple drunk by grace and by system
And many more than a thousand times you did not believe yourself

[69]

Saint Francis brimming with grotesque songs
Danced in Italy in the eyes of naughty children
Just as King David foolish patriarch
Who leapt around in his nightshift and span before the ark
They both thus pretended to be delirious
And depreciated themselves to be admired
They were as full of pride as that Diogenes
Spread out in the sun in his obscene misery
Where he found Alexander opaque, and, comely and handsome
Said to him: you are casting your shadow on the lip of my barrel!
Diogenes at least was not a hypocrite;
Modesty was hardly his favourite virtue,
And against the abuse, the abuser revolted,
He will never sin by too much humility.
But these blessed monks with squinting lids
Chewing on verses and pursing their lips

But all these swindlers shaven or hairy
The Carmelites shaven, the Capuchins bearded
These people belted with twine and their feet in rags
The skull without thought and the neck without cravat

Having for God the Devil and the fear of the law
The unfortunates! many are of such good faith
These people have more pride more bile, more hatred
With it you could armour the human carapace
They honour God by their abasement
Their eternal filthiness must serve them as ornament
They make a luxury of Heaven with their sterile efforts
Of their unquestioning faith in their useless old things
They carry all of Hell upon their beaten brow
And the Devil smiles in creating their virtue

[70]

The Dispute Between Jesus Christ and the Devil

One day gentle Jesus on the summit of the mountains
Encountered Mephisto, the prince of demons
Who seemed very reluctant to meet with each other
And here are the words that they rhymed together
So that we never say again the Christian universe
That sacred dogma rhymes with nothing:

Jesus
All the poor in spirit are happy upon the earth
Because they possess the reign of my father

Mephisto
Yes, the poor in spirit are happy down here
As long as we mock them they don't understand.

Jesus
Happy is he who weeps, we shall dry his tears

Mephisto
Having a dry eye in the first place would have more charm

Jesus
Happy are those who are gentle, for they shall reign.

Mephisto
Upon wolves, if the wolves deign to save themselves

Jesus
Happy are those who hunger for love and for justice

Mephisto
They will die under the table or stuff themselves with vice

Jesus
Happy those of clement heart, we shall pardon them

Mephisto
Yes, forgive always, always you'll be beaten

Jesus
Happy is the pure of heart he shall see God without confusion

Mephisto
And the world in laughter shall crush it in the mire

[71]

Jesus
Happy is the peacemaker he is the child of God!

Mephisto
And God with battles sets the sets the world on fire

Jesus
Happy is the humble and oppressed that we shall proscribe what is just!

Mephisto
He shall die friendless in his august distress

Jesus
If they take your robe offer your cloak

Mephisto
We shall release the hounds to have your skin

Jesus
If someone strikes you on the cheek offer him the other

Mephisto
You will get two slaps then good apostle
And the crime insolent shall stay upon its cart

Jesus
Give unto Caesar that which belongs to Caesar

Mephisto
If Caesar gave you a cross as recompense
What did your children owe to Caesar? power!

Jesus
Be quiet son of Satan you know what is written
You must not tempt the Lord Jesus Christ

Mephisto
The Lord Jesus Christ seems to me hardly credible
If he has not the good sense to refute the Devil

Jesus
It is not to a demon that I deign to speak
Here is the truth that I have just revealed
Man that I have chosen shall be docile by grace
And reject with suspicion that which surrounds you

[72]

If you want to belong to me jump up in a single bound
Hate your father and your mother and live as a vagabond
Don't wear sandals or a baton or a belt
God provides for the needs of all of nature
As the lily of the field Heaven shall clothe you
Feed yourself with the wheat ears that your hand steals
Bless your enemy so that God will curse him
Love your attacker so that God may punish him
Your gentleness irritating the wraths of God
Piling upon Him the furnaces of fire
Ignore your parents, live a celibate life
My best friend is a voluntary eunuch
I did not come here to bring peace
But the sword, hatred and bloody forfeits

I have obscured to my please my salutary dogmas
By fear of correction and of saving my brothers
The world detests me, they shall detest you

But one day beneath your eyes the world shall burn
And to take you away to my holy heritage
I shall descend from Heaven seated upon a cloud
Then the human race almost all criminal
Shall fall forever into the eternal abyss
Whilst waiting flee, go from town to town
Eat when you may and preach the gospel
Will they refuse to believe in and listen to you?
Shake that which I have taken pains to bring:
Your supporters and know that one day this dust
Will use your mockers to enflame the whole town

Mephisto
Well touché! You are seeing my bad side
And your teachings that I have invented
Seeming to strip me of all my power
I shall never reach an equal delirium

[73]

You have dispossessed me, it is a treachery
But in your place I would speak truth
Man, that nature may always be dear to you
Open your house, support your father and mother
Do not believe that bread falls from the sky
Look at ants and honey flies
Resist injustice, to good stay faithful
But never dream of eternal vengeance
Love well your companion and the people of the universe
Without preoccupying yourself with Heaven nor with Hell.
When religions give birth to hatred
They are the sewers for the human family
All bloody altars are horrible altars
Do not believe in gods who damn mortals

Leave freedom even to your adversaries
And, most of all if they are wrong, do not belittle your brothers

Do not tell them what is right just to harm them
Do not pin your hopes on a final disaster
All perishes in this world and all regenerates
The eternal stays calm and has no fury
Keep you soles clean, but when they are dusty
Do not throw the powder into our eyes
And do not plunge us into the lake of asphalt
For having misunderstood your hypocritical speech

Jesus
You have spoken well. It was by forcing you to it
That by taking from error that I wished to begin
Listen now to the foundation of my doctrine
And finally confess that it is wise and divine
Prefer justice of all that is dear to you
And duties of the soul over pleasures of the flesh
Give yourself without reserve to those whom your soul loves

[74]

For your own it is kind to set fire to yourself
Take good for evil, love your enemies
Deprive yourself of happiness and permitted pleasures
To dry away tears and help your brothers
Keep yourself from pride, from bitter words,
Give without calculating what is given to you
Give even your life and God will return it
The heroism of good is the duty of the just
More than anything sermons make your words august
Do your duty first, God watches over your rights
Walk the straightest righteous paths
Never take on the dreaming of a pale anchorite
But wash your face and perfume your head
Do not be too hasty to judge your neighbour
That no hand shall be held out to you in vain

Never abandon your legitimate wife
For two separated spouses adultery is a crime

Love God most of all, your neighbour more than yourself
Love and support then, this is the whole of the law

Mephisto
Lord, just this once I have no more to say
Your first discourse was a satire
Of imposturous priests and I understand it well
But following those people there I feel myself very Christian
I shall therefore by their hand be baptised
To then oppose your true system
Because God has condemned me to propagate evil

Jesus
No, God never created the infernal genius
Your critique has the force of a lever upon ideas
By resistance still strong and fertile
Go, you shall be too proud of your damnation
Receive therefore despite yourself… my benediction

[75]

With these words Mephisto the archangel with a savage look
Made himself into a heap, turned over and disappeared;
Screaming like someone burnt, exploding as he ran amok
He ran towards Veuillot hiding himself whilst growling
Don't be surprised by this anachronism
Because the anti-papist man, the bitter man, the man of schism
By the Devil already in the invented Hell
Hatched then his egg infallibility
The elves with pleasure fashioned his throne
With thick lip and a drunkard's nose
Reserving with care this good spirit made flesh
For the century of rust after that of iron.
For the time when France had its liveried bandits
To the Bagne it went down from livery to livery

And had to in order to find a moment of respite
Bend before Thiers decrepit Talleyrand
For the century oh Trochu made his boastings
Or Bicêtre came to burn the Tuileries

In the time when d'Arboy taken by I know now whom
By Pilate forgotten perished for Blanqui
Don't hide from me the horror of this unclean world
It is corruption, it is the end of the old world
But where such injustice strikes with impunity
That it is not yet the final judgement!

[76]

Before the Council of Rome

Concessions and Confession

Paintings are for the eyes an agreeable lie
Poetry is the art of interpreting the dream
The Mystic Symbol is the veil of the gods
The umpire of fate hides from all eyes
All history is lost in the web of fables
The world hungers for incredible recitals
There is not one mortal in this importune world
Not a king, not a god who is not fooling someone
The most tender mother with her treats
Propagates in her infant loveable untruths.
All love is a liar when it fears to injure
And in the order of love to betray is to caress
We caress the hope of the vainest chimeras
And there is the secret of priests and of mothers.
It is necessary to know how to treat with a wise doctor
People of feeble spirit and badly made brain

And when the truth too forceful or too cruel
To our affections may become lethal
Once we wish to avoid that which it makes foreseen
To speak is a lie and be quiet a duty.
Let us leave to the afflicted the happiness of maybes
And see as false all that should not be
Jesus condemns the man zealous to say all
Who says to his equal you are nothing but insane
Because all men as we know have their grain of madness
Let us never remember that which we should forget
The world's full of fools and whosoever does not wish to see them
Should stay in his chamber and break his mirror
Who said this then? I do not know the poet
But it is like a proverb and everyone repeats it

Now Jesus put in their place the denied pleasures
Of speaking of the rope in the house of the hanged
But the priests still wish us to remember
Sins speak of them and commit them again

[77]

Let us scribe these errors in an eternal book
Let us admit at their feet a criminal desire
To make a true crime from an error we confess to
To immortalise our traces in the mire
Ah then because you should shall I make a vow
At their feet? No truly, but in the face of God
I am going in my youth to claim dementia
Do not mistrust me, I have done my penance
I accuse myself oh my God of having for twenty years
Worshipped as true revolting dogmas
Of having believed from a god in paternal hatred
Keeping for his children eternal torture
And of having, not though without shame and without combat
Burnt away my youth in impure celibacy
That feeds in our senses infertile debauchery
And delivers our sleep to sordid nightmares
Then of having it close to the bed in which my father died

Without modesty, without mercy, without regrets without remorse
Burned that which he loved: a book of Voltaire
Of this noble old man august relic and dear!
I accuse myself of having doubted reason
To have had from fanaticism saved of its poison
And of having regretted the dreadful belief
Of which dumbing terror affected my childhood!
My God! In this pain of which I feel myself pressed
To which Christian priest should I be confessed?
Which bishop to implore who is not my accomplice?
Which Pope will understand my tormented thoughts?
Alas! All these crimes that alone I dare to cry for
Are the virtues of the saints that they made me worship

I am a pariah not being able to be a bonze
And I have nothing to say to these souls of bonze

[78]

The world disdains me and wants to bring me to nothing
Not for my crimes, but for my repentance
They say that I am impious, a rebel
Ah well in my exile my destiny is lovely
I like better their Hell than their insolent Heaven
Singing Hallelujah upon a burning chasm
We are twisted forever sworn to the sufferance
Of my Unfortunate brothers the immense multitude!
Oh my God take pity on these born blind
Who mistake You Lord for the god of the damned
My God, close the mouths of the priests who insult You
Liberate your altars, Your moral and Your religion
These priests of Moloch are not Christians
They have judgements that are not Your own
Do not apply to them the laws that they made for us
Remind yourself of Jesus the most gentle of the prophets

Who said, all bleeding from his members and his brow
The wicked Oh my father forgive what they do
Now they are dragging before the council of Rome
The Pope has made himself God ; me I say to this man
Cursed by forever malediction
Cursed be forever all damnation
Any priest who speaks a curse condemns himself
It is upon the false pastor that anathema falls
The true priest of God is he who blesses
And religion is that which unites us.
Denied be forever the hatred that divides!
Extinguished be this hell that consumes the church
Bonzes, llamas, jurors, the future elect

[79]

You shall all be Christians when you know how to bless!
It's daybreak, the cock crows, go and say your prayers
And put your sword back in its sheath, Saint Peter
Tell your cardinals they have eaten enough
That their reign is over, that the world has changed
That in their chassepots too much marvel sparks
And that they have too much blood upon their scarlet robes.
Consult your past and you shall understand why
The fools in Paris assassinated Darboy
It is because all parties have their equal rages
It is because the chassepots made marvels again!
Ah you have damned us, enemies of our rights!

[80] - *verso*

And me, I bless you in the name of the Albigensians
Of Jan Huss, of Wiclet and of Savoyard
And of all the martyrs of the Holy word!
Yes, we bless you!... not to approve you
But so that you know we wanted to save you
From your foolish pride, from Hell, from yourself
And from your bastard execrable anathema!
We wanted to save you who condemned us,
We wanted to save you monsters who damned us!
Therefore, we declare in the name of Galileo
The sentence of the Inquisition annulled,
In the name of Vanini all the majesty
Of God in nature and in humanity
In the name of Fénélon that men are brothers
That you should keep the bitter words

[81]

Then in the name of good sense and of truth
That annoyance is not holiness.
You are the prelates, you have the tiaras

The crosses, the palliums, the mitres, the simars
You are all-powerful, and me who is nothing more
Than a man having suffered, poor, sober, a Christian
I dare to speak firmly to you and I am infallible
I have for myself truth stronger than the bible
I have for myself a good sense of all human nature
Vaster and better armed than the interests of Rome
And was I to be chained in the courtyard of the pontiff
As before was my master insulted by Caiaphas
I would go and proclaim without fear and without retreat
The law of science and the law of love!

A Painting by Zurbaran

A cadaverous saint, dreadful, horrible
Surprised in a tomb death that he made visible
He sketched it he held it in his fleshless arms
It seemed that the worms were already eating his nose
In their dark orbits his eyes barely gleamed
He had for a robe a sack, for a belt a chain
He had renounced all, science, love, reason
Nothingness is his god the grave is his house
He is already rigid and as cold as stone
The silence eternal fears his prayers
The tears upon his cheek have worn furrows
A permanent mark of ashes stains his rags
We see his teeth dirtied under drawn back lips
And the bones poke holes in his macerated flesh
Death pale skeleton is less cold than him

[82]

And seems to be looking near the wall for a handhold
To get from his hands implacable pincers
That would petrify a belly without entrails
With an awful modesty the bald one argues with himself
It is an abominable and terrible conflict
The man as vampire that has the fanatical desire
To absorb even Death itself and make it his life
And Death powerless to triumph over him
Fears to share his immortal ennui
That he pushes away with a dreadful laugh
And believes himself to already feel that he has eaten it alive

The Genesis of Love

I

Tears of azure give birth to periwinkles
The wise virgin Moon has made her white robes
The rays of the sun germinate in the ditch
The flower flying away becomes a butterfly
Force makes the law and the law makes harmony
Throughout the Universe genius is at work
Tender capricious or cruel by turn
Merciless and gentle, it is called love
It is by this Him the snow at the mountain summits
Melting into long streams sates the countryside
It is by Him that groups were made in the Universe
By the attractions of so many diverse stars
For Him the nestling sing and the bee buzzes
He forms from the grape libertine sap
He tames the lions and makes bulls bellow
Interlaces the beaks of young doves
He made the Sun, He made the stars

[83]

Of the modest Moon, He whitened the veils,
He made the treasures of the night and of the day
God made only one masterpiece: He created love!
Before God awoke from His eternal sleep
In the chaos the force had drained its power
The force without love that we call Satan
Created the behemoth and the leviathan
From the phosphorus of the waters, from silt of the caves
He brought forth solitary monsters
Giant aborted ones, without females, dreadful
That soon, famished devoured each other
The Earth where deformed ferns rotted
Mired in with its gravel enormous bones

Mountains of putrefying flesh
Escaped the fœtus of corruption
Toads, snakes, rats, millipedes
The slimy slug cold salamanders

Scaled dragons green crocodiles
Nightmares destined to populate hell
A thick smog infecting the atmosphere
And flames coming out of chasms in the land
Then one day in the sky uncovered for an instant
Appeared in the dawn a brilliant cloud
The air seemed to purify in its metamorphosis
And the cloud had the form of a rose
Slowly it opened, a radiant infant
Came out and with grace enchanted the heavens
A golden quiver trembled upon his naked shoulder
His candour, his beauty unknown until then
Filled with desire the vermillion clouds
And made in space suns hatch forth
The monsters readied themselves to make war upon him
But he with a light touch louder than thunder
Drawing a divine bow that in his hand whistled
He made them all tremble, twist, turn

[84]

Lost in the fog of smoke and sulphur
They all disappeared in the mouth of the abyss
And the infant their victor the spirit that makes us love
Put his foot on the ground and told it to germinate
Thus delving himself into twin sources
His smile pulled forth two brotherly forms
More beautiful than fables could ever dream of
One was Adam and the other Eve

II

They were born as children as was love their father
And their sex was for them for a long time a mystery
In the Garden of the world they played together
Without love ever entering into their games
They grew up together and their adolescence
Seemed to be foremost a second childhood
But whilst they slept the breath of love
Came to caress them and trouble them one day
Adam burst into tears he felt he was in a dream
His heart palpitating he went towards his Eve
And being unable to suffer the absence of his heart
He searched in Eve for his life and his happiness
Now Eve trembled to the bottom of her soul
She dreamt then that like a tract of flame
Adam penetrated her by a Divine effort
And came rejuvenated to live again in her breast
When they awoke in their arms they still held each other
A great curtain of flowers let filter in the light of dawn
That allowed them to seek each other's eyes
Love their creator who smiled close to them
They blushed then understanding the mystery
And the woman sensed she would become a mother

III

Wanting to keep it with them for more than a day
They plaited flowers to capture love

[85]

Love told them: lose this false hope
And do not touch me, I die when I am captive
I shall be close to you invisible or present
My eternity I have made a gift to you
With the condition though that you are faithful

And that you never taste mortal substance
There are in this garden two trees the fruit of which
One makes you be reborn the other destroys
One is called Life and the other Science,
The science of evil that flattens innocence!
If you approach them your heart is lost;
Therefore never touch this forbidden fruit.
And embracing again the two sworn spouses
Love caressed them the heavens admired them
And the birds sought to imitate
The insects under the grass hide together
The flowers bending swelling their sepals
All seemed to breath the delicacies of love

And nobody foresaw the cruel future
Of love taking flight never to return

IV

Too much happiness produces weariness
And fatigue likes solitude
Adam sometimes on the summit of the mountains
Went to contemplate upon the deep heavens
He observed the rising of the planets
And their setting, the path of comets
The time or the nights of the waning of the lamp
Twice digging itself into a double crescent
In the depths of the sky like meteors
He watched the egregores pass
Without wondering if his wife thought he was late
And that Eve awaited him.
Poor Eve believing herself abandoned
Conceived one day of a sad thought
It seemed to her that Adam no longer loved her.
Love claims absolute rights
He does not like it when we joke with him

[86]

When we neglect him and mostly when we are absent
Doubt finally, the poisonous doubt
Of both spouses came to bite happiness
Like a serpent that slithers into the soul
He invaded the poor woman first
He betrayed her, made her already imagine
Freeing herself, maybe seeking revenge.
He showed her the Tree of evil
Made her taste of the apple of vice
To keep and hold her husband
She dreamed of making him jealous…
Jealous of whom? but jealous of herself.
It is after all only herself that she loves;
To go and see herself in the crystal waters
She left him and turned her back on him.
When he embraces her she sulks and murmurs
That he has crumpled the flowers in her hair.
Adam restrained his unhappy desires
Whenever he is absent he takes longer to return

One evening when he finally came home
He noticed his wife who was crying
She held an already bitten fruit
She said to him: it is the forbidden fruit
For a long time we have suffered being together
Let us finally break the bind that holds us
This fruit shall separate us with no return
It is a poison that cures love
I received it as a celestial gift
I ate of it, I saved you the rest
Thank you said the man and with a brutal gesture
He took and also ate of the fatal fruit
Then separated and hiding themselves in the shadows
One far from the other they passed the dark night
At daybreak both came out
Without saying a word of repentance

When a charming and well-known voice
Seemed to them to come down the road

[87]

Adam my son and you my gentle Eve
I am love I have come to see how it goes
In your household and if your alliance
With a nearby fruit gives you hope
Upon this discourse they both hid themselves
Not daring to appear and doubly ashamed
For not having imagined in their anger
Of this child of which Eve would be mother

V

Saddened, Love said why are you leaving each other
You were lovers, you were spouses
I shall leave you in turn to never reappear
But you shall see me again in the child who shall be born
Work if you must live suffer for him
Work shall chase away dispute and boredom
Your childhood has passed you must dream of the other
That of your son shall become your own once more
Your eyes shall henceforth smile with his eyes
Your heart shall hear his little cries of joy

At his first mistakes you will tremble with alarm
His games shall be your games and his tears your tears
If pride in a lover had been able to fight standing
The mother would have crushed the head of the serpent
Let us go Adam return close to your companion
That throughout your exile your strength shall accompany you
The world around you is no longer paradise
That God in your childhood planted in the far past
You shall never return to your idolatry
You must with the human race conquer the fatherland

You must to virtue submit desire
Because duty begins where pleasure ends
Having thus spoken Love armed with a sword
Closed paradise then took the hand of Eve
And into the hand of Adam gently placing it
He said: support each other that is your punishment
Work without weakening and suffer in silence
I shall with you travel in hope

[88]

Claim the universe you shall be the kings
Come, let us embrace for the last time
Adam found himself back in the arms of his wife
The kiss of love penetrated their souls
A new future was revealed to them
Pressed together they both left
And love went back up to the starry vaults
Where shall be seated one day our consoled souls
Having reached the inaccessible and pure sanctuary
That hides the eternal in a night of azure
Lord said he I have made peace and war
I have given work as a remedy on earth
Does the supreme being command anything of me?
And God replied: Is what you do good?

VI

Such was the narrative primitive and sincere
That Moses received from the ancient sanctuary

And which distorted by the Hebrew priests
Has become to us absurd and tenebrous
I found this fable elegant and flowered
Amongst the first Christian teachers of Alexandria
Who gentle as Socrates and proud as Cato
Made the saints speak in the language in the language of Plato

When science still believed in the true Messiah
And when Synesius listened to Hypatia
Alas those times are long gone, they will never return
Must you flower again beautiful dreams that I loved
When a new Lucius in an ungodly time
I hid my knowledge under the ears of an ass?
Happily I have since transformed myself
Content to be a poet and proud to have loved
When the magician with half-closed lips
Made me become a man by giving me a role

[89]

Death

Recuperating sleep of eternal life
Death is of the phoenix the new birth
A corpse is nothing it is old clothes
That wants neither regrets nor mourning nor monument
Souls like a note upon a broken string
Lose into infinity their recovered strength
They are not in the air in water nor in the fire
And widowed of their corpses they sleep in God
I love in a museum an ancient mummy
Skeletons are beautiful for their anatomy
I even have upon my desk a skull
That shows me its teeth but never bites me
Wandering phantoms are the product of our imaginations
Nature in the grave does not offer truces
Magic has created superfluous rites
And the dead here below reappear no more

Death, for the unfortunate immortal hope
Is the golden-eyed nymph of the fountains of youth
She will take up into her maternal arms
The old and decrepit, the young criminals
And in her clear waters absolve, age
Shall find again innocence and youth together.
She sows at random flattened bones
From which come loves and blooming roses
Her head is crowned in poppies and crowned ears
She imposes silence upon fettered suffering
She tears the slave from the yoke of his oppressors
She comes to soothe devouring worries
She has the gentle regard of a veiled dawn
Her feet are cold and white, her robe is starry
Her long hair is black like a veil of mourning
And to eternity her hand covers the doorway

Wanting to keep us from too bright lights
And protecting our eyes in closing our eyelids

[90]

An Engraving by Albrecht Dürer

Théophile Gautier, most regrettable master
You that I was once fortunate to meet
Your clever uplifting spirit sees all there is
Engraved in the drawing of Melancholia!
Of old Albrecht Dürer this masterly work
Shows us science in royal robes
Following his problem and dream of the ideal
Near a great monument still unfinished
Of which it shrank the keystone
Two deep-thinking eyes survey behind the lids
And its vigorous fist sign of willingness
Seems to press upon its head with authority
To gush out eternal things
Peaceably she sits and knows that she has wings
A childish genie under strokes of love
Writes the truths that she wishes to make known
The grindstone of a mill can be used by an infant as a seat

To show that the book is the bread of college.
Suffering this old dog that devours our days
That we chase away in vain and who follows us still
Bent upon itself and sleeping close to her
Her brow is crowned in immortal verbena
Her victorious hand that never trembles
How fixed upon a point the hand of a compass
She dreams without doubt of the circumference
Before her the heavens stretch into the immense space
And beneath the heavens the sea that other immensity
Receives from the golden sun torrents of clarity
The rainbow analyses with its eyes the light
It has the instruments of each first work
The saw and the plane the hammer the crucible
Nails, the microscope and the crystal ball

The great King Ptolemy and the strong pincers
That save Prometheus and shape his entrails
She is rich, her coffers are full of treasures
She has the keys to all, knows all the locks
Beside her is the clock and further on the scales

[91]

The knell of death that of birth
Waiting to speak their sovereign signal
Her problem is annotated on a square of tin
And the bat that from her flies far away
And carries upon its open wing as a banner
The Greek and Latin word for Melancholia
Meaning to say that never shall a thinker bend
Under black depression and melancholy
Whilst there is reason to chase away folly
Study and work to occupy the days
And divine books to satisfy loves.
Master have you seen in this serene work
The discouragement of human thought
We were not there in the time of Albrecht Dürer
Faith was still alive in the works of Luther
The souls were not fading or dead
We liked work and in-depth study
Your charming spirit that doubt oppressed
Interpreted Melanchton by Alfred de Musset
Supposing that by reason of the vices of our age

The inscription of the monster is that of the page
And in this lovely design fatally understood
He confused the angel and the bat.
Now that you see the good the true, the just
You understand the august symphony of the heavens
You know that to change Hell into a holy place
Art amongst humans is God's dream
You have guessed the great word of the riddle
That we love beauty only for beauty itself

Beauty is the law that illustrates duty
It is the crowing of eternal knowledge
Whilst you live amongst beautiful things
Those who loved you grow their own wings
Tell them to hope and wipe away their tears
Because God doesn't leave emptiness between hearts
And between Earth and Heaven he fills the distance
They will come to listen to your great poem
Between these golden stars paradise without hell
That shall around you create the universe!

[92]

Concerning Man

Epigrams

Man is a bipedal animal
And bimanual who laughs sometimes
Incoherent, invents laws
And foresees death without remedy.
But he declares himself immortal;
Me for my part I believe it to be such;
It is obvious that we are
Immortals upon the dark edges,
Because it is certain that men
No longer die when they are dead
Pain is what we share
Folly is our element
Errors are our nourishment
And worms are our heritage

Still though we are triumphant
And we raise our children
In respect of our hardships
We spoil their appetites
In the hope that these little dears
Will be stupider than their fathers
At birth we know nothing
In dying not much more
Either for truth or for good
An eternal doubt devours us
But we love absurdity
And with our beliefs
We enrich the churches
It is clear that the jealous God
Shall become a God worthy of us
When we lend him drunkenness

If some sages by our blows

[93]

Expose him, it shall be the most foolish
Of all the dreamers on the Earth
And the proof that their reason
May say nothing of any good to us
Is that they have been forced to say nothing

Does the Devil exist or not?
Shall we find after trespass
Someone to judge our life If it shall be followed by another?
One tells us yes the other says no
One laughs the other gives a sermon
And we do not know which to listen to
But God who is always right there
Enlightened us upon all this Is we had taken time to learn.

That which does not seem obvious

Is that it is well to be prudent
And to classify all systems
Almost like poems
This seems nicer to us
One seems old the other new
This does not seem to be true
Let us conclude with Rabelais
That we should take it to task to drink it cold
It is the moral of the fable

Let us love, sing, be happy
And let us ourselves become old
Old age is a wealth
That time increases incessantly
Youth does not exist
It is erased with every step
It is to age that we come into the world

Spring is in our heart
When we make our own happiness
In conserving deep peace

[94]

Marginalia: *Risqué* Things – School of Victor Hugo

Honour is an umbrella
That we shake off
And that we put back in the corner
And glory a candle
Eternal
Of which the dead have no need

History is a power
That throws
Cadavers into the air
And the poet a Gavroche
That clings
To the hanged eaten by worms!

Victor, poet without rules
Is an eagle
Double of a man and of a bullock
And his hippogriff songs
Have the claws
Of a lion who makes the handsome

Ezekiel who feasts
Or who fasts

And has in these circles of fire
Seen we say in this form
Truly enormous
The resemblance of God

Phoebus is a wig
Upon the neck
Of the radiant firmament
And the stars, the planets
The comets

Crawl in his hair

The horizon of concord
Is the cord
By which in her flirtatious game
The moon upon the obelisk
Places her disc
Ball of this cup-and-ball

[95]

The pantheon of glory
Is the market
Of fetishes from the Congo;
And my poem is an ape
Under the liens
Of Monsieur Victor Hugo!

The Retraction of Galileo

A Dramatic Fragment

Adoring the cross and chalice of the Saviour
In the presence of all and of this Holy office
Hand upon the evangelist in nomine dei
Myself, I say Galileo son of Galilei
I declare by the spirit that resides within you
That the Earth stays and the Sun turns
Even by your grandeurs if it is the fatal end
I believe the Earth is flat and the heavens made of crystal
That you do not have brows of the same matter
They let pass life and light
And by your great reflections the universe is lit
Submit yourself without suffering to your sacred order
It is therefore not in vain that the very Holy Bible

[96]

Says that to triumph in a terrible combat
A prophet stopped the sun with one hand
And constrained the moon from brushing its path
I conjure you therefore great pastors of Europe
To absolve me and to absolve as well my telescope
Even though such a great pardon cannot be due
(getting up and striking the ground by foot)
Let us go, and not turn! You are protected from this!
My Lords before me you burned my book
I felt it turn because I was drunk
Science is a wine that goes to our heads
I swear I have observed nothing new
Brought to me of the remains of your prudishness
And in the sacred books looking for astronomy
I shall write no more, no longer think anything
As such might I live and die a good Christian!

Note we could make of this monologue a show
Very gripping, joining it with a pantomime

From which we thus dispose of the setting of the scene
A church lit by a multitude of
Candles, a numerous congregation, inquisitors
Soldiers, black penitents in hoods
A platform upon which an evangelist, near
To which a brazier and instruments of
Torture. The organ plays funeral airs
The procession enters the church and each
Takes their place, Galileo seems loaded
With chains. The organ stops, the Grand
Inquisitor exorcised Galileo with
Holy Water and silently showed him
With one hand the platform and the prie-dieu
With the other the torturers placing
Their pincers in the fire. Galileo hesitates
He takes one step towards the torturers

[97]

Groaning getting louder in the crowd
A woman hurries to the feet of the
Scholar showing him two young
Children, a priest gives Galileo the
Crucifix to kiss Galileo kisses the crucifix
Embraces the two children and after having
Raised his arms to Heaven he climbs slowly
Upon the platform and pronounced in a firm voice
The words of retraction
Whilst holding his hand upon the book of the Evangelists.
When he had finished his chains are removed
The organ plays joyous airs and the procession
Starts again to leave the church. Everyone
Bows before Galileo, a few
Men in the costume of scholars turn away
Solely with contempt. Women cry

And even a man wipes away his tears
With an impatient gesture

At the rising of the curtain and before the entry of the
Procession a bailiff of the Inquisition reads
To the people the monitory here:

So that the Holy Church shall finally be consoled
We bring to this place the one named Galileo
Certain of having said and having even written
Contrary to the laws of the Lord Jesus Christ
Who wishes for his Church to be always respected
Upon all teachings shall always be consulted
This obvious lie horrible and without equal
That the Earth at present turns around the Sun
And this without respect for the Infallible Church
Of Joshua himself and of the Holy Bible
The Holy Office therefore the established crime
Almost in flagrante delicto the guilty arrested
He who without violence and almost without torture
Has himself confessed his dark felony

[98]

Ordain that on this day he shall before us
Be brought to make honourable amend on his knees
And hear him condemned of such penitence
So that the Holy Tribunal may rule indulgence
By default or to have him feel the pincers
Then a Holy Confessor shall again exhort
That if he wishes to persist in his awful blasphemy
He shall take measure and his own blood shall fall upon him
A pyre in the square is already prepared
Upon which this villain of separate Christians
With all his writings shall perish in the flames
That is justice! And may God have mercy on his soul

The organ plays the Dies Irae and the procession

Enters the church
After the abjuration the Grand Inquisitor says to Galileo:
Return to prison, I shall let you know
Your verdict that the Church shall perhaps lessen

But let us hope above all for God's clemency
We shall before you throw the book into the flames
Come light bearer let the fire be lit
And the impious writings shall be wholly consumed Galileo
Well done, throw the ashes to the winds
Let them always in these scholarly centuries
Tell of the efforts taken to control my reason
And acknowledge the laws of the Church!

When Galileo will embrace the crucifix and
Will climb upon the platform the Grand Inquisitor will say:
It is well: you escape damnation
Pronounce now your abjuration
Then Galileo:
Worshipping the Saviour's cross (etc) as
The Highest.

[99]

Voices in the crowd whilst Galileo was brought
Out of the church
The scholars
Ah feeble character!
The women
Ah sadly an old man
Students come before the theatre
And shake hands with an energetic gesture
One amongst them said to the others:
Friends we shall look back upon these charges here later
But let us not condemn this man of genius
Of whom we have understood the sublime irony
His book is spread amongst other nations
We do not renounce his demonstrations

And just as this God of whom he is the prophet
He may rest, because the light is made!

Great Good Sense

Or Simple Discourse

Ignore or know, neither doubt nor belief
Here is the right path that prudence teaches
I may doubt myself, my skill
Never reason nor truth
And what matters it to the Sun if the blind man sees him?
He shines still and always he burns
And if he was a judge, being sure to do well
He shall not punish those who know nothing
Of the things that Heaven does not deign to teach me
I seek to guess at that which I cannot understand
But never being sure of having guessed correctly
I do not serve the God that I gave to myself
It is a sketch of myself that I pin above my hearth

[100]

From my conception I have feared being an idolator
I hold to it, since I have not found anything more pleasing
But if it was made of gold I would eat my calf
What I do well know is that the Iman the Bonze
Brahmins, Fakirs naked and bronze-coloured
The Catholic priest and the stripped Rabbi
Say that for them alone the Eternal has spoken.
Having heard nothing of these multiple discourses
Of none of these pastors am I a disciple;
Of these contradictions I make no case
Knowing that the Eternal doesn't contradict itself.
I know nothing, whilst waiting for God to deign to teach me
If He does not speak to me I have nothing to say to Him,
Not knowing Him never having seen Him,
And the life to come is for me unexpected.

If I had a bastard in the back of China
Completely ignorant of his higher origin
And if somebody made me aware that he said in Peking:
Either I have no father or he is an old rascal
To have never made the effort to write to me
Because of his existence he should have told me
I would reply that by my faith the Chinese one would be right
I would not accuse him of high treason
If I had anything I would have him take his share
He shall receive a letter with his inheritance
Whilst waiting, could he worry about me?
And if to distract him, a pact, a wizard
A bonze a mandarin reclaiming their salary
Saying to him one after the other I know your father
He is white, he is black, he is red, he is blue
Should he believe in them all as we believe in God?

[101]

Should he choose one as the most veritable
Because he admits no doubt nor critic
Myself I don't believe it will displease our sainted confessors
If he told all of them: you are comedians.
And you want God whom we invoke in Rome
To have less intelligence and good sense than a man
Who imposes a law that must be guessed at
And who to blind man's buff wishes to condemn us?
No, I do not believe that at all, I am sure it is not stupid.
I know perfectly well that it is necessary to be honest
To honour our parents and to love our neighbour
But it is necessary to gild a fetish, a thing
A divine little fellow of some kind and one we worship
Without rhyme or reason no matter what the Devil thinks
Because it is written without knowing why
Frankly I do not know is this a fault of my own?
Doubt! Why doubt? nature is visible
I understand the evidence and admit the possibility

But whenever an ignoramus expresses this by chance
I reverse my right to examine later
If of all examination the means refuse
My good will suffices and excuses me
I act as I know we should act and then
I count upon teaching myself to do better if I can
Speak to you of faith Mother of Hope
But I know that faith is merely confidence
I believed in my mother in times when my needs
Forced me every day to seek her attentions
I made proof so often of her maternal bounty!
But I humbly swear that I would have been afraid of her
If ever before me she had into a great fire
Thrown my little brother in honour of the Good God
Catholic Church to you the parable

[102]

I find beauteous things in your obscure symbol
But I know your religion is a religion of blood
And that you make a god of a weak pontiff
I don't believe therefore, I know: I condemn you
In laughing at a lamb who shouts and damns
I know that nature has admirable laws
I know to weep for the just dying upon the cross
I know of the meritorious works of Saint Vincent
I know the arguments of all the consistories
I know one can be an honest man and Christian
And that an excellent priest is a man of good
But I do not know why a miserly priesthood
Preaches poverty whilst taking our money
Why cardinals have such insolent luxury
And why we absolve the violent writer
Who profanes the spirit in praising drunkenness
Manipulates injury and compromises the Church

I do not know how the Pope, this teacher
Custodian of the dogma and not the creator

By a invention Jesuitical and laughable
Can worship himself and believes himself infallible
It matters not to me after all, I am not Luther
But I know that the Devil would execrate Hell
If the Devil existed such as the world loves him
More elegant, finer, more alive than even God
I know that had Joshua done the same to God
Being unable in its course to stop the sun
Without breaking the bonds of the whole of nature
And without making the fall the stars as dust
And that Samson victor over a terraced people
With a broken and bloodied bone
Could not get out for his parched mouth
From this ridiculous bone a trickle of filtered water

[103]

All is possible to God do not say zounds
Ridicule is missing from the attributes of God
God has never signed your profane lies
And leaves you the juices of your ass's jaws
I return to what I say and claim that down here
A thinker is stronger when he does not doubt
Scepticism being impossible in science
Is just the probing of drunken ignorance
I see, I know, I seek and walking step by step
I believe nothing that we do not know
I do not presume things that I know not of
Seeking is not doubting it is still not to know
I survey the problem and when I have found it
I shall say I know and not that I have dreamt it
Whilst waiting I admit that I need to be shown the way
That is confidence and it is not doubt
Of a clairvoyant guide I may follow the steps

If I know that he knows that which I do not
But follow blindly the blind man who staggers
But have by a fool my cradle governed

It is because I claim to not admit for a while
He be Pope and mostly if he says he is God
Whether we are sad or content, they approve of me or blame me
Always with difficulty I want to make the effort
And say to my friends do you want to live in peace?
Learn, believe little, but never doubt

[104]

Theological Reason

Or Reasonable Theology

There exists a supreme inexorable law
That protects the just and punishes the guilty.
The profound sentiment of immortality
Comes to us from nature and humanity.
Life is collective as much as personal
The great foyer projects and receives sparkles
Good should be done only for good
Without hope of payment or fear of chastisement
Moses and Mohammed proclaim theism
God in humanity is Christianity Rome is duty with authority
Geneva is the law with liberty.
Now these diverse dogmas complete each other
The God of Muslims and of Jews is ours
It is in all our equalness that we must love him

Abuses are an evil, they must be reformed
Order demands however free obedience
It is not by duties that the law is balanced
Therefore, Jew and Muslims, Christians united with the Pope
Protestants divided accepted or banished
Are our brothers in God, composing all together
This religion of which the spirit assembles us;
Such is the Catholicism of the universe
That illuminated two words: justice and charity
The other life is unknown to us, the maybe
We live, we die just as God made us born
Does He reward the sheep for being docile?
Does He punish wolves for being wolves?
Do the long struggles of the trapped fly
Make us torment in Hell the spider?
The universe is a field of battle and of death

Where the feeble are always eaten by the strongest

[105]

The great man succumbs oppressed by envy
It is fatality, it is the law of life.
You would have us believe doves of love
That a hell exists for the souls of vultures?
Nero was merely a tiger escaped from his cage
But God himself would be a more savage Nero
If He offered the spectacle to an appalled Heaven
Of a tiger cooked alive for eternity
An eternal ordeal wants a god as a victim
And the rebellious angel, Satan would be sublime
Accepting Hell as terrifying tomb
Rather than admiring his eternal tormentor
Hell would be pride inexorable and sombre
Having God brood upon death in his shadow
It is the negation of the glories of the Saviour
It is of charity eternal dishonour
Of triumphant sin it is an apotheosis

Of God himself as demon it is metamorphosis.
Man, free amateur and creator of evil
Becomes a vanquished god that God treats as an equal
Now being the strongest if God strikes He is a coward
He is vile if he takes revenge, He is wrong if He is angry
A crime cannot be eternal and punished
And evil would be God if it was infinite
God changes into fury His paternal bounty
Relishing of humans the eternal torture
Becoming so complacent for the man of Hell
That we weep whilst admiring the martyr Lucifer.
O let us not dwell forever of hatred and blasphemy
The eternity of God burns because it loves
God will never change; how therefore can we suppose
That an insect irritates and cannot soothe?
Under pain of death, the most serious of punishments

Before he was subjected to human foolishness

[106]

The tomb is peace with liberty
Supreme equality and fraternity.
Does the worm discern the innocent or guilty
And decaying rich of the last unfortunate?
How does the friend of the dead go into the fire
Without legs and without feet having neither body nor connection?
What becomes of the ray that colours the rose
When the robe is withered? It colours something else
You blow on a torch, the flame disappears
Is it extinguished? A child would believe so.
Is the flame a being or simply a phenomenon
An analogue of human thought?
It can only die by lack of nourishment
And the verb is silenced when it's missing an instrument.
My broken violin is no longer of use to me, it matters not
The eternal music with it is not dead

All shall crumble, palaces, graves, temples, altars
But in the great expanse we are immortal
Upon the faith of Christians the text teaches us
So that to do evil we incessantly fear
That a judgement awaits and that on a day to come
We must all be reborn… with memory!
Thus what cries cf horror what terrifying gulps
Nero recognizes Agrippina alive
Who forced him to suckle her crazed black blood!
Ugolino vomited the child he had eaten
Troppman… but I must stop myself, being afraid of the horrible
Lightning is useless against this dreadful picture
The impious from their remorse cannot escape
God would honour them too much if He deigned to strike them
Misfortune to he who sleeps with a stain
He shall awaken damned by nature
And shall no longer inspire fear nor pity…

I would like it better though if all was forgotten

[107]

And do not presume that God substance pure
Will to preserve it salt rottenness
Therefore if he wants to conserve his dirtied work
He shall soak it again in the river of forgetfulness.
Otherwise God is not as we represent Him
And never needs to inspire terror
There is nothing about Him that resembles the caprices of a king
He does all for the law, within the law, by the law
His impalpable substance fills the immensity of space
Where the shape ends infinity restarts
All lives, all is transformed in a fatal progress
And that which always dies is the dream of evil
God is the eternal order, the infinite force
He is the regulator of the great harmony
He is, but He is not that which Man had dreamed of
He is that which the priests have never proven
He is the living law, soul of everything
The reason, the means, the principle and the cause

God in eternity is the knowledge that can
The law that is preserved and the power that wants
Man is a defective god that remembers the Devil
Of Christian mysteries the Gospel is the fable
The Bible is the secret of the pyramidal sphinx
Obscurely engraved upon its ancient pedestal
Catholic dogma is the shadow of these shadows
It is the eagle that Patmos who beneath its sombre wings
Hatches an immortal egg, Holy Charity!
Destroying indulgence with authority,
In its communion that it calls universal
It proclaims the real presence of God.
Yes, upon all altars, in all costumes in all places
It is communion that makes God real
Jesus said: love each other! Let faith bring you together

At the table of Heaven take communion together
And you shall feel me being immortal within you

[108]

Rich and poor beside each other kneeling
Eat the same bread that shall make you immortal
This bread shall be my body returning to life in church
Because I wanted to die to unite humans
And the salvation of the world is the work of my hands
It is in this sublime and simple metaphor
That from the religion to come already shines the dawn
And our wise teachers only saw in this brightness
Bread that transmutes and becomes flesh
They believed to prove their anthropophagy
That from vermillion blood they could still see the cloth redden
Silence virtue!.. the shadows pass
The nights of ignorance shall one day brighten
And man guided by the same light
Shall recognise themselves as children of the same Father!

A Prophetic Vision

I was imprisoned for free speech
And for having divined the symbols of the goals
When the spirit lifting the veils of my flesh
Had me make a tour of Heaven and Hell
Then in the shadow above the most sublimely made
Further away than the teachers, higher than the prophets
He left me standing on a steep rock
Where the serpent of Eden had never crawled
Upon my head a star appeared in silence
And filled the whole sky with an immense aureole
Then I threw myself trembling onto my knees
And I cried: Lord have mercy upon us

[109]

Why did you choose in this incurable world
Of the most obscure sinners me the most unfortunate
To show me suddenly on an unforeseen day
That which even Moses and Saint Paul have not seen?
The spirit replied to me the light in the temple
Is not subordinate to the eye that can contemplate it
Whilst the other repairs itself its accustoming light
Reveals itself to the bird awake first
The star appears therefore, not to your genius
Not to your virtues but to your insomnia.
Something though pleases the Lord in you
You have never through fear been subjected to the infamous law
Fed by the teachers of false Christianity
You push away the yoke of their Pharisaicism.
Abusing you with their authority
From the heights of the temple thus they hurried away
It was thus good that God cut away your swaddling clothes

And had you held up by the hands of his angels

The Poet

I would have been Lord your beloved son
If my mouth falling had not blasphemed
I wept, I suffered and then in my rage
I drank of impure intoxication and I broke my glass
The goddess Astarte without modesty and without faith
One Christmas morning came and offered herself to me
She had the regard of an ingenuous virgin
And beneath her black hair her shoulder half-naked
She spoke softly saying that she loved me
And her looks were beautiful and her voice charmed me
And braving the austere jealousy of a sermon
I said to the demon: come you shall be my wife.
The fatal mystery sadly was accomplished
I had placed insanity and hell into my bed
Astarte claimed that I had diminished her
She abandoned me! then I…I cursed her.

[110]

The Spirit

No, I know your heart, for her it prayed
Then towards God for a long time your pains cried
You shrivelled yourself so that she could be free
This effort in your soul put back the balance
And when you invoked me I came towards you
I speak therefore, listen and be silent before me
This glorious star with a brilliant diadem
It is reason that speaks and lives by itself
The divine phantoms, Jupiter, Jehovah
Are the illusions of a dream that parts
Me, I am the thinking enclosed in your soul
You lend me eyes and wings of fire
And in a movement of nervous eroticism
You felt yourself lifted by one of your hairs
Know that God resides where reason dominated
And that love is not the divine light
Love is a need of the soul or of the flesh
It is a golden husk that hides a bitter fruit

Love ennobles only by sacrifice
Overcome pain is its divine sepal
Abraham of Hell could brave the challenges
When God had him contemplate being ready to smite his son
Still serene peace is painful for a mother
And Jesus triumphant was born upon Calvary
Look around you at the world revolted
It loves with a fury the virgin liberty
But this Holy Virgin with veiled head
Wants us to marry her and die as soon as she is violated
Or sooner she flew when we wish to offend her
And the fatal empire rushes to avenge her
And those whom fury pursues and offends
Betrayed as Ixion only kissed a cloud

Then tied to the wheel of fatality
They climb incessantly and on the other side

[111]

Fall back down to climb and fall again
With revolutions the abyss devours them
Hell awakens then the triumphant vanquished
And tells them that Saturn has eaten his children
The larvae of the grave of avid vengeance
From a used diadem fill their empty skulls
And germinate all at once the field of Ezekiel
And of a corpse-world terrify heaven.
Vain anachronism! their skeleton legs
Click when they walk like castanets
And hit into oblivion the reminder of the past;
They shall no longer find their erased Kingdom
But to liberty wishing to bar the doors
They pass alas by weakened latches
Their powdery radius their chilled tibias
We hear the sharp sound of broken bones
The door pushes them back in opening itself
And the skeleton crumbles with its diadem!

It should be thus as long as authority
Has made no pact with liberty
As long as a scholarly faith to reason submitted
Has not made loved church dogma
As long as the bewildered man struggles without knowing
That we buy the laws at the cost of duty
That inequality rules in nature
That fraternity shall be an imposter
If the men delivered up to the dreaded pell-mell
Could without any brake tear each other apart
If the masses still must be guided
And the blind crowd obey the ideas
That the Pope is not an idol and that God
Does not throw the spirit and knowledge into the fire

That the Church would be stronger and more sincere
In its fair criticism to encourage Voltaire

[112]

And of charity showing the talisman
Gains the author of Alzira to the true God of Guzman
But these disputers, Jesuits, Jansenists
Patouillet furious Nicole and Pascal sad
Offering their pedantry to this divine mocker
Must by amusing him uplifted his heart
Look now at the Church and the apostles
In ink and in bile dipping their paternosters
A pitted face with a facetious nose
Spitting upon humans the filth of the heavens
His style full of stench the gutters walks
And the filth in fact overflows his fountain
Baby Jesus wipes his nose with the white flag
The God of the universe is a great bleeding heart
We conjure pride from human wisdom
With the followers of Saint Philomena…
Thus I looked at the spirit that spoke to me
The star in the sky slowly went away

I doubted the spirit; because within me, unfortunate,
A memory of the abbot murmured: it is the Devil.
Then I awoke drenched in sweat
My temples beat furiously, I was afraid
Afraid of the truth, my God! of justice!
Afraid of Saint Dominic and of his Holy Office
Because of threads of red iron artistically woven
My memories were the robe of Nessus.
Reason when we sleep is never the strongest;
Always towards the past dreams take us,
And the poor thinker prouder than Jehovah
Confused in his foolishness shall finally find himself again

Epilogue

Of this vision I will explain the problem
I feel asleep reading foolish books
And as a glutton mediating the poem

[113]

I have for my supper eaten pork with cabbage

Conclusion
Let us drink it cold
Song
Air of Calpigi

Friends, let us leave the patriarch
By the wind to navigate the ark;
The favourite bird of loves
Promises us still happy days (repeat)
Noah conqueror of the bitter wave
Planted the vine upon the land;

[114]

Care for the vine, and let us drink it cold
This is the advice of the old Rabelais (repeat)

Swelling her nourishing breasts
The earth is fat with its delights
She has for hair the harvests
The woods murmur with songs (repeat)
Her tears make the flowers bloom
Her laughter makes the roses flourish;
Let us pick the rose and let us drink it cold!
This is the advice of old Rabelais! (repeat)

Let us love wine when it flows

And a woman as long as she is beautiful
Let us gather the flowers without crushing them

And pleasures without thinking about it (repeat)
Unfaithful in the morning even
Rose says: it is you alone I love
Let us believe the thing and let us drink it cold
This is the advice of old Rabelais

Which is the most divine system
The last word of the great problem?
Which party makes for us the law
Republicans or the King? (repeat)
What is the sense of the words civicism
Fraternity, patriotism?
It means to say: let us drink it cold!
This is the advice of old Rabelais (repeat)

[115]

You ask if the comets
May meet with the plants?
But if the heavens must be governed
To what end then serve the gods? (repeat)
I can without lens or globe
See the wine meet my glass!
It is the comet! and let us drink it cold
This is the advice of old Rabelais (repeat)

That Nicodemus in the moon
Engineered to seek his fortune,
So high I shall never place
My red eggs to eat them (repeat)
As long as I have in my purse
Enough to fill my humble bowl
I am content, and let us drink it cold!

This is the advice of old Rabelais (repeat)

When we have done with our buffooneries
Worn our last shirts
God takes us back, of us down there
What does he do, what does he not do, (repeat)
What does he do with melted snow,
With old expired moons?
I know nothing; but let us drink it cold
This is the advice of old Rabelais (repeat)

The End

Dedication

Amongst the two-legged animals without feathers
That of the human race usurp the language
There exist few stripped of common sense
And Solomon from a thousand hardly found one.
I have never worked for these vulgar beings
Who of humanity are the supernumerary
Degenerate monkeys presented at the contest
But who to lack of reason still lay claim
These people do not at all love verses nor ideas
Their souls by the spirit are never obsessed
They need Rocambole and the airs of Offenbach
Women, horses gold and tobacco
I write for the thinkers there are no longer any in the world
Who taste wisely of the fruit of Eve the blonde

And who of Mnemosyne opening the altars
We might have the right to believe immortal
If my verses are kept and may survive me
If for some friends we make of them a good book
My muse will dedicate to them a fraternal salutation
With the happy wish of an eternal smile
To glory, to oblivion without fear I resign myself
Loving sometimes their tears, especially those of the vine
I let myself by judged as an ecce homo:
Therefore, my dear readers vel duo vel nemo

Éliphas Lévi
November 1871

LES POÈMES D'ÉLIPHAS LÉVI

Français

1 Ms 1799

« Rimes et raison »

par Éliphas Lévi

Folioté 1 à 116

[2]

La liberté

Iambe

À Auguste Barbier

La bouche aux vils jurons peut se noircir de poudre
Et se crisper en rugissant,
Les mains aux sales doigts peuvent lancer la poudre
Puis se laver avec du sang
L'aveugle multitude a ses jours de victoire ;
Mais quand le peuple est déchaîné
Il se rue au désastre et jamais à la gloire
Le tocsin n'a jamais sonné
Pour annoncer la paix source d'abondance
Le peuple épuisé de fureur
Cherche et trouve toujours une tête qui pense
Malheur alors, trois fois malheur
A tous, si par hasard, la tête qui remplace

Le désordre par l'attentat
Et s'improvise un corps avec la populace
Est la tête d'un scélérat !
C'est alors que l'empire appartient à l'audace
Alors les titans furieux
L'un de l'autre en luttant escaladent la place
Comme s'ils assiègeaient les cieux
La politique affreuse est un concours de crimes
Tibère instruit Caligula
Claude enhardit Néron, l'on flétrit les victimes
Marius fait rimer Sylla
Tallien d'un poignard menace Robespierre
Les rostres sont ensanglantés
Le glaive du bourreau balancier Populaire
Frappe et tranche des deux côtés.

[3]

La suprême raison c'est le dernier supplice
Le bon droit c'est l'impunité
Et tous également ignorant la justice
Méconnaissent la liberté
La liberté n'est pas une fille des rues
La crinière et les seins au vent
Qui prend dans les ruisseaux les hideuses recrues De la révolte au flot mouvant !
Ce n'est point une large et sordide javotte
Qui, dans un délire sans nom
Ceinte du drapeau rouge et retroussant la cotte Grimpe à cheval sur un canon
ô d'Auguste Barbier singulière démente qui, calomniant notre amour pour notre liberté, pour l'ange de la France prend Théroigne de Méricourt !

Certes, la liberté n'est pas une comtesse
Du noble faubourg Saint Germain, Mais c'est encore moins cette infâme drolesse S'enivrant le sabre à la main !....
Elle a de Jeanne d'Arc la mission divine
Et la sévère chasteté
Elle venge toujours le droit qu'on assassine
Elle est forte de vérité
Elle fait protéger le corps dans chaque membre
Et sa balance aux plateaux d'or
Rejette également les piques de septembre Et le couteau de Thermidor.
Elle n'a point voulu le sang de Louis Seize
Ni celui de l'affreux Marat
Devant son tribunal il faut que tout s'apaise

[4]

Elle ne signe de contrat
Qu'entre la fierté digne et la loi souveraine,
Frappe-t-elle, c'est pour sauver.
Mais elle est sans faiblesse et pas un capitaine
Ne se fait jamais enlever.
Quand les plus vils instincts les meutes dévorantes

Ont cru sous les flèches du mal
Et dans le noir filet des haines délirantes
Voir tomber le corps social
Quand de sourds grognements les chenils retentissent
Et quand la trompe du chasseur
A sonné la curée aux limiers qui bondissent
Hurlant la faim, flairant l'horreur
Les aboyeurs pressés alors s'entre déchirent
Se poussant, se mordent entr'eux
Sans arriver jamais à la chair qu'ils aspirent

Car la vierge aux terribles yeux
L'austère liberté près du mort qui sommeille
Pâle mais la couronne au front
Et dans la main le fouet, inexorable veille
Pour le garder d'un lâche affront,
Puis lorsque la cohue à la gueule béante
S'étrangle en un dernier effort
Elle se dresse alors courroucée et géante
Et touchant le prétendu mort
Elle le galvanise, éveille la chair vive
Lui commande au nom de la loi
Sur son front essuyé souffre pour qu'il revive
Et dit : Lazare, lève toi !
Et le vrai peuple enfin, le peuple qui travaille
Le peuple de l'humanité

[5]

Du pouvoir abattu relève la muraille Et reconstruit l'autorité.
La nation s'étonne et sort de son ivresse,
Tous les rangs se donnent la main
On maudit l'anarchie, on cherche la sagesse
Le progrès poursuit son chemin
Et le soldat montrant les lauriers qui fleurissent
Sur son fusil discipliné
Le fermier réparant ses granges qui l'emplissent
La mère offrant son nouveau né

Le laboureur mettant la main sur la charrue
Le pasteur comptant son bétail
Et le peuple marchant paisible dans la rue
Avec les armes du travail,
Le riche sans orgueil, le pauvre sans envie
Tous, et chacun de son côté

Disent en exhibant leurs titres à la vie :
Voici ma part de royauté !

[6]

La mort de Galilée

Le dieu qu'a formulé la vulgaire croyance
Lisait au fond du ciel des livres de sciences
Car l'éternel peut bien s'émanciper un peu
Bien que Rome ait réglé ce que doit faire dieu
Dieu donc, ce dieu borné par des prêtres ignards
Se trouvait à l'endroit dans leurs dogmes barbares
Et se sentant lié par les inquisiteurs
Par décence, disait : ces livres sont menteurs
C'est le soleil qui tourne et la terre immobile
Soutient ma vielle Rome infaillible Sybelle
Rome n'a pas senti le sol qui remuait
Et quand Rome a parlé dieu doit rester muet !
Muets aussi restaient les anges des étoiles
Mais de l'espace immense ayant percé les voiles
Copernic s'écria : vous vous trompez, Seigneur !

A ces mots insolents les élus eurent peur
Mais dieu toujours serein dans la nuit étoilée
Dit : pour le mieux savoir, consultons Galilée
Qui d'un beau désaveu confus et repentant
Dit en frappant la terre : elle tourne pourtant !
Que l'ange de la mort descende et le ramène.
Or Galilée alors malgré sa foi romaine
Braquait son télescope au fond du firmament
Et l'ange n'osa pas le prendre en ce moment
Mais d'un inquisiteur trainant la robe noire
Il apparut au seuil de son observatoire
Le savant tressaillit, fit un signe de croix,
Le celeste instrument s'echappa de ses doigts
Et la mort triompha ; ce n'était plus qu'un homme.
Galilée arriva devant le dieu de Rome
Et il cria : seigneur je consens à l'enfer
Oui, malgré satan même et ses griffes de fer

[7]

Elle tourne, Seigneur, elle tourne, la terre !
Et vous le savez bien malgré votre colère ;
Je le démontrerai pourtant si vous voulez.
Alors dieu s'adressant aux papes assemblés
Leur dit que voulez vous ? il parait qu'elle tourne.
Dès longtemps à regret parmi vous je séjourne
Galilée est damné, je le suis avec lui
Je vous laisse le ciel tout plein de votre ennui
Et pour que votre foi demeure immaculée
Je suivrai dans l'enfer le pauvre Galilée.
Alors dieu descendit dans l'abîme de feu
Le diable dans le ciel prit la place de dieu
Et tout se retourna ; le paradis fut sombre
La science avec dieu du gouffre éclaira l'ombre
Socrate et Vanini devinrent des élus
La vérité dicta des dogmes absolus
La conscience eut droit de grade et de franchise…
Mais le pape infaillible est resté dans l'église !

A Monseigneur Dupanloup

Sur son histoire de Jésus

Vous avez, Monseigneur, dans un noble langage
Tracé de l'homme-Dieu la poétique image
Mais ne sentez vous pas que tant d'humanité
Est un secret reproche à la divinité ?
Le pardon c'est sa vie, et l'enfer sa croyance.
A son père pourtant il prêche l'indulgence
En disant : sauve les de ton gouffre sans fond
Les hommes ô mon père ignorent ce qu'ils font
Dans le beau sentiment qui dicte sa prière
Le fils n'est-il donc pas plus humain que son père ?
Le cruel dieu des juifs n'est-il point dépassé ?
Et dieu comprendra-t-il ce que l'homme a pensé ?
Le cruel dieu des juifs étant le dieu de Rome

[8]

Rome doit en Jésus excommunier l'homme
Car l'homme a déchiré le voile du Saint lieu
Et dans le sauveur l'homme est plus grand que le dieu !
Ainsi dans votre écrit plein d'une foi subtile
Vous humanisez tant le divin évangile
Qu'on sent l'homme d'esprit sous le prédicateur
Vous effacez le diable avec le bon pasteur
Et chez vous, cher orgueil de ma bibliothèque
L'élégant moraliste est meilleur que l'évêque

Paris

À Auguste Barbier

Il est sous le soleil une cité superbe
Aux squares verdoyants pleins de fleurs et plein d'herbe
Une Babel dorée aux splendides contours
S'ouvre de clochers de chars et de tambours
Où des mondes passés la renaissance active
Semble avoir entassé Thèbes Rome et Ninive
Et qui, de l'univers présidant le congrès
Sur les rayons de fer lance au loin le progrès
C'est le cerveau du monde et l'ame de la terre
Rivale du soleil, fileule du tonnerre
C'est le cœur gigantesque où tout vaisseau conduit
Qui dévore l'idée et qui la reproduit.
C'est Paris, c'est le ciel, c'est l'enfer, c'est le monde

[9]

C'est un temple bâti sur un cloaque immonde
Là, règne l'impudeur sur un trône d'argent,
Là travaille et conspire un peuple intelligent
Là, se cache et se tait la misère terrible
Vieux sphinx toujours debout au bord du vice horrible
Et le pâle voyou moqueur et demi nu
Est le visage humain de ce monstre inconnu.
Paris splendeur du vice et candeur du cynisme
Bétise du savoir, farce de l'héroïsme
Spartacus en faux col, Homère en abat-jour
Comédie ou souvent le sublime fait pour
Où les sanglots mélés font un éclat de rire
Où la gaîté renait quand la partie expire
Hopital de Gilbert, forum de Mirabeau
Où le carosse trinque avec le tombereau
Parthénon, lupanar Panthéon, Gémonies
Succès honteux, trafics sublimes agonies !

Le viellard qui jamais ne se lasse en courant
Et qui sans l'attrapper poursuit le juif errant
Le grand semeur d'oubli des choses disparues
Le temps devient flaneur en passant dans les rues
Car il n'a jamais vu résister à la loi
Rien de si florissant et de si beau que toi !
La race de Paris c'est la race vivante
L'instinct divinateur, la paresse savante
C'est Platon raisonnant la hotte sur le dos
C'est Voltaire incarné dans la foi des badauds
C'est Chauvin sans frayeur, Prudhomme sans reproche
Le diable et figaro résumés dans gavroche
C'est la froide cocotte au chignon bousoufflé
Au jupon monstrueux par des cerceaux enflés
Qui se vautre au soleil par deux poneys trainés
Et grimé d'un lorgnon sa joue enfarinée
C'est le petit crevé mannequin bien appris
Qui juge les chevaux et les femmes au prix

[10]

Et qui sait grasseyer dans la langue fleurie
Les termes les plus purs... d'un valet d'écurie
C'est le boursier ventru ganté de beurre frais
Qui du désastre escompte à son profit les frais
Et se frotte les mains puisque la bourse monte
Quand s'abaisse l'honneur et quand grandit la honte
Mais c'est aussi, plus haut que ce lâche bétail
L'étude ingénieuse éclairant le travail
C'est le penseur dictant des lois à la tribune
C'est le mérite enfin corrigeant la fortune
Le poète Barbier prendrait-il par hasard
Pour le cœur de Paris le quartier Mouffetard ?
Où donc va-t-il chercher son infernale étude
Et sa fouge en travail bouillonnant dans la cuve ?
A-t-il pour inspirer les étranges dégouts
Botté jusqu'à la cuisse exploré les égouts ?
Pleine d'une eau noirâtre et qui remue à peine

prend-il dans sa fureur la Bièvre pour la Seine ?

Laissons la pourriture à l'ancien Montfaucon
La morgue est loin du Louvre et vadé d'Apollon
D'un réalisme abject évitons la folie
Au vin délicieux ne métons point de lie
Si Paris est la cuve où les raisins foulés
Versent du vin nouveau les flots encore troublés
Dans ses flancs orageux le nectar surabonde
Et la gloire par lui déborde sur le monde.

[11]

La chute de la colonne

Iambe

Lorsque Vitellius comme un porc sur la paille
Agonisait ensanglanté
Et lorsqu'autour de lui la romaine canaille
Bavait sa lâche cruauté
Lardé par les couteaux ratissé sur les pierres
Enflé, livide, violet
Il n'essuya dit-on ni larmes ni prières ;
Soufflant comme un bœuf il râlait
Puis à l'instant suprême il redevint un homme
Et relevé par la douleur
Il murmura les mots qui stigmatisaient Rome:
J'étais pourtant votre empereur !

C'est l'homme de Sédan qu'on traine aux gémonies
Voilà le gâteux, le crétin
Qui vendit notre France à tant d'ignominies
Voilà l'excrément du destin
Voyez quel nez ! quels yeux ! quel front patibulaire
Voyez ses moustaches en crocs
C'était le roi des grecs le prince des galères
Le Napoléon des escrocs
Il s'est fait prisonnier ; la troupe était vendue
Il combattait pour la livrer !
Notre honneur est flétri la patrie est perdue
La Prusse va nous dévorer
Il régnait par le vol le meurtre et l'adultère
Il nous a pourris jusqu'au cœur !...
C'est bien, nobles français j'aime votre colère
C'était pourtant votre empereur !

[12]

Vous l'avez acclamé teint du sang de décembre
Vous l'avez mis sur le pavois
Les francs ont reconnu pour chef ce fier Sicambre
Avec sept millions de voix !
Vous avez oublié les folles équipées
Et de Boulogne et de Strasbourg
Paris lui coutera ses palais, ses épées
Et les bras nus de son faubourg :
Car c'était le neveu du chapeau légendaire
Si redouté de l'étranger,
Du grand homme de bronze à jamais populaire
Dans les chansons de Béranger ;
La colonne était là pour raconter la gloire
Dont il devenait l'héritier !
L'univers préparait ses crayons, sa mémoire
Et le pape son bénitier.

Malheur ! cet homme a pris Olivier pour ministre !
Sept millions de fois malheur
Cet homme était fou, cet homme était un cuistre
C'était pourtant votre empereur !
Ah colonne maudite a dit la populace
C'est donc toi qui nous a trahis
Trochu nous a berné l'ennemi nous enlace
Et nos foyers sont envahis
Courbet nous disait bien que ton tube en spirale
N'était qu'un mirliton géant
Va porter aux enfers la gloire impériale
Désormais vouée au néant
Que du neveu proscrit l'onde soit solidaire
A bas le mensonge d'airain
De la gloire abaissons le fait jusqu'à terre
Et place au mépris souverain !

[13]

Allons ingénieurs , du fumier des cordages
Des échafauds, des cabestans
Déboulonnez le bronze et brisez les visages
De nos pères vieux combattants
Entaillez en sifflet le pied de la colonne
Puis tenez vous prêts au signal
Et toi, viens répéter grande ombre de Cambronne
Ton mot héroïque et brutal !
C'est bien, tournez, tirez ; les cordes sont tendues
Voilà les lilliputiens
Qui du grand Gulliver tranquille au sein des rues
Tourmentent les tristes liens
Le cotoffe a peu l'air d'aspirer à descendre
Pourtant après un craquement
Dans la foule attentive un cri s'y fait entendre
On voit branler le mouvement

C'en est fait le césar se déplace… il se penche
La colonne se brise en l'air
Sous le bronze en tronçons on voit la pierre blanche
Comme des os perçant la chair
Puis avec un bruit sourd une immense poussière
Tout le mouvement écroulé
S'abat en cent débris et fait trembler la terre
L'égout même en est ébranlé :
Des mains de l'empereur s'échappe la victoire
Adieu Napoléon premier !
Jamais on n'avait vu tant de bronze et de gloire
Tomber sur autant de fumier !
Et vous n'étiez pas le soldat des pyramides
Pour défendre un ancien soldat !
Tu n'as point pris le deuil donc des invalides
Après ce stupide attentat
Les enfants ont craché sur la croix de leurs pères

[14]

[Dans la marge :]
Allez ! que la colonne en lambeaux vous poursuive !
Qu'elle vous morde les talons
Que son relief le grave en creux dans la chair vive
qu'elle ensanglante ses boulous

Et l'étranger les regardait !
Ah ce jour suit le comble aux ignobles misères
Que la fortune nous gardait
Décapiter des morts, déconsommer la cendre
Est-il rien de plus monstrueux ?
Et vous qui jusque là nous avez fait descendre
Parlez anarchistes hideux
Que vous a fait le spectre insulté dans la tombe ?
Rien, disent-ils avec fureur
Mais son nom nous révolte et nous voulons qu'il tombe
C'est l'oncle de votre empereur !
Eh bien votre empereur dans sa lâche démence
Fut digne de vos lachetés
On dit qu'il a vendu les martyrs de la France
Et vous les avez souffletés
Que ce bronze vengeur en tous lieux accompagne
Vos forfaits jamais expiés
Qu'on le fonde en boulets et qu'on vous fasse une bague
Trainer la colonne à vos pieds !

Le tableau de Chenavard

Grand Sphinx de la peinture, oracle de tombeau
Votre énigme est à jour ; voici votre tableau :
Dans la nuit du mystère où le christ agonise
De nos illusions le nuage se brise
Les cultes éperdu se livrent des combats
La terre monte au ciel, le ciel descend en bas
Un crépuscule obscur à la teinte livide
Étale sa pâleur dans l'immensité vide.
D'ormuz et d'Ariman les fantômes sans nom
Se battent sur le corps de Jupiter ammon.
La fable antique veut sous les traits d'une muse
Fixer le temps rapide en lui montrant Meduse,
Le temps tient sous la fausse Venus et les amours
Et la face voilée il va frappant toujours.

[15]

Mercure emporte au ciel d'où le faucheur s'élance
Pandore morte en couche hélas de l'espérance !
Prométhée est captif d'un autre Jupiter
Et regarde le christ sans espérer Luther.
La justice à l'envers, aveugle magnanime
A faussé sa balance en frappant sur le crime
Marsyas écorché règne au sacré vallon
Et chaude insolemment sous le pied d'Appollon
À la droite de dieu sont la force et l'adresse.
Les parques dans le ciel filent en paix leur tresse.
Pour couronner un dieu masqué comme le sort
Voltigent des esprits à la tête de mort
Ivre du fiel divin, mais rêvant l'ambroisie
Dans un cercle fatal tourne la poésie
Que la chimère emporte autour de l'idéal
Et de l'invasion donnant l'affreux signal
La France, ivre sans doute, avec un cor bizarre

Semble appeler odieu dieu du monde barbare
Et l'on voit luire au loin brûlant sans éclairer
Les yeux du loup feuris prêt à tout dévorer.
Vous n'étiez Chenavard qu'un sinistre poète
Et les événements vous ont sacré prophète
Il semble que Jésus Jupiter Jehovah
La nature, l'amour, tout est mort tout s'en va
Les sauvages du nord se partagent la France
La vie est sans attraits, la mort sans espérance
De son prestige ancien l'autel s'est dépouillé
Et l'encens des mortels par le meurtre est souillé !
Paris se remplissant d'indignes funérailles
A de sa propre main déchiré ses entrailles
Le loup Feuris sorti de ses autres germains
S'est engraissé de sang et de membres humains
Hélas tout est perdu tout jusqu'à l'honneur même
Les chiens dans le ruisseau trainent le diadème

[16]

La liberté sanglante a sali son drapeau
La mort ne compte plus son horrible troupeau
Car d'une multitude immonde et revoltée
On lave avec du sang la trace ensanglantée
Le bon droit n'est plus rien, la force fait la loi,
Le pouvoir est sans maitre et le temple sans foi !
ô maitre, je comprends la tristesse profonde
De votre grand tableau qui faisait peur au monde !
Les rois le repoussaient, Paris n'en voulait pas ;
La critique sifflait en l'admirant tout bas ;
De nos palais pour lui la porte était murée ;
Et dans le Luxembourg pour qu'il fit son entrée,
Il fallait le canon de nos envahisseurs,
Les obus révoltés de nos vils oppresseurs
Et l'ordre impitoyable écrasant leur audace !
Dans les écroulements les géants se font place
Pour vous ô Chenavard le tonnerre a parlé
Votre tableau remplit le palais ébranlé

Et la prédiction qu'on taxait de démence sera pour nos neveux notre épitaphe immense !

Ormuz et Ariman

Dirigeant des saisons le convoi solennel
Ormuz était assis dans son calme éternel
A ses pieds la nature allaitait en silence
Les mondes suspendus à sa mammelle immense
Quand soudain se dressant de toute sa hauteur
Ariman dit : je suis comme toi créateur
C'est moi qui fait le mal ! et dieu qui m'encourage
Admirant mon audace et fier de mon courage
Pour occuper l'ennui de son éternité
Créa du châtiment l'horrible majesté.
Je dis : plus de justice ! et lui : plus d'espérance
Alors Dieu souriant répondit : ma vengeance
C'est de te laisser même insulter à mon nom
J'écrase ta fureur d'un éternel pardon
Ton supplice c'est toi ton tourment c'est ta haine.

[17]

Ton trésor dévorant c'est la folie humaine
L'abîme est tout entier dans le cœur des pervers
Et ma miséricorde opprime les enfers.
Torturant de mon jour leur nuit qui se lamente
Je fais paisiblement le bien qui les tourmente
L'ordre éternel s'impose à leur orgueil moqueur
Mes bienfaits renaissants leur déchirent le cœur
Mon règne en s'étendant renverse leur empire
Et pour les foudroyer je ne fais que sourire !

Croire en dieu

Croire en dieu c'est penser qu'il est bon, juste et sage
Que le travail l'honore et que la peur l'outrage
Qu'il veut par la raison se laisser adorer
Sans lui poser d'énigme et sans la dévorer.
C'est des êtres en lui reconnaitre le père
Qui modère le fort, en qui le faible espère
Qui règne sans caprice et dans son avenir
Garde l'éternité pour cesser de punir.
 Le connaitre et l'aimer tel est donc son vrai culte
De tout dogme cruel l'obscurité l'insulte
Son symbole est écrit dans l'immense univers
Traduit chez les humains par des signes divers
Mais pour la raison pure au fond toujours le même
L'humanité le sert la haine le blasphème
Et malgré les enfers inventés en son nom
Pour ne jamais l'absoudre il pardonne à Néron

[18]

Comme il doit pardonner même au prêtre homicide
Même au croyant superbe, au pharisien perfide
Mais comme il est sans haine il sera sans pitié
Et sa bonté jamais ne punit à moitié
La peine c'est le mal provoqué par nos crimes
C'est le désordre enfin dont nous sommes victimes
Et dont le rédempteur n'est jamais attristé
Car pour tout rétablir il a l'éternité
ô dieu que dans mon cœur je sens penser et vivre
Je ne chercherai point tes arrêts sans un livre
Les livres sont menteurs les mots tout impuissants
Le temps change toujours les dogues vieillissants
Ton nom ne sonne pas dans la part de l'humain
Toute voix pour le dire est inhabile et vaine
Ton nom n'est pas un bruit et ton culte Seigneur
N'est pas un appareil, c'est un soupir du cœur !

Tes demeures de pierre emprisonnent mon âme
Qui pour les renverser fait éclater sa flamme

Que dis-je ? mon cœur même en se gonflant d'espoir
Sent le ciel se serrer vers lui comme un pressoir
Les bourdonnements sourds des hymnes de la terre
Se perdent en montant dans la voix du tonnerre
Et le tonnerre meurt, chant d'orgues solennel
Dans le temple muet du silence éternel
des formes et des voix, des cieux et des images
Mon âme a vu la borne et touché les rivages
Et dans le sombre azur de ton immensité
Mon désir éperdu tombe précipité
Ah des cultes humains qu'importe l'édifice
Ou des langues souvent se confond l'artifice
Daigne tu voir mon dieu les erreurs de Babel
Quand ton regard s'égaie au sourire d'Abel ?
La fleur dont un rayon sollicite la bouche
Boit amoureusement le soleil qui la touche
Et de ses doux soupirs elle embaume le ciel

[19]

Notre âme est une fleur dont ta grace est le miel
Nos pleurs sont la rosée où ton soleil se mire
Et ton amour est l'air que notre sève aspire !
Nous laisserons en toi nos erreurs s'oublier.
T'aimer, Seigneur c'est vivre et vivre c'est prier.
Nous vivrons pour aimer, nous aimerons pour vivre
L'univers est un temple et le ciel est un livre
Où nous lisons ton nom mille fois adoré
Tandis que sur le seuil de ton parvis sacré
De cent cultes divers le symbolisme étrange
Semblable aux cent couleurs des ailes d'un archange
Nuance le reflet doré sombre ou vermeil
De la même lumière et du même soleil !

Eternelles amours

Eternité ! toujours ! Ces mots, erreur suprême
Ou vérité d'un jour veulent dire : je t'aime !
Aimer c'est l'absolu. Le temps n'est pas l'amour
Un instant de bonheur rend éternel un jour.
L'éternité c'est dieu, c'est la beauté, c'est l'âme
C'est le feu créateur dont le temps est la flamme
Elle nous apparait puis se cache à nos yeux
Heureusement pour nous car nous serions des dieux
Et les dieux trop souvent amoureux des mortelles
Ont déserté l'Olympe ou les enfers pour elles.
Eternité grand tout que divise un instant
Epouse de ce dieu qui se montre inconstant
Pour créer une fois, si toi-même, féconde
Tu n'es pas la nourrice et la mère du monde
Au sein de l'empyrée et des soleils flottants

[20]

Ta durée infinie est l'espace des temps
Comme l'immensité de l'espace sans voiles
Est une éternité d'étoiles et d'étoiles…
Le temps poursuit l'amour l'amour dompte le temps
Et quand deux cœurs émus touchés par le printemps
Caressent du bonheur l'éphémère espérance
C'est l'eternel amour qui fait son œuvre immense
Alors on dit : toujours ! à jamais ! et souvent
Cet espoir infini s'enfuit avec le vent
Mais il n'est point perdu : sur des rives nouvelles
Il aime à voyager comme les hirondelles
Quand un amour finit c'est un hiver qui vient
Puis germe un autre amour et le cœur se souvient
Amour, secret divin qu'un baiser nous révèle
Vague pressentiment d'une vie immortelle
Gage déjà certain d'un splendide avenir
Ou d'un jour qui n'est plus lumineux souvenir

Eprouver ta chaleur c'est vivre ! te connaitre
C'est être homme et t'aimer c'est être dieu peut-être
Oui, t'aimer à jamais, comprendre ta beauté
C'est le ciel ; en jouir voilà l'éternité
Car tu n'es passager que dans nos mauvais songes
Et même leur pinceau coloré de mensonges
Qui t'ébauche au hasard sur le tissu des jours
Nomme encore éternels les fantômes d'amours
Ah le poète André, ce fier et doux génie
Ce nouvel Arion de l'antique Hellénie
Que brisa sans pitié malgré sa lyre d'or
Contre un écueil sanglant l'orageux Thermidor
Le chantre de Neere et de Fanny, mon maitre
Eut évité la mort s'il l'avait pu connaitre
Son cœur de désespoir et de colère armé
Trop altéré d'amour ne fut jamais aimé
Les chants mélodieux dont son exil nous berce
Sont les pleurs de Tibulle essuyés par Properce
Sa Camille lascive, amante sans beauté
Décourage bientôt l'ardente volupté

[21]

Elle n'a même pas courant de veine et veine
La fièvre de Délie et sa fureur romaine
C'est une courtisane aux baisers ennuyés
Au teint de plâtre aux yeux dans les vapeurs noyés
Je donnerai Lesbie et Camille et Délie
Pour un seul cheveu d'or de la pâle Ophélie
Qui vivante d'amour et folle de douleurs
S'endort dans le trépas en caressant des fleurs
J'aime de Roméo la compagne sublime
ô du celeste amour passion magnanime
Si chenier t'eut comme il n'eut dans l'univers
Pour consoler son cœur pour inspirer ses vers
Aimé suivi que toi ! ses colères viriles
N'eussent pas affronté les tempêtes civiles
Avare de ses jours et s'envolant plus haut

Il n'eut pas de son sang décoré l'échafaud.
Et qu'importe à l'amour que les trônes chancellent
Qui des vieux préjugés les débris s'amoncellent
Qui des peuples errants le flux et le reflux
Jette à l'echo des noms et des cris superflux ?
L'amour est un sommet qui ne craint pas la foudre
L'amour c'est l'aigle altier qui secouant la poudre
De son aile superbe abaissée un instant
Remonte vers son aire où le bonheur l'attend
Au dessus du nuage et dans le ciel paisible
Cette aire est suspendue au roc inaccessible
Et là, l'oiseau des dieux aux dieux même pareil
S'appaise les regards fixés sur le soleil.

[22]

Le poète et le réaliste

Le poète

ô vallons de Tempé, solitudes profondes
Bord que le Sperchios anime de ses ondes
Fleuves musiciens et bois mélodieux
Qu'habite et fait chanter le souvenir des dieux,
Grands tombeaux fleurissant sous le ciel d'Italie
ô Venise la rouge, ô Nice le jolie
Lieux vantés, lieux chéris, exils inspirateurs
Non, je ne rêve pas vos sites enchanteurs.
J'aime mieux ma retraire obscure et solitaire
Pleine d'un souvenir et d'un tendre mystère
J'aime mieux le bouquet désséché qu'oublia
En me quittant hier ma blanche Ophélia

Le réaliste

Les bouquets désséchés ne sont point mon affaire
Je voudrais une belle et bonne menagère.
Les vers sont ennuyeux.. mais c'est quand on les lit
Je voudrais quelque chose à palper dans mon lit
Mais je veux un amour qui soit une ressource
Et mette quelque chose à palper dans ma bourse

Le poète

Je ne sais quel regard a fasciné mon cœur
Un doux songe d'enfant de mon âme est vainqueur
ô vierge n'es-tu pas Aphrodite la blonde ?
Est-ce toi que la nacre allait bercer sur l'onde
Quand le ciel à la rose empruntant ses couleurs
Enflamma son azur et fit pleuvoir des fleurs ?
Serais tu Galatée au jeune Acis trop chère
Ou simplement la sœur de la blanche Néere

Et les dieux arrêtés à contempler tes yeux
Ont-ils à l'abandon laissé rouler les cieux

[23]

En sorte que l'hiver prolongeant son empire
Ne laisse de printemps qu'où ta bouche respire ?

Le réaliste

Quel galimathias ? ma belle écoutez moi
Je ne suis ni banquier ni poète ni roi
Mais dès que je vous vois, foi de menteur honnête
La caboche me tourne et je me sens tout bête
Si vous avez aussi je ne sais quel désir
En mélant tout cela nous aurons du plaisir.

Le poète

Les fleurs de la prairie étaient toutes écloses
Un rossignol chantait le cantique des roses
Les feuilles frémissaient ivres de vert nouveau
Sous des souffles de brise et des ailes d'oiseau,
L'onde claire ou flottaient des mourantes corolles
Murmurait au gazon d'amoureuses paroles.
Les grillons prolongeaient leur cri soufflant et doux,
Des gouttes d'eau pendaient aux épines des houx
Les rives de cressons étaient toutes couvertes
Les moucherons dansaient, et les grenouilles vertes
Montraient pour écouter les sons lointains du cor
Leur corset d'émeraude et leur lunettes d'or
Moi je vous demandais à la brise amollie
Au rossignol des bois je disais Ophélie
Aux feuillages émus je répétais tout bas :
Est-elle auprès de vous ? ne me la cachez pas.
Je poursuivais dans l'eau le reflet de mon rêve
A la feuille de houx, pour vous belle enfant d'Eve
Je disais durcissez la pluie en diamants

Je disais ; grondez les petits grillons charmants
De n'être pas ici quand mon cœur le réclame
Moucherons argentés que le soleil enflamme
Sifflez, volez, dansez, dites lui de venir.
Son du cor dans les bois fais la resouvenir
Qu'un oiseau familier désire être sa proie
Reinettes des marais sautez pour que je crois

[24]

Que vous la pressentez, que vous avez souci
D'annoncer sa présence et de la voix ici :
Que c'est en son honneur que vous vous faites belles
Que les blancs nénuphars sont vos fraiches ombrelles
Et que vous avez mis pour voir mon doux trésor
Vos corsets d'émeuraude et vos lunettes d'or.

Le réaliste

C'est peut être joli, mais la fillette est sage
Je viens de demander ta belle en mariage
Et je la prends, mon dieu, je te le dis tout bas
Pour faire des enfants et repriser des bas
Elle est fort raisonnable et comprend qu'il faut vivre
Qu'un ménage à son aise est meilleur qu'un beau livre
Elle sait qu'un beau vers ne vaut pas un écu Adieu poète.

Le poète

Adieu cocotte... adieu cocu
Passez moi le gros mot en faveur de la rime
Adieu Madame, adieu, vous êtes ou sublime
Ou stupide et l'amour rira sous son bandeau
De trouver Ophélie au lit de Coquardeau.

Sagesse d'amour

On peut aux passions abandonner les rênes
Quand l'âme resplendit de clarté souveraines
Lorsqu'on sait s'oublier et souffrir comme un dieu
Lorsqu'on a des mains d'or on peut toucher au feu.
Le vulgaire ignorant de mes amours peut rire
Et siffler Jupiter qui se change en satyre
Mais la foudre dormante et voilant son éclair
Sait bien que le satyre est encore Jupiter !
Le taureau ravisseur qui fend la rue profonde
Par ses mugissements fera trembler le monde
Le cygne de Léda peut à l'aigle pareil
L'œil fixe et radieux monter vers le soleil
Alcide est bien plus grand quand sa main triomphale
Assouplit sa vigueur sur le fuseau d'Omphale
Qu'armé de la masse et par des nœuds de fer

[25]

Trainant le chien du gouffre aux portes de l'enfer.
J'aime à voir le géant qu'un petit enfant mène
L'abaissement d'amour c'est la grandeur humaine
L'amour qui se soumet n'est que plus indompté
Et l'on n'est jamais vil aux pieds de la beauté
C'est pour plaire à l'amour qu'on recherche la gloire
La guerre pour l'amour dispute la victoire
L'amour contraint la nuit à nous rendre le jour
On est noble, on est fier, on est grand par l'amour.
Krishna, le dieu pasteur, le conquérant des âmes
Attirait au désert les vierges et les femmes
Et le son de sa flûte avait tant de douceur
Qu'en leur charmant l'oreille il ravissait leur cœur
Alors il leur disait : ô vierges trop légères
Pourquoi délaissez-vous la maison de vos mères ?
Femmes, pourquoi quitter le toit de votre époux
Les mères vont pleurer, les hommes sont jaloux.

Et les vierges disaient, et les femmes charmées
Répondaient : d'un mortel si nous étions aimées
Et si pour l'écouter nous mettions en oubli
Nos mères, nos époux, notre cœur avili
Mériterait le blâme et la peine sévère
Mais ton chant est plus doux que la voix d'une mère
Ton amour est plus beau que celui d'un époux
C'est pourquoi, fils du ciel, aime nous et prend nous
Les accords enchantés de la flûte divine
D'un soupir éternel gonflent notre poitrine
Ils pénétrent l'esprit de lumière et de feu
Et nous voulons mourir sous les baisers d'un dieu !
Ah qu'importe au bonheur ce que le monde en pense
Lorsqu'il est partagé, l'amour c'est l'innocence
Pour tous ceux que son charme à jamais entraina
L'amour est à jamais la flûte de Krishna

[26]

Mais d'un amour menteur craignons la voix impure
Faisons taire l'orgueil écoutons la nature
Ne jettons pas l'espoir de notre éternité
Dans un gouffre insolent de stupide beauté
Redoutons de Seylla la ceinture aboyante
Et que notre folie au moins soit prévoyante
Au plaisir passager tendons toujours la main
Sans déserter pour lui jamais le droit chemin !
Attaché comme Ulysse au mot de ma carème
J'écoute, je regarde et j'aime la sirène.
Ma sirène est jolie, elle a les cheveux blond
Les yeux bleus sont frangés de cils dorés et longs
Toute entière elle sort pour moi de l'onde bleue
Et je sais que d'un phoque elle n'a point la queue
Puis elle disparait et semble m'oublier
Je suis heureux alors de m'être fait lier
Car autrement, lancé dans le gouffre à la nage
Je voudrais la chercher de rivage en rivage…
Mais elle reparait quand je n'y songe plus

Riant de mes transports de mes pleurs superflus
Elle approche et retient la coupe d'ambroisie
Elle aiguillonne encore mon âpre jalousie
Je me prête à ses jeux, je jouis de souffrir
Je suis triste parfois jusqu'à vouloir mourir
Et je sens un parfum dont son baiser m'enivre
Que souffrir et mourir ainsi d'amour… c'est vivre
Je retrouve mes vers, mes rêves de vingt ans
Mon hiver refleurit, ma neige est un printemps
Je suis heureux de voir cette Aphrodite blonde
S'élever tout à coup sur l'écume de l'onde
Pendant que mon vaisseau doucement emporté
Vogue vers la science et l'immortalité !

[27]

Anacréon

Le vieil Anacréon disait aux jeunes filles
Venez à moi venez mes colombes gentilles
De tendresse et de fleurs je veux vous parfumer
Je ressemble à l'hiver mais mon foyer pétille
Et toutes les saisons ont droit de vous aimer
Vous dont pour moi la vue est une renaissance
Oh ne souriez pas de ma seconde enfance
Et craignez d'afficher dans son bonheur d'un jour
Ce poète joyeux si vieux pour l'espérance
Et si jeune pourtant, si jeune pour l'amour
A l'heure où du sommeil la douceur est si forte
J'ai reçu Cupidon qui frappait à ma porte
L'enfant en grelottant riait d'un air vainqueur
Je réchauffais ses doigts, lui préparait ses armes
Et dans l'espoir trompé de me causer des larmes
D'une flèche cruelle il a blessé mon cœur

A son cher triomphant je m'attelais sans crainte
Et lui me flagellant d'un rameau d'Hyacinthe
Dieu courroucé tout nouveau semblait toujours s'armer
Puis me voyant lassé, suant à grosses gouttes
Marcher à pas pesants et confondre les routes
Il me disait : vieillard tu ne sais plus aimer
J'ai bu des pleurs amers sur sa lèvre vermeille
Lorsqu'il allait criant piqué par une abeille
Dans le sein de Vénus cacher son désespoir
Je lui disais : enfant cette abeille me venge.
L'enfant parmi les pleurs riait d'un air étrange
Je lui disais adieu ; lui m'a dit : au revoir !
Ce soir là j'ai fermé ma fenêtre et ma porte
Je me suis cuirassé d'une armure très forte
En disant Cupidon ne sera plus vainqueur
Mais lui se moquant fort de ce vieil invincible

A pris la forme alors d'une flèche invisible
Et le monstre emplumé s'est glissé dans mon cœur

[28]

Eh bien je veux aimer j'ai chanté la victoire
Les Atrides, Cadmus, les héros et leur gloire
J'essayais de mon luth les cordes tour à tour
L'une disait amour l'autre disait je t'aime
Adieu donc les héros adieu la gloire même
Ma lyre ne veut plus répondre qu'à l'amour
Que l'amour retroussant sa tunique légère
Me verse un vin joyeux sur un lit de fougère
De nos ans passagers le cours est incertain
Apportez des parfums, donnez des fleurs écloses
Je veux tout aujourd'hui me consonner de roses
Qui sait si je pourrai me parfumer demain ?
Vous riez lycoris oh voyez jeune fille
Tous ces petits amours ils sont de ma famille
Ils boivent dans ma coupe et grignotent mon pain
Venez voir le soleil dans mon flacon qui brille
Qui sait si nous pourrons nous enivrer demain ?

Si mes cheveux sont blancs et si vous êtes blonde
Venus blonde a fleuri dans l'écume de l'onde
Qui du père océan forme les blancs cheveux
Les lys blancs par contraste embellissent les roses
Et les rougeurs de l'aube apparaissent encloses
Dans les nuages blancs du matin radieux
Bien des volcans de neige ont la tête couverte
Bien des fleurs au front blanc ont une tige verte
La colombe au bec rose aime le ramier blanc
L'hymen donne à la vierge une couronne blanche
Et du saule amoureux qui sur l'onde se penche
Un doux reflet blanchit le feuillage tremblant
Aphrodite au milieu des vagues ses sujettes
Apparait comme un lys parmi des violettes
La lune blanche aux fleurs se montre tous les soirs

Sur votre sein charmant qu'argente la jeunesse
Laissez ma tête folle oublier sa vieillesse
Et près de votre sein mes cheveux seront noirs

[29]

Et pendant ce temps les vieux sages de la Grèce
Vous cultiviez l'ennui pour fêter la sagesse
Et vous mettiez la mort dans votre panthéon
ô sages croyez moi votre mélancolie
Vos livres oubliés, votre docte folie
Ne valent pas un vers du fol Anacréon

Guillot le franc-maçon

Guillot le franc-maçon n'est pas un sot vulgaire
Il marche le corps droit et les pieds en équerre ;
Il est dans son faux col raide à faire plaisir
Il est incorruptible à l'endroit du silence
Montrez lui l'échafaud, montrez lui la potence
C'est toujours l'échafaud qu'on lui verra choisir
En argot franc-maçon l'échafaud c'est la table
Là ce frère terrible et le convive aimable
Manie habilement la hache et le poignard.
Le poignard c'est l'eustache à découper la viande
La hache est un couteau d'une longueur plus grande
Et l'assassin d'Hiram est souvent un canard

[30]

Avec la poudre rouge, avec la poudre blanche
Il sait faire long feu quand revient le dimanche
Il garde des secrets connus depuis cent ans.
Il a juré d'ailleurs de ne jamais nous dire
Qu'en hiver les frimas exercent leur empire
Et que le temps est beau quand revient le printemps
Il a splendidement accompli son épreuve ;
Il sait crier : à moi les enfants de la veuve
Quand un profanateur lui prête un coup de poing
Il a des mouvements où le mystère perce
Et son nom sur la planche où son esprit l'exerce
Est précédé d'un F avec un triple point.
Il fait de Salomon la parole sacrée
Et garde dans sa poche une chose dorée
Où l'équerre s'oppose à l'angle du compas.
Il a des mots hébreux qu'il ne sait pas écrire ;
Demandez lui tout bas ce que cela veut dire

Je puis vous assurer qu'il ne réponde pas
Au fond de sa commode il conserve en cachette

Un large ruban bleu paré d'une cosette
Où l'on voit Mac Bénac écrit en abrégé
Qu'est-ce que Mac bénac ? un irlandais peut-être
Silence malheureux ? c'est le secret du maitre
C'est pour cela jadis qu'Hiram fut égorgé.
Ces gens là sont-ils fous ? se moquent-ils du monde ?
Non, d'une allégorie admirable et profonde
Leur chef fut autrefois le confident discret.
Ses successeurs naïfs se contentent d'y croire
Et ne savent plus même au fond de quelle armoire
Il a caché la clé du cabinet secret.
(X) *placer ici la strophe oubliée*
Guillot le franc-maçon n'est pas un sot vulgaire ;

[31]

Il marche le corps droit et les pieds en équerre
Il est dans son faux col raide à faire plaisir.
Il est incorruptible à l'endroit du silence
Montrez lui l'échafaud, montrez lui la potence
C'est toujours l'échafaud qu'on lui verra choisir !
(X) *strophe oubliée par le copiste*

Mais ils n'en ont pas moins soit compagnon soit maitre
Des gestes de guignol pour mieux se reconnaitre,
Avant l'apprentissage ils étaient Moabon :
Puis ils ont eu dépit de la foudre de Rome
Leur grand maitre écossais nommé Joseph Prud'homme
Et Guillot qui prétend s'appeler Gabaon.

L'enfer des amoureux

I

Ah les grands vers ! franchement je m'étonne
Qu'on puisse en lire une page à la fois
Tant leur cadence est triste et monotone !
De Despréaux les rigoureuses lois
Les mots choisis, le nombre, la mesure
Et le repos qu'on nomme la césure,
Et le pathos, enfin ce qu'il louait
Nous fait bailler et lui même avouait
Que les grands vers ont des succès tragiques
Et qu'on ennuie en termes magnifiques.
Avez-vous vu le front olympien
Et la pâleur de Leconte de l'Isle
Le froid dédain de sa lèvre immobile
Et son regard qui ne croit plus à rien ?
Il a le spleen des anglais le pauvre homme
En méditant ses vers marmoréens

[32]

Les désespoirs sont hyperboréens
Il est glacé comme un faux dieu de Rome.
Victot Hugo du moins est amusant
Il sait tirer de l'idéal-fantôme
Des cauchemars pour l'univers atome
On rit on tremble on pleure en le lisant
Il est sublime à force de démence
Et nous saisit par son absurde immense
Et puis des vers il renverse les lois
Il est grotesque et terrible sans choix
A des erreurs, à des vérités nues
Il sait mêler des choses saugrenues
Qui dans la nuit crèvent comme un pétard.
Salut à toi gigantesque moutard !

Quasimodo fut crée pour gavroche
Et ta pensée aux comètes s'accroche
Moi qui ne puis les saisir aux cheveux
Je vais chanter l'enfer des amoureux

II

Lorsque de tout les semences premières
Dormaient encore sous un limon bourbeux
Quand du chaos le manteau ténébreux
Flottait sur l'eau des froides grenouillères
Survint l'amour qui grisa le chaos
Et de nectar lui barbouilla la trogne
Le vieux dormeur alors devint ivrogne
Et de la terre il sépara les eaux
Pour les garder plus longtemps sans les boire
Il les sala si l'on en croit l'histoire
Ainsi fut fait cet abîme des mers
Qui vit plus tard naître Vénus plus belle
Que son azur et parfois plus cruelle
Que la tourmente et les gouffres amers.

III

Enfin la terre amoureuse ingénue
A son auteur se fit voir toute nue

[33]

Et la nature aimante au cœur de feu
Se montra prête aux caresses de dieu.
Or du veillard quand la veuve éternelle
De la nature eut élargi le sein
Il fut surpris par un ange rebelle
Qui méditait un amoureux larcin
Pendant six jours à l'épouse embrasée

Dieu prodigua la céleste rosée
Mais le septième il s'endormit enfin
Comme épuisé de tendresse et de force
Le diable alors plus dispos et plus fin
A la nature offrit sa noire amorce
La pauvre mère avait les flancs très chauds
Elle mordit à la fatale pomme
Et le bon dieu fut traité comme un homme
Malgré sa foudre et ses brulants réchauds.

IV

A son réveil scandale et tintamarre !
De son courroux le paradis trembla ;
D'un coup de pied reçu dans la bagarre
Pendant neuf jours Satan dégringola.
Mais du viellard la femme était enseinte
De son époux d'abord, puis du galant.
Elle enfanta d'abord la cité sainte
Où des esprits perche le cœur volant
Ce premier fruit fut la pure semence
De Jéhovah, notre monde à son tour
Vint à faux terme…. Et c'est la médisance
Qui l'attribue au diabolique amour.
Mais dans son ventre empli par la luxure
Et le conflit du diable et du bon dieu
Après sa couche on dit que la nature
Sentait grouiller des avortons de feu
Du beau satan c'était la graine pure

V

A son époux elle cacha son mal

[34]

Mais un beau soir, comme aux jeunes étoiles
Pour s'amuser le ciel donnait un bal
Au firmament elle emprunta ses voiles
Puis se glissa sans lumière et sans bruit
Pour guide ayant sa négresse la nuit Hors du manoir du divin Sganarelle.
Il était temps ; la douleur maternelle
Vint la saisir aux portes du jardin
Que nos ayeux ont surnommé l'Eden
Mais elle avait eu des peurs si terribles
Quand son mari tempêtait dans les cieux
Qu'elle mêla quelques monstres horribles
Aux tendres fruits de l'archange amoureux
Car, à la fois, en se tordant la bouche
Comme un enfant qui crache un fruit amer
Elle enfanta dans sa dernière couche
L'amour la mort le plaisir et l'enfer

VI

Voilà pourquoi les solitudes mornes
Du Sinaï dans un jour solennel
Ont vu Moyse imitant l'éternel
Du mont sacré descendre avec des cornes.
Voilà pourquoi le sombre Jéhovah
Contre nature est si fort en colère
Qu'il fait trouver la pomme douce amer
Aux héritiers du beau péché d'Héva
Contre sa femme hélas trop endiablée
On dit qu'il plaide en séparation
Et le Sénat de la sainte Sion
(c'est le conseil de l'Eglise assemblée)
A dos à dos renvoyé les époux
Et nous soumet aux lois du dieu jaloux
En décidant que madame nature
Sauf son respect n'est qu'une belle impure

Qu'il faut la finir et la contrarier

[35]

Qu'il faut d'ailleurs consoler notre père
En partageant en amour sa misère
Et pour cela qu'il faut se marier.

VII

L'enfer d'amour c'est donc le mariage
Ah si Pyrame eut épousé Thisbé
Sur son poignard peut-être il fut tombé
Pour se soustraire aux ennuis du ménage
Ou si plus tôt de sa vieille aux abois
Il eut trouvé le voile dans les bois
Il eut remis le poignard dans sa gaine
Et de mourir n'aurait point pris la peine
Il aurait dit : ma pauvre femme ! enfin !
Elle n'est plus, c'est une triste fin.
Si j'avais pu je l'aurais délivrée
Mais tout est dit puisqu'elle est dévorée.
Alors Thisbé se hâtant d'accourir
Eut dit coquin tu ne veux pas mourir !
J'ai pour époux un héros je m'en vante !
Pour te punir je suis encore vivante
Allons nous en bras dessus bras dessous
Et gérions nous c'est le droit des époux

VIII

Ah si Saint Preux eut épousé Julie
Il eut été plus bête que Wohmar
Et plus trompé le pauvre diable, car
D'être jaloux il eut fait la folie
Julie alors aurait fait des sermons

A fatiguer des femmes de mormons ;
(mais les mormons n'existaient pas encore)
L'entendez vous cette docte pécore
Lui reprocher ce qu'elle a fait pour lui
Et l'exalter de colère et d'ennui
Alors Saint Preux ou Rousseau (c'est le même)
Dit : quoi ! voilà la bégueule que j'aime !
Elle est d'accord avec mes ennemis

[36]

Adieu bonheur que je m'étais promis
Je plante là cette femme savante
Pour aller vivre avec quelque servante.

IX

Au même fil liez deux tourtereaux
Et l'un de l'autre ils seront les bourreaux
L'un veut voler l'autre rester tranquille
L'un veut aller au bois l'autre à la ville
Ou se tiraille ou se plume le cou
Ou se démanche une patte, ou est fou.
Oui pour guérir deux amants il me semble
Qu'il suffirait de les lier ensemble.
C'est que l'amour n'est pas le pot-au-feu
L'amour n'est pas un acte de notaire
Ratifié sous le ventre du maire…
L'amour est tout : c'est le diable ou c'est dieu
Il est heureux lorsqu'il brise des chaines
Lorsqu'il affronte et suscite les haines
Il est joyeux vainqueur et détesté
Mais il s'endort dès qu'il est accepté

X

Vais-je conclure en haine du notaire
Pour les larçins de l'infâme adultère ?
Non l'adultère est une lâcheté
C'est une ignoble et basse impureté.
Celle qui prend un joug indigne d'elle
Doit se punir en lui restant fidèle.
Estimez vous ce récureur d'égouts
Qui du partage affrontant les dégouts
D'un vieux pourceau vient essuyer la place
Et que souvent à coups de pied l'on chasse ?
Heureux amants sachez en vérité
Que le bonheur aime la liberté
Cachez longtemps votre bonheur au monde
Fuyer les nœuds de l'intérêt immonde
Mais si pourtant un maternel espoir
De vous unir vient vous faire un devoir

[37]

S'il faut monter l'amour qui vous ressemble
Soumettez vous pour acheter la paix
Mariez vous pour vos enfants.. oui.. mais
Pour être heureux ne vivez pas ensemble
Fermez les yeux et ne plaidez jamais !
A quoi servent les vers
Et vous me demandez à quoi servent les vers !
Demandez à l'oiseau sous les feuillages verts
A quoi sert la chanson que toujours il répète
Demandez lui pourquoi la nature est poète
Demandez au Zéphyr demandez aux rameaux
Pourquoi leur bruit s'accorde au murmure des eaux
Demandez au soleil paré d'or et de flammes
A quoi sert sa clarté qui fait chanter les armes
Et l'oiseau répondra je chante sans savoir
A quoi sert ma chanson de l'aurore et du soir
Et l'arbre répondra dans sa vaste ramure

Je frémis sans savoir à quoi sert la verdure !
Et le soleil dira je réjouis les fleurs
Sans savoir à quoi sert ma féconde chaleur
Et le rosier dira montrant les fleurs écloses
Je fleuris sans savoir à quoi servent les roses.

[38]

Le vin de Chypre

Chanson

Un soir Bacchus aux bras de Cythérée
Ayant du jour surpris le dieu vermeil
Il enchaina leur paresse enivrée
Et de ses feux dépouilla le soleil.
Puis fécondant les beautés immortelles
De la déesse au sourire enchanteur
Il la remplit d'une double chaleur
Et d'un vin pur lui gonfla les mamelles.
Le vin de Chypre est fils du soleil d'or
Ma coupe est vide, amis versez encore
Oui de Vénus c'est le fait qui s'épanche
Elle a pressé les roses de son sein
D'Anacréon la messagère blanche
Vient s'abreuver à ce ruisseau divin
Puis pour rêver son innocent délire
Elle s'endort sur le luth enchanté

Et son plumage ivre de volupté
En palpitant fait soupirer la lyre.
Le vin de chypre est fils du soleil d'or
Ma coupe est vide amis versez encore
L'aigle qui boit la vendange éternelle
Loin du nectar tourne un bec oublieur
De Chypre il voit une envie nouvelle
Et pour en boire il déserte les cieux
A l'empirée il préfère une treille
Et laisse fuir le tonnerre altéré
Qui s'enroulant comme un serpent sacré
Va se noyer au fond de la bouteille !
Le vin de Chypre est fils du soleil d'or
Ma coupe est vide amis servez encore

[39]

De vin de Chypre encore tout embaumé
D'Anacréon l'ivresse soupirait
Il sommeillait livrant sa bouche aimée
A mille amours que son souffle attisait
Puis à l'entour de ses lèvres vermeilles
Des fleurs du monde apportant les moissons
Sur les raisins des essains de chansons
Se suspendaient ainsi que des abeilles
Le vin de Chypre est fils du soleil d'or
Ma coupe est vide amis versez encore
Le vin de Chypre embellit ma pensée
Ce que je cherche il le dit sans efforts
Il fait jaillir mon âme cadencée
A mon doux rêve il prête des accords
Il fait en moi refleurir le jeunesse
Des souches dieu il éteint le courroux

Et sa folie a des charmes si doux
Qu'elle rendrait jalouse la sagesse
Le vin de Chypre est fils du soleil d'or
Ma coupe est vide amis versez encore
Dans notre sang la lumière circule
Escaladons l'Olympe radieux
Entre nos pieds la terre s'accumule
La table monte et nous sommes des dieux
Chacun s'embrasse en se disant je t'aime
Et l'on ignore en ce conflit divin
Si le baiser n'est pas encore du vin
Le vin n'étant qu'un baiser de dieu même !
Le vin de chypre est fils du soleil d'or
Ma coupe est vide, amis versez encore !

[40]

A Victor Hugo

Après une première lecture de ses chansons
Des rues et des bois
Des soleils décrochant les chaines
Mettre au vert le cheval ailé
Qui courbe le front des grands chênes
Sous son pied bleu d'ombres voilées
Puis faire la figure à Virgile
En célébrant Jarnicoton
Et palper le mollet agile
De Lisbeth ou de Janneton
Dans le baquet des blanchisseuses
Culbuter l'amour barbouillé
Et faire des taches mousseuses
A son sourire encanaillé
Ce n'est point cueillir l'harmonie

De la nature au cœur de feu
C'est blaguer avec le génie
C'est polissonner avec dieu.
Hugo, ce livre où ta vieillesse
Le débraille en rire effronté
D'un titan c'est la folle ivresse
C'est un énorme nudité
Et je voudrais prendre les voiles
D'une vierge aux habits plus longs
Et son manteau fermé d'étoiles
Pour t'en couvrir à reculons.
La muse n'est pas une fille
Et c'est affligeant, par le ciel,
De voir trinquer à la courtille
Le grand prophète Ezéchiel

[41]

Ton sourire à l'air d'un sarcasme
Tes soupirs sont des calembours
Ta gaité tousse comme un asthme
Tes rêves brulants sont des fours
Tes pieds éventrent tes savates
Et ta joie a l'air d'un lion
Qui donne de grands coups de pattes
Pour attraper un papillon
Tu n'es point gaulois cher grand homme
Tes sauts défoncent le chemin :
Quand tu veux cueillir une pomme
L'arbre te reste dans la main
Et je trouve mieux la démence
Et le bon sens de l'homme gris
Dans les gros pont-neufs de colmance
Que dans tes fiers amphigouris

Après une seconde lecture
Je mets de l'eau dans mon vin.
De l'auteur des misérables
Ce nouvel ouvrage est plein
De bêtises adorables
C'est trivial et divin
C'est du génie à plein verre
Et la raison cherche en vain A rider son front sévère.
Un mot baroque est laché
Et Prud'homme tout morose Croit que c'est un gros péché
Mais il en sort une rose
Parfois les baisers fleuris

[42]

De cette fée en délire
Semblent pondre une souris
Et c'est toujours un sourire.
C'est risqué, mais c'est joli

C'est choquant mais plein de verve
A la page on fait un pli
Et des cornes à Minerve !

Sérieusement

Ne dédaignons jamais la nature éternelle
Toujours jeune toujours éblouissante et belle
C'est notre illusion qui cause la laideur
Il n'est point de Satan dans l'œuvre du seigneur
Dieu fait la vérité l'homme dit le mensonge
Et l'erreur qui s'endort se traduit par un songe
Une araignée est belle en ses proportions
Le ciel en la créant eut ses intentions
Mais vous offenseriez la nature indignée
En prétant à l'abeille un ventre d'araignée
Chaque chose d'ailleurs en son lieu doit rester
Et rien hors de saison ne doit se présenter
Des cheveux sont de l'or autour d'un beau visage
Mais ils sont de l'ordure au milieu du laitage
On ne fait point rimer Sylvie avec Goton

[43]

Ni l'âme de Virgile avec Jarnicoton
On peut voir sa servante avec un œil cupide
Mais on ne fera pas qu'un torchon soit splendide
Turlurette a des yeux comme Callirhoé
Ninie a des seins blancs aussi bien que Chloë
C'est bien : mêlez Ninie a des airs d'opérette
Pour un refrain joyeux réservez Turlurette
Mais ne prétendez pas que les chats du grenier
Miaulent de plus beaux vers que ceux d'André Chénier
Chaque musique est douce en sa propre harmonie
Et l'art de bien choisir est le don du génie
La rue a ses pont-neufs pleins de grosse gaité
Les bois sont éloquents dans leur simplicité
Mais les oiseaux perchés sous la verte ramure
Ne font point de chansons de grotesque structure
L'Appollon quoi qu'on dise est plus beau qu'un magot
Que dit le rossignol ? il ne dit point Margot.

Si dans quelque boutique obscure et mal soignée
On voit par aventure un beau fil d'araignée
Provoquant le plumeau s'étendre dans son vol
Du profil de Minerve un crâne de saint Paul
Le fil à mon avis orne peu les images
Si je trouve des fleurs parmi de vieux fromages
Je n'en trouverai pas leur parfum plus exquis
Un rustre est après tout moins propre qu'un marquis
Je vous permets d'aimer dans leur simple nature
Les femmes de satin sous des robes de bure
Mais ne cousez jamais poète libertin
Une rime de bure a des vers de satin
Parfois dans un quatrain rocailleuse merveille
En enchantant l'esprit vous écorchez l'oreille
Dans une fleur qu'on voit doucement remuer
Vous jettez du tabac qui fait éternuer
Je crains quand vous mêlez et les ris et les farces
Que vous n'alliez changer les graces pour des garces

[44]

Et poutant qui pourrait s'irriter contre vous ?
Vous mêlez au fumier d'adorables bijoux
Vous semez sous nos pieds les trésors de l'Asie
Avec la feuille morte et la paille moisie
Racine près de vous n'est plus que de l'orgeat
Et racine pourtant n'était point un goujat
Comme lui ménageant l'harmonie et la rime
Vous êtes simple et doux quand vous êtes sublime
Ah vous avez des vers qui raviraient le ciel
Vous prêtez à l'amour des paroles de mielOn ne critique plus, on pleure et l'on vous aime Et vous embelliriez jusqu'à la laideur même !

Le roi d'Israël

Hymne hébraïque (x)

Le dieu de l'univers dit au roi d'Israël
Viens t'assoir à ma droite et dépose ton glaive
Tes ennemis tombés dans un sommeil sans rêve
Garderont sous tes pieds le silence éternel
Ton sceptre est dans Sion ton règne est sur le monde
Ton empire a soumis les rois épouvantés
Regarde autour de toi tes ennemis domptés
Et règne triomphant dans une paix profonde
Les lois de ton pouvoir gouvernent le destin
Le front de tes élus à l'éclat du tonnerre
Et je t'ai fait sortir du ventre de ta mère
Avant de réveiller l'étoile du matin
(x) qui croirait que ce chant grandiose et sauvage
Est un psaume que nous chantons à vêpres et
Que les docteurs catholiques prétendent avoir été
Fait pour Jésus-Christ ?

[45]

Le seigneur l'a juré par l'honneur de la gloire
Et les serments de dieu ne s'effacent jamais
Tu seras devant lui prêtre de la victoire
Comme Melchisédech fut le roi de la paix
L'éternel dans ta droite a remis sa puissance
Israël doit régner par les mains de son roi
Il brisera les chefs au jour de sa vengeance
Et leurs sceptres vaincus tomberont devant toi
Lui même jugera ceux qui te font le guerre
Pour finir leur désastre il ira les chercher
Puis il viendra te prendre et te fera marcher
Sur les fronts écrasés des maitres de la terre
Qui donc marche si fier sous un ciel dévorant ?
C'est le roi d'Israël qui jamais ne s'arrête

Il puise avec sa main l'eau fraiche du torrent
Et toujours plus superbe il relève la tête !

Le renard et le corbeau

Eh quoi lecteur intraitable
Tu veux toujours du nouveau !
Eh bien soit : voici la fable
Du renard et du corbeau
C'est nouveau comme les fables
Nouveau comme le pont neuf
La grenouille avec le bœuf
En sont témoins véritables
Mais on a tant critiqué
La fable de la fontaine
Rousseau la trouve si pleine
D'un enseignement risqué
Que pour ce juge sévère
Dont je comprends l'argument
Je vais tâcher de la faire
Non pas mieux, mais autrement

[46]

Un corbeau sur une fenêtre
Soulevait un fromage, un renard l'avisa,
Et contre le mur se rasa
En disant : salut ô mon maitre !
Vous êtes magnifique avec cet habit noir !
Si c'est un plaisir de vous voir
Que serait-ce de vous entendre ?
Vous devez avoir une voix
Forte et gracieuse à la fois,
Une voix formidable et tendre !...
Crouah ! dit le corbeau, le fromage tomba
Et maitre renard le goba.
Voilà de nos flatteurs tout ce qu'il faut attendre

Les deux étoiles

Fable

Deux étoiles brillaient dans un ciel sans nuages,
Un invincible aimant les faisait se chercher
On les voyait se rapprocher
Et de leurs doux rayons confondre les mirages
L'une disait : je t'aime ! et l'autre répondait :
Je t'aime ! un seul désir toutes deux les guidait
Il le semblait du moins : mais des deux la plus belle
En voyant de sa sœur les rayons l'envahir
S'arrêta tout à coup, se prit à tressaillir
Et dit en reculant vers la nuit éternelle :
Je cherche le bonheur, mais je crains le trépas ;
Dans ta lumière confondue
Si je m'unis à toi je vais être perdue !...
L'autre lui répondit : va tu ne m'aimes pas

[47]

En amitié lorsqu'on songe à soi-même
Il ne faut pas dire qu'on aime
L'échange en amitié n'a rien de hasardeux
L'intérêt d'autrui c'est le nôtre
On était tout seul, on est deux
Nous nous retrouvons l'un dans l'autre
Ce qu'on donne on ne le perd pas
C'est au fond qu'on économise
Quand même on n'aspirerait pas
Aux fruits de la terre promise
L'amour est l'escompte du ciel
Il n'appauvrit jamais personne
Son caractère essentiel
C'est de s'enrichir quand il donne

Les châtiments de Victor Hugo

C'est pour les dieux surtout qu'il faut être sévère
Les dieux doivent les lois et l'exemple à la terre
L'auréole d'un front vivement éclairé
Le flétrit doublement si c'est un front taré
La muse au sistre d'or doit avoir des mains pures
Et ne verser jamais de fiel dans les blessures
C'est pourquoi le poète aux vils emportements
Doit subir à jamais ses propos châtiments
Quand Juvenal aigri par les cris de l'école
Porta jusqu'à l'excès sa mordante hyperbole
Ses satires gardaient dans leur obsécuité
D'un Jupiter vengeur la sombre majesté
Pour châtier Crispin de sa fortune accrue
Il ne ramasse point l'injure dans la rue
Il voit avec dégout les ignobles romains

[48]

Mutiler ce Séjan qu'encensèrent leurs mains
Et ne va point souillant des grandeurs trop punies
En disputes le reste aux chiens des gémonies
Je comprends qu'un pourceau fouille dans un bourbier
Je ne sais si jamais un infâme barbier
Maitre Olivier le dain dans l'eau blanchâtre et sale
Chercha les résidus de la crasse royale
Mais je ne comprends pas qu'un génie inspiré
Un penseur radieux, un pacte sacré
Plongeant dans les égouts ses mains patriarcales
Traine ses ailes d'or sur des choses fécales
Trop de haine détruit les droits de la raison
On n'exécute pas Mandrin par le poison
Quiconque est en fureur n'est pas une victime
C'est un bourreau jaloux, un juge illégitime.
On ne soufflette pas l'homme qu'on fait mourir
Je comprends qu'en exil ton âme a du souffrir

Victor Hugo, j'admets que loin de la patrie
L'amertume s'exalte et se change en furie
Tant que Napoléon fut un triste César
Je comprends ta colère attachée à son char
Mais quand les châtiments ont terminé leur tâche
Quand César est tombé l'insulte devient lâche
On ne piétine pas sur Claude agonisant
Hugo, voilà pourquoi je souffre en te lisant
En cessant de régner Claude a cessé de vivre
Et plus digne que lui tu supprimais ton livre
Mais si pour un peu d'or ta muse a profité
De la chute du maitre et de l'impunité
Si la haine survit quand la puissance est morte
Ta colère déroge et n'est plus la plus forte
Ta muse est une goule outrageant les tombeaux

[49]

Qui d'un pouvoir-cadavre exhume les lambeaux
Et vend cupidement ses œuvres de vampire
C'est la dernière enfin des hontes de l'empire !

Le chant des captifs

Mélodie hébraïque

Sur les fleuves de Babylone
Au pays de l'exil où dieu nous abandonne
Dans nos barques le soir nous allions pour pleurer
Aux saules du milieu des fleuves
Nous suspendions nos harpes veuves
Qui semblaient pour Sion gémir et soupirer.
Nous nous cachions loin du rivage
Pour ne plus entendre la voix
De l'oppresseur lâche et sauvage
Qui disait : chantez nous vos hymnes d'autrefois.
ô Jérusalem ô ma mère !
Comment chanterions sur la terre étrangère
Les hymnes du dieu d'Israël ?

[50]

Jérusalem si je t'oublie
Qu'au palais ma langue se lie
Que ma main desséchée éprouve un froid mortel !
Que jamais je ne te revois
Si tu n'es l'espoir de mon cœur
Et le principe de ma joie
Et le rêve de mon bonheur !
Souviens toi, dieu de la vengeance
Des fureurs des enfants d'Edom
Le jour où blasphémant ton nom
Ils renversèrent ta puissance !
Ils criaient : anéantissez !
Brulez Jérusalem entière !
Anéantissez, renverssez,
Arrachez la dernière pierre !
Courtisanne des nations

Malheur ! malheur à toi Babylone l'impure !
Heureux qui doit un jour payer avec usure
Tes lâches profanations !
Bienheureuse la main guerrière
Du vengeur juste et triomphant
Qui doit sur ta dernière pierre
Ecraser ton dernier enfant !
Aux saules du milieu des fleuves
Nous suspendions nos harpes veuves
Qui semblaient pour Sion gémir et soupirer
Sur les fleuves de Babylone
Au pays de l'exil où dieu nous abandonne
Dans nos barques le soir nous allions pleurer

[51]

L'échelle de Jacob

Aux suprêmes hauteurs l'esprit doit toujours tendre
Mais l'infini l'épuise et le force à descendre.
Il tombe dans l'enfer sitôt qu'il se fait dieu
Deux cercles aimantés de lumière et de feu
Du grand axe divin sont les pôles extrêmes
De leur attraction les forces sont les mêmes
L'enfer attire l'ange et le ciel les démons
Les hauteurs tour à tour sont des gouffres profonds
Car le monde absolu tourne comme la terre
Pendant l'éternité les esprits sont en guerre
Pour changer de demeure et semblent conquérir
Le passage central qu'on appelle mourir.
L'enfer grandit le ciel, le ciel creuse l'abyme
On est triomphateur tour à tour et victime.
Tous luttent dans Caïn tous meurent dans Abel.

Le monde des esprits c'est la tour de Babel
Qui plonge son reflet dans l'eau noire et dormante
Quand je monte joyeux mon ombre se lamente
Et descend vaguement dans mon reflet perdu
Jamais nul n'est monté sans être descendu
Les âmes ont leur nuit leur sommeil et leur rêve
Leur soleil noir et blanc soir et matin se lève
Les réprouvés du blanc sont les élus du noir
Et l'espoir grandissant grandit le désespoir :
Mais c'est le même Dieu que notre œil clair ou sombre
Revêt de la lumière ou couvre de son ombre
Il étend ses deux bras l'un dans l'ombre où ses doigts
Tracent avec du feu de formidables lois
L'autre dans la lumière où ses doigts trempés d'ombre
Ecrivent sur le jour un dogmatisme sombre
Et l'âme universelle immense balancier

[52]

Au travail créateur voulant s'associer
Refait du noir au blanc sa course à moitié ronde
Et devient le moteur de l'horloge du monde
Jamais l'ange vainqueur ne monte vers les cieux
Sans entrainer captif un démon furieux
Et jamais réprouvé dans la sombre demeure
Ne tombe sans damner un bel ange qui pleure
Tout damné dans l'enfer souffre pour un élu
Qui le remplacera, son cycle révolu ;
Et tout élu jouit pour absoudre le crime
D'un damné tour à tour rédempteur et victime
Dieu veut être offensé pour devenir sauveur,
Et le diable a sa place au conseil du seigneur.
De Job sur son fumier les larmes condensées
En étoiles au ciel seront un jour placées.
Un insolent bonheur est le crime des dieux,
(x) Et c'est être innocent que d'être malheureux
(x) vers de Lafontaine

Ainsi l'ombre et le jour trompent notre œil débile
Et dieu ne permet pas la souffrance inutile
Qui souffre s'enrichit, souffrir c'est amasser
Qui se repose perd, jouir c'est dépenser
Lorsqu'on est ruiné l'on retourne à l'ouvrage
Qui souffre plus pourra dépenser davantage
Puis après chaque jour de travail accompli
L'âme avant de dormir se baigne dans l'oubli
Telle est la grande loi, la loi de l'équilibre
Qu'on cesse de subir quand l'esprit devient libre
Il se transforme alors, il change de milieu
Il est dans l'infini créateur avec dieu
C'est Prométhée enfin que Jupiter adore
Et Lucifer vainqueur devient un égrégore
Il est l'âme et le roi d'un astre radieux
Car dieu fait les soleils pour y loger les dieux

[53]

Le nôtre est la demeure où Jésus se rallie
Aux esprits immortels de Moyse et d'Elie
Hénoch les précéda dans ce brillant séjour
Sur la terre qui souffre ils reviendront un jour
Quand par les éléments tour à tour épurés
La terre par le feu sera transfigurée
Alors dieu dans le ciel n'aura que des élus
La souffrance, la mort l'enfer ne seront plus
La cité transparente et pure comme un verre
Déjà bâtie au ciel descendra sur la terre
Alors nous gouterons le bonheur et la paix
Toute la rue doit être essuyée à jamais
Un ciel nouveau luira sur la terre nouvelle
Et nous nous souviendrons de la vie éternelle
Telle est la vision qu'avec sa plume d'or
Saint Jean l'évangéliste écrivit au Thabor

Et qu'il continuait au bruit des sept tonnerres
Dans l'île de Patmos entre les sept lumières
Notre âge ne croit plus aux visions des saints
Le ciel a la science a voilé ses desseins
L'autel est ébranlé la foi s'est obscurcie
Des mortels fatigués l'âme s'est endurcie
Quelque chose pourtant doit bientôt transpirer
A travers le rideau prêt à se déchirer.
N'abjurons pas, prions, la foi c'est l'espérance
L'homme doit avant tout croire à son ignorance
Constater ce qu'il sait, chercher la vérité
Et se dire ignorant sans incrédulité
Puis sans approfondir l'insondable mystère
Dormir comme l'enfant dans les bras de sa mère.

[54]

Anacréon à sa colombe

Péleïa, ma colombelle
Vous êtes amoureuse et belle
Votre bec rose a de l'éclat
Votre plumage est délicat
Vous roucoulez d'un air si tendre
Que c'est plaisir de vous entendre
Lorsqu'avec de petits frissons
Vous sommeillez à mes chansons
Je chante d'une voix plus douce
Le ruisseau sous un lit de secousse
Ne fait pas plus discrètement
N'a pas un babil plus charmant
Car il me semble, oiselle blanche
Que pour vous voir Vénus se penche
Et qu'en venant vous admirer
Elle m'écoute soupirer.
Quand doucement ma main vous touche
Quand je vous presse sur ma bouche

Je respire avec volupté
Tous les parfums de la beauté.
Mais quoi ! vous cherchez la fenêtre !
Désirez vous un nouveau maître ?
Aimez vous quelque jouvenceau
Frisé, paré, volage et beau,
Qui vous prendra, ma colombelle,
Pour faire un présent à sa belle ?
Hélas ma mignonne autrefois
Vous preniez du pain dans mes doigts
Autrefois vous m'étiez fidèle
Etes vous comme l'hirondelle
Qui fuit au déclin des beaux jours ?
Faites vous la chasse aux amours

Avez-vous la soif des voyages
Comme tous les oiseaux volages ?
Allez, vous vous repentirez
Un jour, trop tard vous reviendrez
Poudreuse et peut être blessée
Vers ma demeure délaissée

[55]

Anacréon n'y sera plus
Vos regrets seront superflus
Votre poète sans colombe
Se sera couché dans la tombe
Il ira sur les sombres bords
pleurer ses amours chez les morts
Et se consonner d'asphodèle
Loin de la colombe infidèle.

L'amour du vieillard

L'amour chez le vieillard c'est l'amour paternel
Son plus tendre désir n'a rien de criminel
Et jamais l'oubli ne l'étonne
Il a tout ce qu'il veut ne voulant que le bien
Son cœur n'est point jaloux et sans exiger rien
Il accepte ce qu'on lui donne
La sagesse tardive appaise enfin son cœur
Un pur attachement succède à la fureur
Des passions désordonnées
Son âme se remplit de calme et de soleil
Et les heures pour lui d'un sourire pareil
Passent l'une à l'autre enchaînées.
Ainsi quand l'éternel créa les éléments
Du chaos amoureux les longs soulèvements

[56]

Déchirèrent l'espace immense ;
Tous les mondes rivaux bondirent désunis
Et leurs bruits éclatants des gouffres infinis
Epouvantèrent le silence
L'incendie à la main les étoiles couraient
Les astres furieux entre eux se dévoraient
Des jours les nuits étaient jalouses.
Les rochers s'écroulaient pour violer la mer
Les volcans s'élançaient et prenaient dans l'ether
Les comètes pour leurs épouses
Mais la terre vaincue enfin se reposa
Sous un baiser du ciel le monde s'appaisa
L'univers eut l'amour pour base.
L'eau féconda la terre et réprima le feu
Et la création put contempler son dieu
Dans une imperturbable extase

Sait-on pourquoi nos cœurs palpitent agités
Et pourquoi nos printemps vers les brûlants étés
En secouant leurs fleurs s'élancent
Pourquoi l'inquiétude étreint nos plus beaux jours
Et pourquoi nous marchons sur de faibles amours
Que nos désirs toujours devancent ?
C'est que notre âme a soif d'harmonie et de paix
Elle a soif du bonheur qui ne tarit jamais
L'amour ! l'amour sans injustice.
L'amour qui par l'orgueil n'est jamais combattue
L'amour pur, l'amour vrai, l'amour par la vertu
Elevé jusqu'au sacrifice !
Cet amour qui rayonne et qui n'absorbe pas
Cet amour dont l'espoir affronte le trepas
Car il tient les clés de la vie

[57]

Son abnégation s'enrichit à donner :
Il ne s'occupe pas de plaire ou d'étonner
Aimer est toute son envie.
La jalousie est vaine à vouloir le garder
Il est beau sans le voir et sans se regarder
Est-ce que le soleil se mire ?
Il est riche à jamais de son propre trésor
Il est celui qui creuse, il est la mine d'or
Il est le monarque et l'empire
Celle qu'on aime ainsi peut s'éloigner de nous
Loin d'elle on peut souffrir mais on n'est point jaloux
On l'aimerait même infidèle
Nous lui gardons toujours nos bienfaits oubliés
Tout prêt à revenir, à mourir à ses pieds
Si jamais son cœur nous rappelle.

Mais n'assombrissons point des rêves superflus ;
Les cœurs unis ainsi ne se séparent plus.
Non, tu n'es pas une chimère
Amour dont l'idéal rendrait les dieux plus doux

Amour dont la grandeur prête même à l'époux
Les sublimités de la mère !

[58]

Dialogue d'Jakoub et d'Adonaï

Ou la lutte de Jacob avec l'ange

Adonaï
Je suis Dieu je commande au ciel comme aux enfers

Jakoub
Je suis homme et je veux savoir pourquoi je sers

Adonaï
Tu sers pour obéir à la loi de ton maitre

Jakoub
Qui veut me commander doit se faire connaitre

Adonaï
Tu me connais assez quand je te fais trembler

Jakoub
C'est qu'à la fièvre alors tu prétends ressembler

Adonaï
Je suis plus fort que toi tombe à genoux rebelle

Jakoub
La raison du plus fort n'est jamais la plus belle

Adonaï
Ecoute le tonnerre il parlera pour moi.

Jakoub
Le tonnerre est un bruit qui gronde comme toi

Adonaï
J'ai crée le soleil, reconnais ma puissance

Jakoub
Mes yeux de ton soleil n'ont pas vu la naissance

[59]

Adonaï
Je puis t'anéantir

Jakoub
Je ne serai plus rien
Et ton être pour moi sera pareil au mien

Adonaï
Je me fais adorer par la nature entière

Jakoub
Je ne la comprends pas, traduis moi la prière.

Adonaï
Elle dit que ma main du néant la tira

Jakoub
Quand le néant pourra le savoir il rira

Adonaï
Regarde l'infini, tu verras mon domaine

Jakoub
L'infini c'est la fin de la science humaine

Adonaï
Tu sens bien que le ciel n'est pas crée par toi.

Jakoub
Pourquoi le serait-il par un autre que moi ?

Adonaï
Parce que l'univers ne s'est pas fait lui-même

Jakoub
Et toi, qui t'a crée ? c'est le même problème ?

Adonaï
J'existe par moi-même

Jakoub
Et l'univers aussi

Adonaï
Non, c'est moi qui l'ai fait

[60]

Jakoub
Il est mal réussi
L'ignorance et le mal se disputent la terre
La peste, les fléaux, l'injustice, la guerre
Y promènent toujours leurs glaives dévorants

Adonaï
Les hommes sont pervers.

Jakoub
C'est qu'ils sont ignorants
Pour échapper au mal il font le mal eux-mêmes

Adonaï
Tes vains raisonnements ne sont que des blasphèmes
Il faut croire en silence et plier devant moi

Jakoub
Alors tu te fais juge et tu caches la loi

Adonaï
La loi tu la connais.

Jakoub
Chaque peuple a le sienne
Manques tu de moyens pour promulguer la tienne ?

Adonaï
Des moyens, insolent ! tiens voici mon arrêt :
Je vais en le touchant t'énerver le jarret.

Jakoub
Aïe ! Je boite, Seigneur, le fait est véritable
Et vous êtes vraiment l'éternel ou le diable

Adonaï
Va donc prêcher mon nom.

Jakoub
Seigneur je suis honteux
D'avoir à me servir d'un argument boiteux

Adonaï
Sont-ce des gens bien faits qu'il faut que tu combattes
Un boiteux marche droit aux yeux des culs de jattes

[61]

En tête à tête ici nous avons discuté
Sans trouver à nous deux un mot de vérité
Je te bénis Jacob nous sommes deux compères
Tu naquis fort malin pour supplanter tes pères
Tu savais par ton art de champêtre forban
Escroquer des brebis au beau père Laban
Sois le père des juifs, brocante et fais fortune
Va rogner le soleil, falsifier la lune
Fais pour moi des billets que je protesterai
Et que tu nommeras ton grand livre sacré

Adieu Jacob adieu mon fils et mon prophète
Toi seul comprend combien l'espèce humaine est bête
Et tu la soummettras toute entière à la loi
D'un dieu plus menaçant mais moins rusé que toi !

Le poète

Rêvant un souvenir de musique éternelle
Le poète est un fou dont la folie est belle
Il a dans son oreille un vague tintement
Il possède un bandeau d'immense enchantement
Qui transforment pour lui les crapauds en génie
Et les cris discordants en douces harmonies
Il ne voit que beautés il ne croit pas au mal
L'amour ce furieux besoin de l'animal
Pour lui n'est qu'un attrait qui rapproche les amis
Quand la cendre s'éteint il voit briller des flammes
Les enfants nouveau-nés ces petits nains affreux
Sortant de l'utérus tout rouge tout glaireux
Les poignets convulsés et les paupières closes
Sont pour lui des amours qui naissent dans des roses

[62]

Les femmes ces miroirs du caprice changeant
Qui n'aiment que l'orgueil les chiffons et l'argent
Ces vampires chéris de la jeunesse folle
Egoïsmes nerveux à l'engouement frivole
Etres que la logique a toujours irrités
Nourrices du mensonge et des absurdités
Sont pour lui des péris des elfes et des fées
Il les voit de pervenche et de myrte coiffées
Dans un vague rayon danser au bord de l'eau
Leurs babils importuns sont des chansons d'oiseau
Un soupir de leur bouche embaume les fleurs même
Les rayons du soleil leur font un diadème
Le doux Zephyre attend leurs baisers créateurs
Le gazon reverdit sous leurs pieds enchanteurs
Lorsqu'elles ont passé l'air frémit et l'épure
Et leur grâce est l'amour de toute la nature

Aussi par tant d'erreurs les poètes charmés
Aiment avec furie et ne sont pas aimés
Le tasse devient fou pour son Eléonore
Le Dante à Béatrix n'a pas pu plaire encore
Pétrarque fut par Laure illustre et dédaigné
Chénier livre Camille au sarcasme indigné
Pour avoir dans les bras d'un malotru peut-être
Surpris cette beauté dont il se croyait maitre
On connait de Rousseau les tableaux enchanteurs
Ses mensonges brûlants enivrent ses lecteurs
Louise de Warens lui préférait un cuistre
Et de l'isolement le délire sinistre
Lui fit choisir Thérèse une sale goton
Qui pour un palfrenier le trahissait dit-on
Moi-même j'ai chéri d'un amour insensé
La jeune Noëmie ma belle fiancée
Qui dans ma pauvreté qu'elle me reprochait
Un jour m'abandonna pour un vieux qui couchait

[63]

Quand Faust de sa prison veut sauver Marguerite
Qu'il n'a point délaissée après l'avoir séduite
Puisque c'est Valentin le brutal aggresseur
Qui vient en expirant déshonorer sa sœur
Faust est contraint de fuir mais au moment suprême
Il vient la délivrer en se perdant lui-même
La folle se détourne alors avec fureur
Et lui dit : laissez moi, vous me faites horreur
Et de supplier, heureux de l'avoir retrouvée
Les hypocrites voix chantent : elle est sauvée.
Ah c'est que le poète est le grand paria
Le jour de sa naissance un ange lui cria
Marche sous les mépris de la foule imbécille
Sois exilé toujours va-t-en de ville en ville
Et que tout seul pour toi soit inhospitalier
Platon te banniera couronné de lauriers
De sourires pour toi la fortune est avare

Et l'hopital des fous peut t'attendre à Ferrare

Si comme Camoëns sans asile et fièvreux
Tu ne meurs pas perdu parmi les malingreux
Les femmes t'aimeront après ta mort peut-être
Quand parmi des bijoux un butor un vieux reitre
Leur offrira tes vers richement illustrés
Sous une couverture et des fermoirs dorés
Si jamais un libraire ayant su te comprendre
A trouvé quelque argent à tirer de ta cendre !
Chante pour la nature et comme les oiseaux
Perd tes gazouillements à travers les rameaux
Fais comme Lafontaine ; aime les solitudes
Les longs sommeils sans bruit, les faciles études,
Mais ne prodigue pas facilement tes vers
Sache que le poète est seul dans l'univers
On aime à l'insulter même quand on l'admire
On veut empoisonner son innocent délire
Et le monde jouet des viles passions
Voudrait le dépouiller de ses illusions
S'il souffre c'est bien fait pourquoi rimeur superbe

[64]

Cultive-t-il encore les rôles de Malherbe
Quand le siècle blasé de sarcasmes nourris
Retourne aux vieux chardons de l'âme Scudéry ?
Qu'il devienne amusant s'il veut qu'on l'applaudisse
Qu'il soit le saltimbanque ou le pantin du vice
Et que d'un barbarisme étrange et colossal
Il émaille parfois son vers paradoxal
Le nombre harmonieux, l'expression choisie
La sagesse en un mot n'est plus la poèsie
Il faut faire sentir en style réchauffé
La rosée a des vers qui boivent du café
Il faut suspendre au nez de Minerve indignée
Des poèmes tissus de toiles d'araignées
Faire de son génie un jet d'eau sans pareil

Avec des diamants lapider le soleil
Pour jouer à la boule arrondir les étoiles
Préférer des torchons aux plus célestes voiles
Affubler la pudeur d'un bonnet de coton
Débrailler Arthémise ennoblir Margotton

Et tout cela pour plaire à qui ? mon dieu que sais-je ?
A des petits crevés qui sortent du collège
Et qui pour se venger de virgile oublié
Et dans leurs versions souvent estropié
Ont besoin d'une muse héroïne à moustaches
Capable d'enhardir leurs amours de potaches
Merci ! j'aime encore mieux poète d'autrefois
Chercher comme Gilbert l'exil riant des bois
Ou contempler rêveur près du bon Lafontaine
Le soleil découper des ombres dans la plaine
Voir nicher les oiseaux sur les clochers bénis
Poursuivre dans l'azur des rêves infinis
Et même aux Margottons prêtant de la décense
En ne leur parlant pas croire à leur innocence
Errer comme l'abeille autour des frais buissons
Pour les petits enfants composer des chansons
Et négliger, d'oubli mes hymnes consommées
Comme l'arbre abandonne au vent ses fleurs fanées
Je veux de qui m'oublie à mon tour oublier

[65]

Ouvrir toute mon âme aux merveilles des cieux
Sans chercher à savoir si pour d'autres merveilles
Midas le roi Midas a de longues oreilles
Ah malgré les mépris du vulgaire imposteur
Le poète est divin puisqu'il est créateur
Homère mendiant dans sa noble vieillesse
De l'Olympe à son tour fit l'aumone à la Grèce
Les poètes errants insensés radieux
Étaient des immortels puisqu'ils faisaient des dieux
Car tel est du vieux Sphinx le magique problème

L'homme a du créer dieu pour être dieu lui-même
Le sombre Ezéchiel, le prêtre Esaïas
Qui recula le jour sur l'horloge d'Achas
Le lyrique Baruch et les deux rois prophètes
Etaient en Israël d'admirables poètes
David lâche tyran mais psaltruiste inspiré
Fut par la poésie absous et consacré

Salomon tout perdu de débauches infâmes
A laissé des chansons plus belles que les femmes
Ainsi pauvre poète errant sans feu ni lieu
Sois fier de tes haillons qui déguisent un dieu
Tu n'as point de Daoud commis les adultères
Ni comme Salomon fait égorger tes frères
Sois fier d'être poète et de n'être pas roi
Les prophètes étaient malheureux comme toi
Leurs chants ont renversé le sacerdoce antique
D'autres éclairciront le mystère biblique
Chante, le ciel t'entend, tu n'as point de rivaux
Les rédempteurs du monde ont marché tes égaux.
Tu n'as point de valets mais tu n'as pas de maitre
Et du vieux Béranger qui ne voulut rien être
Les refrains goguenards les malignes chansons
Aux bourbous sur leur trône ont donné des frissons
Sois riche de génie et grand d'indépendance
Et tu te trouveras plus glorieux je pense

[66]

Au lieu d'être un valet de Napoléon trois
D'être un enfant d'Adam plus noble que les rois
Et parmi tous les fils de ce mangeur de pommes
Le plus doux, le plus simple et le meilleur des hommes

L'humilité chrétienne

Jamais quand des titans la révolte entassa
Pour se hisser au ciel Pélion sur Ossa
Ou quand Laomédon patron des dieux manœuvre
Les força par son vol à submerger leurs œuvres
Jamais quand de Tantale un bouquet odieux
Livra l'infanticide à l'appétit des dieux
Ou quand de Capanée écrasé par la foudre
Au nez des immortels riait encore la poudre
On ne vit un orgueil aussi démesuré
Aussi risible, aussi sottement assuré
Aussi paradoxal dans son outrecuidance
Aussi victorieux dans sa bêtise immense
Que cette hypocrisie aux yeux faux et baissés
Appliquant son front jaune à des marbres glacés

[67]

Que cette vanité pleurante sur la cendre
Qui s'applatit sans cesse et croit pouvoir descendre
Que cet abaissement de la divinité
Dont les docteurs chrétiens ont fait l'humilité.
Ainsi cet homme, insecte éclos dans la poussière
Croit devoir se baisser pour ramper sur la terre !
De son immensité saintement oublieux
Il incline son front pour ménager les cieux !
De peur d'être splendide il se met dans la fange !
Il cède à l'éternel son auréole d'ange !
Mais tu ne sais donc pas géant aux dieux pareil
Que la terre excrément des cheveux du soleil
Ressemble au parasite à la peau grise et noire
Qu'un enfant fait tomber sous son peigne d'ivoire
Que toi-même perdu sur cette inanité
Tu n'es pas même un pou de la divinité
Que tu n'as ni raison ni mesure ni place
Et de t'humilier tu veux avoir l'audace !

Nous portons avec nous, nous foulons sous nos pas
L'infiniment petit que nous ne voyons pas
Que dirions-nous si nous savions que le volvoce
Le vibrion mobile ou l'acarus féroce
Pour ce faire épargner par notre orgueil jaloux
En se pliant en deux se courbent devant nous
Mais pour nous observer ont-ils un télescope ?
Eh bien si le soleil était un microscope
Et qu'un ange attentif portant sa vue en bas
Nous chercha sur la terre il ne nous verrait pas
Le moindre nous échappe et nous perdons l'immense
L'ignorance finit, le doute recommence
Nous ne savons quel Dieu ni quel diable prier
Et pourtant notre orgueil prétend l'humilier !
Hausse-toi sur tes pieds monte sur des échasses
Trouve pour te grandir les montagnes trop basses

[68]

Monte comme Nadar dans un ballon géant
Gonflé comme un désir qui crève de néant
Mais si ton ballon crève enjambe l'hippogriffe
Vois fuir comme un point blanc le pic de Ténériffe
Monte jusqu'à la zone où l'air manque aux poumons
Tourbillonne plus haut sur l'aile des démons
Et tu seras toujours comme un grain de poussière
Arraché par le vent d'une motte de terre
Et l'ange du soleil portant la vue en bas
Eut-il des yeux de lynx ne t'apercevra pas.
Et tu crois que ton dieu jaloux de se faire homme
Va mourir de douleur pour le vol d'une pomme
Lui dont les grands vergers pleins d'arbres toujours verts
Laissent dans l'infini tomber des univers !
Tu crois que le soleil va suspendre sa marche
Pour des prêtres hébreux qui braillent devant l'arche

Et que, de leur trompette éternisant l'écho
Tomberont devant toi les murs de Jéricho !

Tu crois qu'en te gonflant ainsi qu'une grenouille
Tu rempliras de toi l'abîme que dieu fouille
Ou qu'en t'aplatissant comme un ballon crevé
Tu pourras soupirer ; seigneur je suis sauvé !
Imbécile et crétin ! va, la gloire infinie
Ne se réchauffe point de ton ignominie
Ta grandeur devant dieu se chiffre par zéro
Ne te déprime point, il fait ton numéro.
Saint Cucufin devant une table royale
Orne d'un jaune d'œuf sa barbe déjà sale
Qu'on le croit imbécile il sera satisfait ;
Mais pauvre Cucufin le tour est déjà fait !
Tu n'es qu'un triple sot par grace et par système
Et bien plus mille fois que tu ne crois toi-même

[69]

François guittardant de grotesques chansons
Dansait en Italie aux yeux des polissons
Comme le roi David folâtre patriarche
Qui sautait en chemise et tournait devant l'arche
Ils affectaient ainsi tous deux de délirer
Et se dépréciaient pour se faire admirer
Ils étaient orgueilleux comme ce Diogène
S'étalant au soleil dans sa misère obscène
Qui trouvait Alexandre opaque, et, bel et beau
Lui disait : tu fais ombre au seuil de mon tonneau !
Diogène du moins n'était pas hypocrite ;
Modestie était peu sa vertue favorite,
Et contre les abus, abuseur révolté,
 Il ne pécha jamais par trop d'humilité.
Mais ces moines béats à la paupière louche
Machonnant des versets et se pinçant la bouche

Mais tous ces aigrefins rasés ou chevelus
Les carmes épilés, les capucins poilus
Ces gens ceints d'une corde et les pieds en savates
Le crâne sans pensée et le cou sans cravates

Ayant pour dieu le diable et la crainte pour loi
Les malheureux ! plusieurs sont de très bonne foi
Ces gens ont plus d'orgueil plus de fiel, plus de haine
Que n'en peut cuirasser la carapace humaine
Ils font honneur à dieu de leur abaissement
Leur crasse à l'éternel doit servir d'ornement
Ils font un luxe au ciel de leurs efforts stériles
De leur foi sans raison de leurs vieux inutiles
Ils portent tout l'enfer sur leur front abattu
Et le diable sourit en créant leur vertu

[70]

La dispute de Jésus Christ avec le diable

Un jour le doux Jésus sur le sommet des monts
Rencontra Méphisto, le prince des démons
Qui se ressemble peu très volontiers s'assemble
Et voici les propos qu'ils rimèrent ensemble
Pour qu'on ne dise plus dans l'univers chrétien
Que le dogme sacré ne rime avecque rien :

Jésus
Tous les pauvres d'esprit sont heureux sur la terre
car ils posséderont le règne de mon père

Méphisto
Oui, les pauvres d'esprit sont heureux ici bas
Lorsqu'on se moque d'eux ils ne comprennent pas.

Jésus
Heureux celui qui pleure, on séchera ses larmes

Méphisto
Avoir l'œil sec d'avance aurait bien plus de charmes

Jésus
Heureux ceux qui sont doux, car ils doivent régner

Méphisto
Sur les loups, si les loups daignent les épargner

Jésus
Heureux les affamés d'amour et de justice

Méphisto
Ils meurent sous la table ou s'empiffre le vice

Jésus
Heureux les cœurs cléments, on leur pardonnera

Méphisto
Oui, pardonnez toujours, toujours on vous battra

Jésus
Bienheureux le cœur pur il voit dieu sans mélange

Méphisto
Et le monde en riant l'écrase dans la fange

[71]

Jésus
Heureux le pacifique il est enfant de dieu !

Méphisto
Et le dieu des combats mettra le monde en feu

Jésus
Heureux l'humble opprimé qu'on proscrit quoique juste !

Méphisto
Il mourra sans amis dans sa détresse auguste

Jésus
Si l'on prend votre robe offrez votre manteau

Méphisto
On lâchera les chiens pour avoir votre peau

Jésus
Si l'on vous a frappé sur la joue offrez l'autre

Méphisto
Tu recevras alors deux soufflets bon apôtre

Et le crime insolent restera sur son char

Jésus
Il faut rendre à César ce qu'on doit à césar

Méphisto
Si César te donnait la croix pour récompense
Que devraient tes enfants à César ? la potence !

Jésus
Tais toi fils de satan tu sais qu'il est écrit
On ne doit point tenter le seigneur Jésus Christ

Méphisto
Le seigneur Jésus Christ me parait peu croyable
S'il n'a pas le bon sens de réfuter le diable

Jésus
Ce n'est pas au démon que je daigne parler
Voici la vérité que je viens révéler
Homme que j'ai choisi sois docile à la grace
Rejette avec mépris tout ce qui t'embrasse

[72]

Si tu veux être à moi lève toi d'un seul bond
Hais ton père et ta mère et vis en vagabond
Ne porte ni souliers ni baton ni ceinture
Dieu pourvoit aux besoins de toute la nature
Comme le lys des champs le ciel t'habillera
Nourris toi des épis que ta main volera
Bénis ton ennemi pour que dieu le maudisse
Aime ton agresseur pour que dieu le punisse
Tes douceurs irritant la colère de dieu
Entasseront sur lui des fournaises de feu
Ignore tes parents, vis en célibataire
J'ai pour meilleur ami l'ennuque volontaire
Je ne suis pas venu pour apporter la paix

Mais le glaive, la haine et de sanglants forfaits
J'obscurcis à plaisir mes dogmes salutaires
De peur de corriger et de sauver mes frères
Le monde me déteste, il vous détestera

Mais un jour sous vos yeux le monde brûlera
Et pour vous emporter dans mon saint héritage
Je descendrai du ciel assis sur un nuage
Alors le genre humain presque tout criminel
Tombera pour jamais dans le gouffre éternel
En attendant fuyez, allez de ville en ville
Manger quand vous pourrez et prêchez l'évangile
Refuse-t-on de croire et de vous écouter ?
Secouez ce que j'ai défendu de porter :
Vos soutiens et sachez qu'un jour cette poussière
Fera de vos moqueurs flamber la ville entière

Méphisto
Bien touché ! tu me prends par mes mauvais côtés
Et tes enseignements que j'aurais inventés
Semblent me dépouiller de toute ma puissance
Je n'arriverais pas à pareille démence

[73]

Tu m'as dépossédé , c'est une trahison
Mais à ta place moi je vais parler raison
Homme, que la nature à jamais te soit chère
Ouvre ta maison, soutiens tes père et mère
Ne crois pas que le pain te tombera du ciel
Regarde les fourmis et les mouches à miel
Résiste à l'injustice, au bien reste fidèle
Mais ne rêve jamais la vengeance éternelle
Aime bien ta compagne et peuple l'univers
Sans te préoccuper du ciel ni des enfers.
Quand les religions n'enfantent que la haine
Elles sont des fléaux pour la famille humaine
Tous les autels sanglants sont d'horribles autels

Ne crois pas à des dieux qui damnent les mortels
Laisse la liberté même à tes adversaires
Et, surtout s'ils ont tort, ne maudis point tes frères

Ne leur dis pas le bien pour leur faire du mal
Ne fais point ton espoir d'un désastre final
Tout périt en ce monde et tout se régénère
L'éternel reste calme et n'a point de colère
Tiens propres tes souliers, mais lorsqu'ils sont poudreux
Ne nous en jette pas la poudre dans les yeux
Et ne nous plonge pas dans le lac asphaltique
Pour n'avoir pas compris ta parole hypocrite

Jésus
Vous avez bien parlé. C'est pour vous y forcer
Qu'en prêtant à l'erreur j'ai voulu commencer
Ecoutez maintenant le fond de ma doctrine
Et confessez enfin qu'elle est sage et divine
Préfère la justice à tout ce qui t'est cher
Et les devoirs de l'âme aux plaisirs de la chair
Donne-toi sans réserve à ceux que ton cœur aime

[74]

Pour les siens il est doux de s'immoler soi-même
Prends le bien pour le mal, aime tes ennemis
Prive-toi du bien-être et des plaisirs permis
Pour essuyer des pleurs et secourir tes frères
Garde toi de l'orgueil, des paroles amères,
Donne sans calculer ce qu'on te donnera
Donne même ta vie et dieu te la rendra.
L'héroïsme du bien c'est le devoir du juste
Plus que tous les serments rend ta parole auguste
Fais ton devoir d'abord, dieu veille sur tes droits
Marche dans les sentiers du bien les plus étroits
Ne prend point l'air rêveur d'un pâle anachorète
Mais lave ton visage et parfume ta tête
Ne sois point téméraire à juger ton prochain

Que nulle main vers toi ne soit tendue en vain
N'abandonne jamais ta femme légitime
Des époux séparés l'adultère est un crime

Aime dieu plus que tout, ton prochain plus que toi
Aimer et supporter, voilà toute la loi.

Méphisto
Seigneur, pour cette fois je n'ai plus rien à dire
Votre premier discours était une satire
Des prêtres imposteurs et je le comprends bien
Mais suivant ces gens là je me sens très chrétien
Je vais donc de leur main recevoir le baptème
Pour m'opposer ensuite à votre vrai système
Puisque dieu me condamne à propager le mal

Jésus
Non, dieu n'a point crée le génie infernal
Ta critique est l'appui du levier des idées
Par la lutte toujours fortes et et fécondées
Va, tu serais trop fier de ta damnation
Reçois donc malgré toi… ma bénédiction

[75]

A ces mots Méphisto l'archange au regard fauve
Se ramasse en un tas, se renverse et se sauve ;
Hurlant comme un brulé, ruant pétaradant
Il court près de Veuillot se cacher en grondant
Ne vous étonnez pas de cet anachronisme
Car l'homme pape-oté, l'homme fiel, l'homme schisme
Par le diable déjà dans l'enfer inventé
Couvait alors son œuf infaillibilité
Les lutins à plaisir lui façonnaient la trogne
Avec la lèvre épaisse et le nez d'un ivrogne
Réservant avec soin ce bel esprit fait-chair
Pour le siècle de rouille après celui de fer.
Pour le temps où la France a des bandits livrée

Au bagne descendait de livrée en livrée
Et devrait pour trouver un moment de répit
Se baisser jusqu'à Thiers Taleyrand décrépit
Pour le siècle o Trochu ferait ses hâbleries
Où Bicêtre viendrait brûler les Tuileries

Dans le temps où d'Arboy pris de je ne sais qui
Par Pilate oublié périrait pour Blanqui
Ne cachez moi l'horreur de cette époque immonde
C'est la corruption, c'est la fin du vieux monde
Mais où tant d'injustice éclate impunément
Que ce n'est pas encore le dernier jugement !

[76]

Devant le concile de Rome

Concessions et confession

La peinture est des yeux l'agréable mensonge
La poésie est l'art de traduire le songe
Le symbole mystique est le voile des dieux
L'arbitre du destin se cache à tous les yeux
Toute histoire se perd dans le tissu des fables
Le monde est affamé de récits incroyables
Il n'est pas un mortel en ce monde importun
Pas un roi, pas un dieu qui ne trompe quelqu'un
La mère la plus tendre avec ses gâteries
Prodigue à son enfant d'aimables menteries.
Tout amour est menteur lorsqu'il craint de blesser
Et dans l'ordre amical tromper c'est caresser
On caresse l'espoir des plus vaines chimères
Et c'est là le secret des prêtres et des mères.
Il faut savoir traiter en sage médecin
Les gens d'un esprit faible et d'un cerveau mal fait

Et quand la vérité trop forte ou trop cruelle
A nos affections peut devenir mortelle
Lorsqu'on veut éviter ce qu'elle fait prévoir
La dire est un mensonge et la taire un devoir.
Laissons à l'affligé le bonheur du peut-être
Regardons comme faux ce qui ne doit pas être
Jésus condamne l'homme à tout dire empressé
Qui dit à son pareil tu n'es qu'un insensé
Car tout homme on le sait a son grain de folie
Ne rappelons jamais ce qu'il faut qu'on oublie
Le monde est plein de fous et qui n'en veut pas voir
Doit rester dans la chambre et casser son miroir
Qui donc a dit cela ? J'ignore le poète
Mais c'est comme un proverbe et chacun le répète

Or Jésus met au rang des plaisirs défendus
De parler de la corde au logis des pendus
Et les prêtres pourtant veulent qu'on remémore
Les péchés pour les dire et les commettre encore

[77]

Qu'on sculpte ses erreurs dans un livre éternel
Qu'on avoue à leurs pieds un désir criminel
Pour faire un crime vrai d'une erreur qu'on avoue
Pour immortaliser nos traces dans la boue
Eh bien puisqu'il le faut je vais faire un aveu
A leurs pieds ? Non vraiment, mais en face de dieu
Je vais de ma jeunesse accuser la démence
Ne me méprisez pas, j'ai fait ma pénitence
Je m'accuse ô mon dieu d'avoir pendant vingt ans
Adoré comme vrais des dogmes révoltants
D'avoir cru que d'un dieu la haine paternelle
Gardait à ses enfants la torture éternelle
Et d'avoir, non pourtant sans honte et sans combat
Immolé ma jeunesse à l'impur célibat
Qui nourrit dans nos sens la débauche inféconde
Et livre nos sommeils au cauchemar immonde
Puis d'avoir près du lit où mon père était mort

Sans pudeur, sans pitié, sans regrets sans remord
Brûlé ce qu'il aimait : un livre de Voltaire
De ce noble vieillard relique auguste et chère !
Je m'accuse d'avoir douté de la raison
D'avoir du fanatisme épargné le poison
Et d'avoir regretté l'effroyable croyance
Dont la terreur stupide énerva mon enfance !
Mon dieu ! Dans la douleur dont je me sens pressé
A quel prêtre chrétien puis-je me confesser ?
Quel évêque implorer qui ne soit mon complice ?
Quel pape comprendra ma pensée au supplice ?
Hélas ! Tous ces forfaits que seul j'ose pleurer
Sont les vertus des saints qu'ils m'ont fait adorer

Je suis un paria ne pouvant être un bonze
Et je n'ai rien à dire à ces âmes de bronze

[78]

Le monde me dédaigne et veut m'anéantir
Non pour mes attentats, mais pour mon repentir
Ils disent que je suis un impie, un rebelle
Eh bien dans mon exil ma destinée est belle
J'aime mieux leur enfer que leur ciel insolent
Chantant alleluia sur un gouffre brûlant
On se tord pour jamais vouée à la souffrance
De mes frères maudits la multitude immense !
ô mon dieu prend pitié de ces aveugles nés
Qui te prennent seigneur pour le dieu des damnés
Mon dieu, ferme la bouche aux prêtres qui t'insultent
Affranchis tes autels, ta morale et ton culte
Ces prêtres de Moloch ne sont pas des chrétiens
Ils ont des jugements qui ne sont pas les tiens
Ne leur applique pas les lois qu'ils nous ont faites
Souviens-toi de Jésus le plus doux des prophètes

Qui disait, tout saignant des membres et du front
Les méchants ô mon père ignorent ce qu'ils font
Maintenant qu'on me traîne au concile de Rome
Le pape s'est fait dieu ; moi je dis à cet homme
Soit maudite à jamais la malédiction
Soit damné à jamais toute damnation
Tout prêtre qui maudit se condamne lui-même
C'est sur le faux pasteur que tombe l'anathème
Le vrai prêtre de dieu c'est celui qui bénit
Et la religion c'est ce qui nous unit.
Soit proscrite à jamais la haine qui divise !
Soit éteint cet enfer qui consume l'église
Bonzes, lamas, jurans, élus de l'avenir

[79]

Vous serez tous chrétiens quand vous saurez bénir !
Il fait jour, le coq chante, allons fais ta prière
Et remets ton épée à son fourreau, saint Pierre
Dis à tes cardinaux qu'ils ont assez mangé
Que leur règne est fini, que le monde a changé
Que dans leurs chassepots trop de merveille éclate
Et qu'ils ont trop de sang sur leur robe écarlate.
Consulte ton passé tu comprendras pourquoi
Des fous ont dans Paris assassiné Darboy
C'est que tous les partis ont des fureurs pareilles
C'est que les chassepots ont encore fait merveilles !
Ah vous nous maudissez, ennemis de nos droits !

[80] - *verso*

Et moi, je vous bénis au nom des Albigeois
De Jean Huss, de Wiclet et de Savouarde
Et de tous les martyrs de la sainte parole !
Oui, nous vous bénissons ! … non pour vous approuver
Mais pour que vous sachiez qu'on voudrait vous sauver
De votre fol orgueil, de l'enfer, de vous-même
Et de votre bâtard l'exécrable anathème !
Nous voulons vous sauver vous qui nous condamner,
Nous voulons vous sauver monstres qui nous damner !
Donc, nous vous déclarons au nom de Galilée
De l'inquisition la sentence annulée,
Au nom de Vanini toute la majesté
De dieu dans la nature et dans l'humanité
Au nom de Fénélon que les hommes sont frères
Qu'il se faut épargner les paroles amères

[81]

Puis au nom du bon sens et de la vérité
Que l'irritation n'est pas la sainteté.
Vous êtes des prélats, vous avez des tiares

Des croix, des palliums, des mitres, des simarres
Vous êtes tout puissant, et moi qui ne suis rien
Qu'un homme ayant souffert, pauvre, sobre, un chrétien
J'ose vous parler ferme et je suis infaillible
J'ai pour moi la raison plus forte que la bible
J'ai pour moi le bon sens de tout le genre humain
Plus vaste et mieux armé que l'intérêt romain
Et fussai-je enchaîné dans la cour du pontife
Comme autrefois mon maitre outragé par caïphe
J'y viendrais proclamer sans crainte et sans retour
Le droit à la science et le droit à l'amour !

Un tableau de Zurbaran

Un saint cadavéreux, épouvantable, horrible
Surprend dans un tombeau la mort qu'il rend visible
Il la presse il la tient dans ses bras décharnés
Il semble que des vers rongent déjà son nez
Dans leur orbite obscur ses yeux luisent à peine
Il a pour robe un sac, pour ceinture une chaine
Il a tout abjuré, science, amour, raison
Le néant est son dieu la tombe est sa maison
Il est déjà rigide et froid comme la pierre
Le silence éternel a peur de sa prière
Les larmes sur sa joue ont creusé des sillons
Une cendre immobile estompe ses haillons
On voit les dents saillir sous les lèvres tirées
Et les os font des trous dans ses chairs macérées
La mort pâle squelette est moins froide que lui

[82]

Et semble vers le mur chercher un point d'appui
Pour sortir de ses mains implacables tenailles
Qui vont pétrifier un ventre sans entrailles
D'une affreuse pudeur la chauve se débat
C'est un abominable et terrible combat
L'homme vampire ayant la fanatique envie
D'absorber la mort même et d'en faire sa vie
Et la mort impuissante à triompher de lui
Craignant de partager son immortel ennui
Qui le repousse avec un rire d'épouvante
Et croit sentir déjà qu'il la mange vivante

La génèse d'amour

I

Les larmes de l'azur font naitre les pervenches
La lune vierge sage a fait les robes blanches
Les rayons du soleil germent dans le sillon
La fleur en s'envolant devient un papillon
La force fait la loi la loi fait l'harmonie
Partout de l'univers travaille le génie
Tendre capricieux ou cruel tour à tour
Impitoyable et doux, il se nomme l'amour
C'est par lui que la neige au sommet des montagnes
Fondue en longs ruisseaux abreuve les campagnes
C'est lui qui fut formé des groupes d'univers
Par les attractions de tant d'astres divers
Pour lui l'oisillon chante et l'abeille butine
Il forme du raisin la sève libertine
Il dompte les lions fait mugir les taureaux
Entrelace les becs de jeunes tourtereaux
Il a fait le soleil, il a fait les étoiles

[83]

De la lune pudique il a blanchi les voiles,
Il a fait les trésors de la nuit et du jour
Dieu n'a fait qu'un chef d'œuvre : il a crée l'amour !
Avant que dieu sortit de son sommeil immense
Dans le chaos la force épuisait sa puissance
La force sans amour qu'on appelle satan
Créait le Béhémoth et le Léviathan
Du phosphore des eaux, du limon des marnières
Elle faisait sortir des monstres solitaires
Des avortons géants, sans femelles, affreux
Qui bientôt, affamés se dévoraient entr'eux
La terre où pourrissaient des fougères difformes
Mélait à ses cailloux des ossements énormes

Des montagnes de chair en putréfaction
S'échappaient les fœtus de la corruption
Les crapauds, les serpents, les rats, les scolopendres
Le limaçon visqueux les froides salamandres

Les dragons écaillés les crocodiles verts
Cauchemars destinés à peupler les enfers
Une vapeur épaisse infectait l'atmosphère
Et les flammes sortaient des gouffres de la terre
Lorsqu'un jour dans le ciel découvert un instant
Apparut dans l'aurore un nuage éclatant
L'air semblait s'épurer dans sa métamorphose
Et le nuage avait la forme d'une rose
Paisible il s'entrouvrit, un enfant radieux
En sortit et de grace enchanta tous les cieux
Un carquois d'or tremblait sur son épaule nue
Sa candeur, sa beauté jusqu'alors inconnue
Peuplèrent de désir les nuages vermeils
Et firent dans l'espace éclore des soleils
Les monstres s'apprêtaient à lui faire la guerre
Mais lui d'un trait léger plus fort que le tonnerre
Armant un arc divin que sa main fit siffler
Il les fit trembler tous, se tordre, se rouler

[84]

Se perdre dans des flots de fumée et de souffre
Ils disparurent tous dans la gueule du gouffre
Et l'enfant leur vainqueur l'esprit qui fait aimer
Mis le pied sur la terre et lui dit de germer
Alors en se mirant dans deux sources jumelles
Son sourire en tira deux formes fraternelles
Plus belles que jamais la fable n'en rêva
L'une fut Adamus et l'autre fut Héva

II

Ils étaient nés enfants comme l'amour leur père
Et leur sexe pour eux fut longtemps un mystère
Dans le jardin du monde ils se jouaient tous deux
Sans que l'amour jamais se méla à leur jeux
Ils grandirent ensemble et leur adolescence
Sembla n'être d'abord qu'une seconde enfance
Mais pendant qu'ils dormaient le souffle de l'amour
Survint les caresser et les troubler un jour

Adam versa des pleurs il sentait dans un rêve
Son cœur tout palpitant s'en aller vers son Eve
Et ne pouvant souffrir l'absence de son cœur
Il cherchait dans Eva sa vie et son bonheur
Or Eva tressaillit jusqu'au fond de son âme
Elle rêvait alors que comme un trait de flamme
Adam la pénétrait par un effort divin
Et venait rajeuni revivre dans son sein
Au réveil dans leur bras ils se serraient encore
Un grand rideau de fleurs laissait filtrer l'aurore
Qui leur fit voir tandis qu'ils cherchaient des yeux
L'amour leur créateur qui souriait près d'eux
Ils rougirent alors devinant le mystère
Et la femme sentit qu'elle deviendrait mère

III

Voulant le conserver avec eux plus d'un jour
Ils tressèrent des fleurs pour enchainer l'amour

[85]

L'amour leur dit : perdez cette espérance vaine
Et ne me touchez pas, je meurs quand on m'enchaine
Je serai près de vous invisible ou présent
De mon éternité je vous ai fait présent

A la condition pourtant d'être fidèles
Et de ne point goûter aux substances mortelles
Il est dans ce jardin deux arbres dont le fruit
Fait renaitre par l'un ce que l'autre détruit
L'un se nomme la vie et l'autre la science,
La science du mal qui flétrit l'innocence !
Si vous en approchez votre cœur est perdu :
Ne touchez donc jamais à ce fruit défendu.
En s'embrassant encore les deux époux jurèrent
L'amour les caressa les cieux les admirèrent
Et pour le imiter les oiseaux se cherchaient
Les insectes sous l'herbe ensemble se cachaient
Les fleurs en s'inclinant fécondaient leurs calices
Tout semblait de l'amour respirer les délices

Et nul ne prévoyait le cruel avenir
De l'amour s'envolant pour ne plus revenir.

IV

Trop de bonheur produit la lassitude
Et la fatigue aime la solitude
Adam parfois sur le sommet des monts
Allait causer avec les cieux profonds
Il observait le lever des planètes
Et leur coucher, la marche des comètes
L'heure ou des nuits la lampe décroissant
Deux fois se creuse en un double croissant
Au fond du ciel comme des météors
Il regardait passer les eggrégores
Sans se douter qu'à sa femme il tardait
De le revoir et qu'Héva l'attendait.
La pauvre Héva se croyant délaissée
Conçut un jour une triste pensée
Il lui sembla qu'Adam ne l'aimait plus.
L'amour prétend à de droits absolus
Il n'aime pas qu'avec lui l'on plaisante

[86]

Qu'on le néglige et surtout qu'on s'absente
Le doute enfin, le doute empoisonneur
Des deux époux vint mordre le bonheur
Comme un serpent qui se glisse dans l'âme
Il envahit d'abord la pauvre femme
Il la trompa, la fit déjà songer
A s'affranchir, peut-être à le venger.
Il lui montra l'arbre de la malice
La fit goûter à la pomme du vice
Pour retenir et fixer son époux Elle rêva de le rendre jaloux...
Jaloux de qui ? mais jaloux d'elle-même.
C'est désormais elle seule qu'elle aime ;
Pour s'aller voir dans le crystal des eaux
Elle le quitte et lui tourne le dos.
Lorsqu'il l'embasse elle boude et murmure
Qu'il a froissé les fleurs de sa coiffure.
Adam restreint ses désirs mécontents
Lorsqu'il s'absente il tarde plus longtemps

Un soir enfin rentrant dans sa demeure
Il apperçoit sa compagne qui pleure
Elle tenait un fruit déjà mordu
Elle lui dit : c'est le fruit défendu
Depuis longtemps nous souffrons d'être ensemble
Rompons enfin le nœud qui nous rassemble
Ce fruit nous doit séparer sans retour
C'est un poison qui guérit de l'amour
Je l'ai reçu comme un présent céleste
J'en ai mangé, je t'ai gardé le reste
Merci dit l'homme et d'un geste brutal
Il prend et mange aussi le fruit fatal
Puis séparé et se cachant dans l'ombre
L'un loin de l'autre ils passent la nuit sombre
Au jour naissant tous deux allaient sortir
Sans s'adresser un mot de repentir
Lorsqu'une voix charmante et bien connue

Semble pour eux descendre de la rue

[87]

Adam mon fils et toi ma douce Héva
Je suis l'amour je viens voir comment va
Votre ménage et si votre alliance
D'un fruit prochain vous donne l'espérance
A ce discours ils se cachent tous deux
N'osant paraitre et doublement honteux
De n'avoir pas songé dans leur colère
A cet enfant dont Héva serait mère

V

Malheureux dit l'amour pourquoi vous quittiez vous
Vous étiez des amants, vous êtes des époux
Je vous quitte à mon tour pour ne plus reparaitre
Mais vous me reverrez dans l'enfant qui va naitre
Travaillez s'il le faut vivez souffrez pour lui
Le travail chassera la dispute et l'ennui
Votre enfance est passée il faut songer à l'autre
Celle de votre fils redeviendra la vôtre
Vos yeux vont désormais sourire avec ses yeux
Votre cœur entendra ses petits cris joyeux

A ses premiers faux pas vous tremblerez d'alarmes
Les jeux seront vos jeux et les larmes vos larmes
Si l'orgueil chez l'amante a pu vaincre en rampant
La mère écrasera la tête du serpent
Allons Adam reviens auprès de ta compagne
Que partout dans l'exil ta force l'accompagne
Le monde autour de vous n'est plus le paradis
Que dieu pour votre enfance avait planté jadis
Vous ne reviendrez plus à votre idolaterie
Il faut du genre humain conquérir la patrie
Il faut à la vertu soumettre le désir

Car le devoir commence où finit le plaisir
Ayant ainsi parlé l'amour armé d'un glaive
Ferma le paradis puis il prit la main d'Eve
Et dans la main d'Adam la plaçant doucement
Il dit : supportez vous c'est votre châtiment
Travaillez sans faiblir et souffrez en silence
Je vais faire avec vous voyager l'espérance

[88]

Défrichez l'univers vous en serez les rois
Allez, embrassons nous pour la dernière fois
Adam se retrouva dans les bras de sa femme
Le baiser de l'amour pénétra dans leur âme
Un nouvel avenir se révéla pour eux
Appuyés l'un sur l'autre ils partirent tous deux
Et l'amour remontant aux voutes étoilées
Où siègeront un jour nos âmes consolées
Vint jusqu'au sanctuaire inaccessible et pur
Qui cache l'éternel dans une nuit d'azur
Seigneur dit-il j'ai fait la concorde et la guerre
J'ai donné le travail pour remède à la terre
Le suprême pouvoir ne m'ordonne-t-il rien ?
Et dieu lui répondit : ce que tu fais est bien ?

VI

Tel était le récit primitif et sincère
Que Moyse reçut de l'ancien sanctuaire

Et qui défiguré par les prêtres hébreux
Est devenu pour nous absurde et ténébreux
J'ai trouvé cette fable élégante et fleurie
Chez les premiers chrétiens docteurs d'Alexandrie
Qui doux comme Socrate et fiers comme Caton
Faisaient parler aux saints la langue de Platon
Quand la science encore croyait au vrai messie

Et quand Synésius écoutait Hypacie
Hélas ces temps sont loin, reviendront-ils jamais
Devez-vous refleurir beaux rêves que j'aimais
Quand nouveau Lucius dans un temps profane
Je cachais mon savoir sous des oreilles d'âne ?
Heureusement depuis je me suis tranformé
Content d'être poète et fier d'avoir aimé
Quand la magicienne aux lèvres demi closes
M'a fait devenir homme en me donnant des rôles

[89]

La mort

Sommeil réparateur de la vie éternelle
La mort est du phénix la naissance nouvelle
Un cadavre n'est rien c'est un vieux vêtement
Qui ne veut ni regrets ni deuil ni monument
Les âmes comme un son dont la corde est brisée
Perdent dans l'infini leur force reposée
Elles ne sont dans l'air dans l'eau ni dans le feu
Et veuves de leur corps elles dorment en dieu
J'aime dans un musée une antique momie
Les squelettes sont beaux pour leur anatomie
J'ai sur mon bureau même une tête de mort
Qui me montre les dents et jamais ne me mord
Les fantômes errants sont issus de nos rêves
La nature au tombeau ne donne point de trèves
La magie a crée des rites superflus
Et les morts ici bas ne réaparaissent plus

La mort, des malheureux immortelle espérance
Est la nymphe aux yeux d'or des sources de jouvence
Elle va ramassant dans ses bras maternels
Les vieillards décrépits, les jeunes criminels
Et dans ses claires eaux le remord, la vieillesse
Retrouvent à la fois innocence et jeunesse.
Elle sème au hasard des ossements flétris
D'où sortent des amours et des rosiers fleuris
Sa tête est de pavots et d'épis couronnée
Elle impose silence à la peine enchaînée
Elle arrache l'esclave au joug de ses tyrans
Elle vient appaiser les soucis dévorants
Elle a le doux regard d'une aurore voilée
Les pieds sont froids et blancs, sa robe est étoilée
Ses longs cheuveux sont noirs comme un crêpe de deuil
Et de l'éternité sa main cachant le seuil

Veut nous en épargner les trop vives lumières
Et protège nos yeux en fermant nos paupières

[90]

Une gravure d'Albrecht Dürer

Théophile Gautier, trop regrettable maitre
Vous que j'eus un instant le bonheur de connaitre
Votre esprit malin tenant voit tout ce qu'il y a
De gravé dans le dessin de Mélancholia !
Du vieil Albrecht Dürer cette œuvre magistrale
Nous montre la science à la robe royale
Poursuivant son problème et l'idéal rêvé
Près d'un grand monument toujours inachevé
Dont elle a dégrossi la principale pierre
Deux yeux profonds penseurs veillent sous la paupière
Et son poing vigoureux signe de volonté
Semble presser sa tête avec autorité
Pour en faire jaillir les choses éternelles
Paisible elle est assise et sait qu'elle a des ailles
Un génie enfantin sous les traits de l'amour
Écrit les vérités qu'elle veut mettre au jour
La meule d'un moulin sert à l'enfant de siège

Pour montrer que le livre est le pain du collège.
La peine ce vieux chien qui dévore nos jours
Qu'on chasse vainement et qui nous suit toujours
Replié sur lui-même est endormi près d'elle
Son front est couronné de verveine immortelle
Sa main victorieuse et qui ne tremble pas
A fixé sur un point la branche d'un compas
Elle rêve sans doute à la circonférence
Devant elle des cieux s'étend l'espace immense
Et sous les cieux la mer cette autre immensité
Reçoit d'un soleil d'or des torrents de clarté
L'arc en ciel analyse à ses yeux la lumière
Elle a les instruments de toute œuvre première
La scie et le rabot le marteau le creuset
Les clous, le microscope et la sphère on lisait

Le grand roi Ptolémée et les fortes tenailles
Qui sauvent Prométhée et forment ses entrailles
Elle est riche, sa bourse est pleine de trésors
Elle a les clés de tout, connait tous les ressorts
Près d'elle est une horloge et plus loin la balance

[91]

La cloche de la mort celle de la naissance
Attendent pour parler son signal souverain
Son problème est chiffré sur un carré d'airain
Et la chauve souris qui loin d'elle s'envole
Et porte sur son aile ouverte en banderolle
Le mot grec et latin de Mélancholia
Veut dire que jamais un penseur ne plia
Sous la tristesse noire et la mélancolie
Tant qu'il eut la raison pour chasser la folie
L'étude et le travail pour occuper ses jours
Et les livres divins pour régler ses amours.
Maitre vous avez vu dans cette œuvre sereine
Le découragement de la pensée humaine
On n'en était pas là du temps d'Albrecht Dürer
La foi vivait encore dans l'œuvre de Luther
Les âmes n'étaient pas défaillantes et mortes
On aimait le travail et les études fortes
Votre charmant esprit que le doute oppressait
A traduit Mélanchton par Alfred de Musset
Supposant qu'en raison des vices de notre âge

L'inscription du monstre est celle de la page
Et dans ce beau dessin fatalement compris
Il a confondu l'ange et la chauve souris.
Maintenant vous voyez le beau le vrai, le juste
Vous comprenez des cieux la symphonie auguste
Vous savez que changeant l'enfer en un saint lieu
L'art parmi les humains est le rêve de dieu
Vous aviez deviné le grand mot du problème
Qu'on n'aime le beauté que pour la beauté même

La beauté c'est le droit qu'illustre le devoir
C'est le couronnement de l'éternel savoir
Pendant que vous vivez parmi les choses belles
Ceux qui vous ont aimé laissant pousser leurs ailes
Dites leur d'espérer et d'essuyer leurs pleurs
Car dieu ne laisse pas de vide entre les cœurs
Et de la terre au ciel il remplit la distance
Ils iront écouter votre poème immense
Parmi ces astres d'or paradis sans enfers
Qui vont autour de vous créer des univers !

[92]

Sur l'homme

Epigrammes

L'homme est un animal bipède
Et bimane qui rit parfois
Déraisonne, invente des lois
Et prévoit la mort sans remède.
Mais il se déclare immortel ;
Moi pour ma part je le croit tel :
Il est évident que nous sommes
Immortels sur les sombres bords,
Puisqu'il est certain que les hommes
Ne mourront plus dès qu'ils sont morts.
La douleur est notre partage
La folie est notre élément
Les erreurs sont notre aliment
Et les vers sont notre héritage

Pourtant nous sommes triomphants
Et nous élevons nos enfants
Dans le respect de nos misères
Nous dépravons leurs appétits
Dans l'espoir que ces chers petits
Seront plus bêtes que leurs pères
En naissant nous ne savons rien
En mourant pas grand chose encore
Soit pour le vrai soit pour le bien
Un doute éternel nous dévore
Mais nous aimons l'absurdité
Et de notre crédulité
Nous enrichissons les églises
Il est clair que le dieu jaloux
Devient un dieu digne de nous
Lorsqu'on lui prête des sottises

Si quelques sages à nos coups

[93]

S'exposent, ce sont les plus fous
De tous les rêveurs de la terre
Et la preuve que leur raison
Ne peut rien nous dire de bon
C'est qu'ils sont forcés de se taire

Le diable est-il ou n'est-il pas ?
Trouvons nous après le trépas
Quelqu'un pour juger notre vie
Qui d'une autre sera suivie ?
L'un nous dit oui l'autre dit non
L'un rit l'autre fait un sermon
Et l'on ne sait auquel entendre
Mais dieu qui toujours se voila
Nous eut éclairci tout cela
S'il nous importait de l'apprendre.

Ce qui ne parait évident

C'est qu'il convient d'être prudent
Et de classer tous les systèmes
A peu près comme des poèmes
Celui-ci nous semble plus beau
L'un parait vieux l'autre nouveau
Celui là n'est pas vraisemblable
Concluons avec Rabelais
Qu'il faut tâcher de boire frais
C'est la morale de la fable

Aimons, chantons, soyons joyeux
Et laissons nous devenir vieux
La vieilleuse est une richesse
Que le temps augmente sans cesse
La jeunesse n'existe pas

Elle s'efface à chaque pas
C'est pour vieillir qu'on vient au monde
Le printemps est dans notre cœur
Quand nous faisons notre bonheur
En conservant la paix profonde

[94]

Marge : choses risquées - école de Victor Hugo

L'honneur est un parapluie
Qu'on essuie
Et qu'on remet dans un coin
Et la gloire une chandelle
Eternelle
Dont les morts n'ont pas besoin

L'histoire est une potence
Qui balance
Des cadavres dans les airs
Et le poète un gavroche
Qui s'accroche
Aux pendus mangés des vers !

Victor, poète sans règle
Est un aigle
Doublé d'un homme et d'un veau
Et ses chansons hippogriffes
Ont les griffes
D'un lion qui fait le beau

Ezéchiel qui déjeune
Ou qui jeûne

A dans des cercles de feu
Vu dit-on sous cette forme
Très énorme
La ressemblance de dieu

Phébus est une perruque
Sur la nuque
Du firmanent radieux
Et les astres, les planètes
Les comètes

Fourmillent dans ses cheveux
L'horizon de la concorde
C'est la corde
Par quoi dans son jeu coquet
La lune sur l'obélisque
Met son disque
Boule de ce bilboquet

[95]

Le panthéon de la gloire
C'est la foire
Aux fétiches du Congo ;
Et mon poème est un singe
Sous le linge
De Monsieur victor Hugo !

La rétractation de Galilée

Fragment dramatique

Adorant du sauveur la croix et le calice
En présence du monde et de ce saint office
La main sur l'évangile in nomine dei
Moi, dit Galiléo fils de Galiléi
Je déclare à l'esprit qui parmi vous séjourne
Que la terre demeure et que le soleil tourne
Même de vos grandeurs si c'est l'arrêt fatal
Je crois la terre plate et les cieux en crystal
Que n'avez-vous des fronts de la même matière
Ils laisseraient passer la vie et la lumière
Et par vos grands reflets l'univers éclairé
Se soumettrait sans peine à votre ordre sacré
Ce n'est donc pas en vain que la très sainte Bible

[96]

Dit que pour triompher dans un combat terrible
Un prophète arrêta le soleil d'une main
Et contraignit la lune à rebrousser chemin
Je vous conjure donc grands pasteurs de l'Europe
De m'absoudre et d'absoudre aussi mon télescope
Bien qu'un si grand pardon ne puisse n'être du
(se relevant et frappant la terre du pied)
Allons, ne tourne pas ! Cela t'est défendu !
Mes seigneurs devant moi vous brûlerez mon livre
Je la sentais tourner parce que j'étais ivre
La science est un vin qui nous monte au cerveau
Je jure de ne rien observer de nouveau
M'en rapportant du reste à votre prud'hommie
Et dans les livres saints cherchant l'astronomie
Je n'écrirai plus rien, ne penserai plus rien
Ainsi puissé je vivre et mourir bon chrétien !
Note on pourrait faire de ce monologue une scène
Très saisissante, en y joignant la pantomine

Dont on disposerait ainsi la mise en scène
Une église éclairée par une multitude de
Cierges, un peuple nombreux, des inquisiteurs
Des soldats, des pénitents noirs en cagoule
Une estrade sur laquelle un évangile, près
de là des réchauds et des instruments de
torture. L'orgue joue des airs funèbres
la procession entre dans l'église et chacun
prend place, Galilée parait chargé
de chaines. L'orgue se tait, le grand
inquisiteur exorcise Galilée avec de
l'eau bénite et lui montre en silence
d'une main l'estrade et le prie-dieu
de l'autre les bourreaux qui mettent
des tenailles au feu. Galilée hésite
il fait un pas vers les bourreaux

[97]

Des gémissements s'élevant dans la foule
Une femme se précipite aux pieds du
Savant en lui montrant deux jeunes
Enfants, un prêtre donne à Galilée le
Crucifix à baiser Galilée baise le crucifix
Embrasse les deux enfants et après avoir
Levé les bras au ciel il monte lentement
Sur l'estrade et prononce d'une voix
Ferme les paroles de la rétractation en
Etendant la main sur le livre des évangiles.
Lorsqu'il a fini on lui ôte ses chaines
L'orgue joue des airs joyeux et la procession
Recommence pour sortir de l'église. Tout
Le monde s'incline devant Galilée, quelques
Hommes à costumes de savants se détournent
Seuls avec mépris. Des femmes pleurent
Et un homme même essuie ses larmes
Avec un geste d'impatience

Au lever du rideau et avant l'entrée de la
Procession un huissier de inquisition lira
Au peuple le monitoire que voici :

Pour que la sainte église enfin soit consolée
On amène en ce lieu le nommé Galilée
Convaincu d'avoir dit et d'avoir même écrit
Contrairement aux lois du seigneur Jésus Christ
Qui veut que son église à jamais respectée
Sur tout enseignement soit toujours consultée
Ce mensonge évident horrible et sans pareil
Que la terre à présent tourne autour du soleil
Et cela sans respect de l'église infaillible
De Josué lui-même et de la sainte Bible
Le saint office donc le crime constaté
Presque en flagrant délit le coupable arrêté
Lequel sans violence et presque sans torture
Lui-même a confessé sa noire forfaiture

[98]

Ordonne qu'en ce jour il sera devant nous
Conduit pour faire amende honorable à genoux
Et l'ouïr condamner à telle pénitence
Que du saint tribunal réglera l'indulgence
A défaut de quoi faire ou le tenaillera
Puis un saint confesseur encore l'exortera
Que s'il veut persister dans son affreux blasphème
Qu'il mesure et que son sang retombe sur lui-même
Un bûcher sur la place est déjà préparé
Sur lequel ce méchant des chrétiens séparé
Avec tous ses écrits périra dans la flamme
C'est justice ! Et que dieu prenne soin de son âme

L'orgue joue le dies ira et la procession
Entre dans l'église
Après l'abjuration le grand inquisiteur
Dit à Galilée :

Retournez en prison, je vous ferai connaitre
Votre arrêt que l'église adoucira peut-être

Mais espérez surtout la clémence de dieu
Nous allons devant vous jetter le livre au feu
Allez porte-flambeaux que le bûcher s'allume
Et qui l'écrit impie en entier se consume Galilée
C'est bien fait, jettez en la cendre à tous les vents
Puisse-t-elle à jamais dans les siècles savants
Raconter les efforts de ma raison soumise
Et faire apprécier les arrêts de l'église !

Quand Galilée embrassera le crucifix et
Montera sur l'estrade le grand inquisiteur dira :
C'est bien : vous échappez à la damnation
Prononcez à présent votre abjuration
Alors Galilée :
Adorant du sauveur la croix (etc) comme
Plus haut.

[99]

Voix dans la foule pendant que Galilée est emmené
Hors de l'église
Les savants
Ah faible caractère !
Les femmes
Ah malheureusement vieillard
Des étudiants viennent sur le devant du théâtre
Et se serrent les mains avec un jeste énergique
L'un d'entre eux dit aux autres :
Amis nous reverrons ces arrêts là plus tard
Mais ne condamnons pas cet homme de génie
Dont nous avons compris la sublime ironie
Son livre est répandu parmi les nations
On ne rétracte pas des démonstrations
Et semblable à ce dieu dont il est le prophète
Il peut se reposer, car la lumière est faite !

Gros bon sens

Ou simple discours

Ignorer ou savoir, ni doute ni croyance
Voilà le droit chemin qu'enseigne la prudence
Je puis douter de moi, de mon habileté
Jamais de la raison ni de la vérité
Et qu'importe au soleil que l'aveugle le voit ?
Il rayonne toujours et toujours il flamboie
Et s'il était un juge, étant sur qu'il fait bien
Il ne punirait pas ceux qui n'en savent rien
Des choses que le ciel ne daigne pas m'apprendre
Je cherche à deviner ce que j'en puis comprendre
Mais n'étant jamais sûr d'avoir bien deviné
Je ne sers pas le dieu que je me suis donné
C'est un dessin de moi que j'accroche à mon âtre

[100]

De ma conception je crains d'être idolâtre
J'y tiens, tant que je n'ai rien trouvé de plus beau
Mais s'il était en or je mangerais mon veau
Ce que je sais très bien c'est que l'iman, le bonze
Les brames, les faquirs nieds et couleur de bronze
Le prêtre catholique et le rabbin pelé
Disent que pour eux seuls l'éternel a parlé.
N'ayant rien entendu de ce discours multiple
D'aucun de ces pasteurs je ne suis le disciple ;
Des contradictions je ne puis faire cas
Sachant que l'éternel ne se contredit pas.
J'ignore, en attendant que dieu daigne m'instruire
S'il ne me parle pas je n'ai rien à lui dire,
Ne le connaissant pas ne l'ayant jamais vu,
Et la vie à venir est pour moi l'imprévu.

Si j'avais un bâtard dans le fond de la Chine
Tout à fait ignorant de la haute origine

Et si l'on m'apprenait qu'il a dit à Pékin :
Ou je n'ai point de père ou c'est un vieux coquin
De n'avoir jamais pris la peine de m'écrire
Car de son existence il aurait du m'instruire
Je répondrais ma foi le chinois a raison
Je ne l'accuse pas de haute trahison
Si j'avais quelque bien j'en ferais le partage
Il recevrait ma lettre avec mon héritage
En attendant, de moi peut-il se soucier ?
Et si pour le distraire, un pacte, un sorcier
Un bonze un mandarin réclamant leur salaire
Lui disaient tour à tour moi je connais ton père
Il est blanc, il est noir, il est rouge, il est bleu
Doit-il croire en eux tout comme l'on croit en dieu ?

[101]

Doit-il en choisir un comme plus véridique
Parce qu'il n'admettra ni doute ni critique
Moi je crois n'en déplaise à nos saints confesseurs
Qu'il doit leur dire à tous : vous êtes des farceurs.
Et vous voulez que dieu tel qu'on l'invoque à Rome
Ait moins d'intelligence et de bon sens qu'un homme
Qu'il impose une loi qu'il faille deviner
Et qu'à colin-maillard il veuille nous damner ?
Non, je n'en doute point, je suis sur que c'est bête.
Je sais parfaitement qu'il convient d'être honnête
D'honorer ses parents et d'aimer son prochain
Mais qu'il faille dorer un fétiche, un machin
Un bonhomme divin quelconque et qu'on l'encense
Sans rime ni raison quoi que le diable en pense
Parce que c'est écrit sans qu'on sache pourquoi
Franchement je l'ignore est-ce ma faute à moi ?
Douter ! Pourquoi douter ? la nature est visible
Je comprends l'évidence et j'admets le possible

Mais lorsqu'un ignorant le formule au hasard
Je reverse mon droit d'examiner plus tard

Si de tout examen le moyen se refuse
Ma bonne volonté me suffit et m'excuse
J'agis comme je sais qu'il faut agir et puis
Je compte en m'instruisant faire mieux si je puis
Vous parler de la foi mère de l'espérance
Mais je sais que la foi n'est que la confiance
Je croyais à ma mère au temps où mes besoins
Me forcaient tous les jours à connaitre ses soins
J'éprouvais si souvent sa bonté maternelle !
Mais j'avoue humblement que j'aurais eu peur d'elle
Si devant moi jamais elle eut dans un grand feu
Jetté mon petit frère en l'honneur du bon dieu
Église catholique à toi la parabole

[102]

Je trouve des beautés dans ton obscur symbole
Mais je sais que ton culte est un culte de sang
Et que tu fais un dieu d'un pontife impuissant
Je ne doute donc pas, je sais : je te condamne
En riant d'un agneau qui fusille et qui damne
Je sais que la nature a d'admirables lois
Je sais pleurer le juste expirant sur la croix
Je sais d'un saint Vincent les œuvres méritoires
Je sais les arguments de tous les consistoires
Je sais qu'on pourrait être honnête homme et chrétien
Et qu'un excellent prêtre est un homme de bien
Mais j'ignore pourquoi le sacerdoce avare
Prêchant la pauvreté de notre argent s'empare
Pourquoi les cardinaux ont un luxe insolent
Et pourquoi l'on absout l'écrivain violent
Qui profane l'esprit en vantant la sottise
Manipule l'injure et compromet l'église

Je ne sais pas comment le pape, ce docteur
Conservateur du dogme et non pas créateur
Par une invention Jésuitique et risible
Peut s'adorer soi-même et le croire infaillible

Que m'importe après tout, je ne suis pas Luther
Mais je sais que le diable exécrerait l'enfer
Si le diable existait tel que le monde l'aime
Plus élégant, plus fin, plus vivant que dieu même
Je sais que Josué fut-il à dieu pareil
N'aurait pu dans sa course arrêter le soleil
Sans briser les ressorts de la nature entière
Et sans faire tomber les astres en poussière
Et que Samson vainqueur d'un peuple terrassé
Avec un ossement sanglant et fracassé
N'a pu faire sortir pour sa bouche altérée
De cet os ridicule un ruisseau d'eau filtrée

[103]

Tout est possible à dieu direz vous non morbleu
Le ridicule manque aux attributs de dieu
Dieu n'a jamais signé vos mensonges profanes
Et vous laisse le jus de vos machoires d'ânes
Je reviens à mon dire et prétend qu'ici bas
Un penseur est bien fort lorsqu'il ne doute pas
Le scepticisme étant impossible en science
N'est qu'un tâtonnement de la sotte ignorance
Je vois, je sais, je cherche et marchant pas à pas
Je ne crois jamais rien se qu'on ne sait pas
Je ne présume pas les choses que j'ignore
Chercher n'est pas douter c'est ignorer encore
Je sonde le problème et quand j'aurai trouvé
Je dirai je connais et non pas j'ai rêvé
En attendant j'admets qu'on me montre la route
C'est de la confiance et ce n'est pas du doute
D'un guide clairvoyant je puis suivre les pas

Si je sais qu'il connait ce que je ne sais pas
Mais suivre aveuglément l'aveugle qui chancelle
Mais faire par un fou gouverner ma nacelle
C'est ce que je prétends n'admettre pour un peu
Fut-il pape et surtout s'il me dit qu'il est dieu

Qu'on soit triste ou content, qu'on m'approuve ou me blâme
Toujours cahin caha je veux tirer ma rame
Et dire à mes amis : voulez vous vivre en paix ?
Apprenez, croyez peu, mais ne doutez jamais

[104]

Raison théologique

ou théologie raisonnable

Il existe une loi suprême inexorable
Qui protège le juste et punit le coupable.
Le sentiment profond de l'immortalité
Nous vient de la nature et de l'humanité.
La vie est collective autant que personnelle
Le grand foyer projette et reprend l'étincelle
Il faut faire le bien pour le bien seulement
Sans espoir de salaire ou peur de châtiment
Moyse et Mahomet proclament le théisme
Dieu dans l'humanité c'est le christianisme
Rome c'est le devoir avec l'autorité
Genève c'est le droit avec la liberté.
Or ces dogmes divers se complètent l'un l'autre
Le dieu des musulmans et des juifs est le nôtre
C'est dans tous nos pareils que nous devons l'aimer

Les abus sont un mal, il faut les réformer
L'ordre exige pourtant l'obeissance libre
Il n'est point de devoirs que le droit n'équilibre
Donc, juifs et musulmans, chrétiens au pape unis
Protestants divisés acceptés ou bannis
Sont nos frères en dieu, composant tous ensemble
Cette religion dont l'esprit nous rassemble ;
Telle est de l'univers la catholicité
Qu'illuminent deux mots : justice et charité
L'autre vie est pour nous l'inconnu, le peut-être
Nous vivons, nous mourons tels que dieu nous fit naitre
Récompensera-t-il le mouton d'être doux ?
Punira-t-il les loups d'avoir été des loups ?
Les longs frémissements de la mouche indignée

Feront-ils qu'on tourmente en enfer l'araignée ?
L'univers est un champ de bataille et de mort
Où le faible est toujours mangé par le plus fort

[105]

Le grand homme succombe opprimé par l'envie
C'est la fatalité, c'est la loi de la vie.
Vous fait-on croire aussi colombes des amours
Qu'il existe un enfer pour l'âme des vautours ?
Néron n'était qu'un tigre échappé de sa cage
Mais dieu serait lui-même un Néron plus sauvage
S'il offrait ce spectacle au ciel épouvanté
D'un tigre cuit vivant pendant l'éternité.
Un supplice éternel veut un dieu pour victime
Et l'ange révolté, satan serait sublime
Acceptant de l'enfer l'effroyable tombeau
Plutôt que d'adorer son éternel bourreau
L'enfer serait l'orgueil inexorable et sombre
Faisant couver à dieu le trépas dans son ombre
C'est la négation des gloires du sauveur
C'est de la charité l'éternel déshonneur
Du péché triomphant c'est une apothéose

De dieu même en démon c'est la métamorphose.
L'homme, libre amateur et créateur du mal
Devient un dieu vaincu que dieu traite en égal
Or étant le plus fort si dieu frappe il est lâche
Il est vil s'il se venge, il a tort s'il se fâche
Un crime ne peut être éternel et puni
Et le mal serait dieu s'il était infini
Dieu changeant en fureur sa bonté paternelle
Savourant des humains la torture éternelle
Devient si complaisant pour l'homme de l'enfer
Qu'on pleure en saluant le martyr Lucifer.
Oh n'éternisons pas la haine et le blasphème
L'éternité de dieu brûle parce qu'elle aime
Dieu ne change jamais ; comment donc supposer

Qu'un insecte l'irrite et ne peut l'appaiser ?
A la peine de mort, la plus grave des peines
D'avance il a soumis les sottises humaines

[106]

Le tombeau c'est la paix avec la liberté
L'égalité suprême et la fraternité.
Le ver discerne-t-il l'innocent du coupable
Et le riche pourri du dernier misérable ?
Comment l'ami des morts s'en irait-elle au feu
Sans jambes et sans pieds n'ayant ni corps ni lien ?
Que devient le rayon qui colorait la rose
Quand la robe est flétrie ? Il colore autre chose
Vous soufflez un flambeau, la flamme disparait
Est-elle anéantie ? un enfant le croirait.
La flamme est-elle un être ou bien un phénomène
Analogue à celui de la pensée humaine ?
Elle ne peut mourir que faute d'aliment
Et le verbe se tait s'il manque d'instrument.
Mon violon brisé ne me sert plus, qu'importe
La musique éternelle avec lui n'est pas morte

Tout s'écroule, palais, tombeaux, temples, autels
Mais dans l'immensité nous sommes immortels
De la foi des chrétiens le texte nous enseigne
Afin que de mal faire incessamment on craigne
Qu'un jugement s'apprête et qu'un jour à venir
Nous devons tous renaître... avec le souvenir !
Alors quels cris d'horreur quels sanglots d'épouvante
Néron reconnaissant Agrippine vivante
Qui le force à téter son sang noir et figé !
Ugolin vomissant l'enfant qu'il a mangé
Troppmann... mais je m'arrête, ayant peur de l'horrible
La foudre est inutile à ce tableau terrible
L'impie à ses remords ne pouvant échapper
Dieu l'honorerait trop s'il daignait le frapper
Malheur à qui s'endort avec une souillure

Il se réveillera damné par la nature
Et n'inspirera plus ni crainte ni pitié...
J'aimerais mieux pourtant que tout fut oublié

[107]

Et ne suppose pas que dieu substance pure
Veuille pour la garder saler la pourriture
Donc s'il veut conserver son ouvrage Sali
Il le retrempera dans le fleuve d'oubli.
D'ailleurs dieu n'est pas tel qu'on nous le représente
Et n'a jamais besoin d'inspirer l'épouvante
Il n'a rien qui ressemble aux caprices d'un roi
Il fait tout pour la loi, dans là loi, par la loi
Sa substance impalpable emplit l'espace immense
Où la forme finit l'infini recommence
Tout vit, tout se transforme en un progrès fatal
Et ce qui meurt toujours c'est le rêve du mal
Dieu c'est l'ordre éternel, c'est la force infinie
C'est le régulateur de la grande harmonie
Il est, mais il n'est pas ce que l'homme a rêvé
Il est-ce que jamais les prêtres n'ont prouvé
Il est la loi vivante, âme de toute chose
La raison, le moyen, le principe et la cause

Dieu dans l'éternité c'est le savoir qui peut
La loi qui se conserve et le pouvoir qui veut
L'homme est un dieu manqué qui se souvient du diable
Des mystères chrétiens l'évangile est la fable
La Bible est le secret du sphinx pyramidal
Obscurément gravé sur son vieux piedestal
Le dogme catholique est l'ombre de ces ombres
C'est l'aigle de Pathmos qui sous ses ailes sombres
Couve un œuf immortel, la sainte charité !
Nuisant l'indulgence avec l'autorité,
Dans sa communion qu'il nomme universelle
Il proclame de dieu la présence réelle.
Oui, sur tous les autels, en tout tenus en tout lieu

C'est la communion qui réalise dieu
Jésus dit : aimez-vous ! que la foi vous rassemble
A la table du ciel communiez ensemble
Et vous me sentirez être immortel en vous

[108]

Riche et pauvre à côté l'un de l'autre à genoux
Mangez le même pain qui vous immortalise
Ce pain sera mon corps revivant dans l'église
Car j'ai voulu mourir pour unir les humains
Et le salut du monde est l'oeuvre de mes mains
C'est dans cette sublime et simple métaphore
Que du culte à venir brille déjà l'aurore
Et nos sages docteurs n'ont vu dans cet éclair
Qu'un pain qui s'escamote et devient de la chair
Ils ont cru pour prouver leur anthropophagie
D'un sang vermeil encore voir la nappe rougie
Silence la vertu !.. les ombres passeront
Les nuits de l'ignorance un jour s'éclaireront
Et les hommes guidés par la même lumière
Se reconnaitront tous enfants du même père !

Vision prophétique

J'étais emprisonné pour la libre parole
Et pour avoir des dieux deviné le symbole
Quand l'esprit soulevant les voiles de ma chair
Me fit faire le tour du ciel et de l'enfer
Puis dans l'ombre au dessus des plus sublimes faites
Plus loin que les docteurs, plus haut que les prophètes
Il me laissa debout sur un roc escarpé
Où le serpent d'Eden n'avait jamais rampé
Sur ma tête une étoile apparut en silence
Et remplit tout le ciel d'une auréole immense
Alors je me jettais tout tremblant à genoux
Et je criais : seigneur ayez pitié de nous

[109]

Pourquoi choisissez vous dans le monde incurable
Des plus obscurs pécheurs moi le plus misérable
Pour me montrer soudain dans un jour imprévu
Ce que Moyse même et saint Paul n'ont pas vu ?
L'esprit me répondit la lumière du temple
N'est pas subordonnée à l'œil qui la contemple
Quand l'autre reparait son éclat coutumier
Se révèle à l'oiseau réveillé le premier
L'étoile apparait donc, non pas à ton génie
Non pas à tes vertus mais à ton insomnie.
Quelque chose pourtant plait au seigneur en toi
Tu n'as point de la peur subi l'infâme loi
Nourri par les docteurs du faux christianisme
Tu repoussas le joug de leur pharisaïsme.
Abusant contre toi de leur autorité
Du haut du temple alors ils t'ont précipité
Il fallut bien alors que dieu rompit tes langes

Et te fit soutenir par la main de ses anges

Le poète

J'aurais été seigneur votre enfant bien aimé
Si ma bouche en tombant n'avait pas blasphémé
J'ai pleuré, j'ai souffert et puis dans ma colère
J'ai bu l'ivresse impure et j'ai brisé mon verre
La déesse Astarté sans pudeur et sans foi
Un matin de noël se vint offrir à moi
Elle avait les regards d'une vierge ingénue
Et sous ses cheveux noirs l'épaule demi nue
Elle parlait tout bas disant qu'elle m'aimait
Et sa vue était belle et sa voix me charmait
Et bravant d'un serment l'austérité jalouse
J'ai dit au démon : viens tu seras mon épouse.
Le mystère fatal tristement s'accomplit
J'avais mis la démence et l'enfer dans mon lit
Astarté prétendait que je l'avais réduite
Elle m'abandonna ! puis moi... je l'ai maudite.

[110]

L'esprit

Non, je connais ton cœur, pour elle il a prié
Puis vers dieu bien longtemps tes douleurs ont crié
Tu t'es flétri toi-même afin qu'elle fut libre
Cet effort dans ton âme a refait l'équilibre
Et quand tu m'invoquais je suis venu vers toi
Je parle donc, écoute et tais toi devant moi
Cette étoile de gloire au brillant diadème
C'est la raison qui parle et vit par elle-même
Les fantômes divins, Jupiter, Jéhovah
Sont les illusions d'un songe qui s'en va
Moi je suis la pensée éclose dans ton âme
Tu me prètes des yeux et des ailes de flamme
Et dans un mouvement d'érotisme nerveux
Tu te sens enlevé par un de tes cheveux
Sache que dieu réside où la raison domine
Et que l'amour n'est pas la lumière divine
L'amour est un besoin de l'âme ou de la chair
C'est une écorce d'or qui cache un fruit amer

L'amour ne s'ennoblit que par le sacrifice
La douleur surmontée est son divin calice
Abraham de l'enfer pu braver les défis
Quand dieu l'eu contemplé prêt à frapper son fils
Toujours la paix sereine à la douleur pour mère
Et Jésus triomphant est né sur le calvaire
Regarde autour de toi le monde révolté
Il aime avec fureur la vierge liberté
Mais cette vierge sainte à la tête voilée
Veut qu'on l'épouse et meurt dès qu'elle est violée
Ou plutôt elle fuit dès qu'on veut l'outrager
Et l'empire fatal accourt pour la venger
Et ceux dont la fureur la poursuit et l'outrage
Trompés comme Ixion n'embrasse qu'un nuage

Puis liés au rouet de la fatalité
Ils remontent sans cesse et de l'autre côté

[111]

Retombant pour monter et retomber encore
Des révolutions l'abîme les dévore
L'enfer réveille alors les vaincus triomphants
Et leur dit que Saturne a mangé ses enfants
Les larves du tombeau de vengeances avides
D'un diadème usé chargeant leurs crânes vides
Font germer tout à coup le champ d'Ezéchiel
Et d'un monde-cadavre épouvantent le ciel.
Anachronisme vain ! leurs jambes de squelettes
Cliquettent en marchant comme des castagnettes
Et battent dans l'oubli le rappel du passé ;
Elles ne trouvent plus leur royaume effacé
Mais à la liberté voulant barrer les portes
Elles passent hélas dans les gâches peu fortes
Leurs radius poudreux leurs tibias glacés
On entend le bruit sec des ossements cassés
La porte les repousse en s'ouvrant d'elle-même
Et le squelette croule avec son diadème !

Il en doit être ainsi tant que l'autorité
N'aura pas fait un pacte avec la liberté
Tant qu'une foi savante à la raison soumise
N'aura pas fait aimer les dogmes de l'église
Tant que l'homme effaré luttera sans savoir
Qu'on achète le droit par le prix du devoir
Que l'inégalité règne dans la nature
Que la fraternité serait une imposture
Si les hommes livrés au pèle-mèle affreux
Pouvaient sans aucun frein se déchirer entre eux
Que les masses toujours doivent être guidées
Et que la foule aveugle obéit aux idées
Que le pape n'est pas un fétiche et que dieu
Ne jette pas l'esprit et le savoir au feu

Que l'église aurait du plus forte et plus sincère
Dans sa juste critique encourager Voltaire

[112]

Et de la charité montrant le talisman
Gagner l'auteur d'Alzire au vrai dieu de Guzman
Mais que ces disputeurs, jésuites, jansénistes
Patouillet furieux Nicole et Pascal tristes
Offrant leur pédantisme à ce divin moqueur
Devaient en l'égayant lui soulever le cœur
Regarde maintenant l'église et les apôtres
Dans l'encre et dans le fiel trempant les patenôtres
Une face grêlée au nez facétieux
Crache sur les humains les ordures des cieux
Son style plein d'odeurs en ruisseaux se promène
Et la salette en fait déborder sa fontaine
L'enfant Jésus se mouche avec le drapeau blanc
Le dieu de l'univers est un gros cœur sanglant
On conjure l'orgueil de la sagesse humaine
Avec les cripeaux de sainte Philomène...
Alors je regardais l'esprit qui me parlait
L'étoile dans le ciel lentement s'en allait

Je doutais de l'esprit ; car en moi, misérable,
Un souvenir d'abbé murmurait : c'est le diable.
Alors je m'éveillai tout trempé de sueur
Les tempes me battaient follement, j'avais peur
Peur de la vérité, mon dieu ! de la justice !
Peur de Saint Dominique et de son Saint office
Car de fils de fer rouge artistement tissées
Mes souvenirs étaient la robe de Nessus.
La raison quand on dort n'est jamais la plus forte ;
Toujours vers le passé le rêve nous emporte,
Et le pauvre penseur plus fier que Jéhova
Confus de sa sottise enfin se retrouva

Epilogue

De cette vision j'explique le problème
Je m'étais endormi lisant des livres fous
Et de tragaldabas méditant le poème

[113]

J'avais à mon souper mangé du porc aux choux

Conclusion
Beuvons frais
Chanson
Air de Calpigi

Amis, laissons du patriarche
Au gré du vent naviguer l'arche ;
L'oiseau favori des amours
Nous promet encore d'heureux jours (bis)
Noë vainqueur de l'onde amère
A planté la vigne sur terre ;

[114]

Soignons la vigne, et beuvons frais
C'est l'avis du vieux Rabelais (bis)

Gonflant ses mammelles nourrices
La terre est grosse de délices
Elle a pour cheveux des moissons
Les bois murmurent des chansons (bis)
Ses larmes font des fleurs écloses
Son rire épanouit les roses ;
Cueillons la rose et beuvons frais !
C'est l'avis du vieux Rabelais ! (bis)

Aimons le vin quand il ruisselle

Et la femme tant qu'elle est belle
Cueillons les fleurs sans les froisser

Et les plaisirs sans y penser (bis)
Infidèle du matin même
Rose dit : c'est toi seul que j'aime
Croyons la chose et buvons frais
C'est l'avis du vieux Rabelais

Quel est le plus divin système
Le dernier mot du grand problème ?
Quel parti nous fera la loi
Les républicains ou le roi ? (bis)
Quel est le sens des mots civisme
Fraternité, patriotisme ?
Cela veut dire : buvons frais !
C'est l'avis du vieux Rabelais (bis)

[115]

Vous demandez si les comètes
Peuvent rencontrer les planètes ?
Mais s'il fallait régir les cieux
A quoi donc serviraient les dieux ? (bis)
Je puis sans lunette ni sphère
Voir le vin rencontrer mon verre !
C'est la comète : et buvons frais
C'est l'avis du vieux Rabelais (bis)

Que Nicodème dans la lune
S'ingénie à chercher fortune,
Si haut je ne vais point loger
Mes œufs rouges pour les manger (bis)
Tant que j'ai dans mon escarcelle
De quoi garnir mon humble écuelle
Je m'en contente, et beuvons frais !

C'est l'avis du vieux Rabelais (bis)
Quand nous avons fait nos bétises
Usé nos dernières chemises
Dieu nous reprend, de nous là bas
Que fait-il, que ne fait-il pas , (bis)
Que fait-il des neiges fondues,
Des vielles lunes morfondues ?
Je n'en sais rien ; mais beuvons frais
C'est l'avis du vieux Rabelais (bis) Fin

[116]

Dédicace

Parmi les animaux à deux pieds sans plumage
Qui de l'espèce humaine usurpent le langage
Il en existe peu dénués de sens commun
Et Salomon sur mille en trouvait à peine un.
Je n'ai point travaillé pour ces êtres vulgaires
Qui de l'humanité sont les surnuméraires
Singes dégénérés présentés au concours
Mais que la déraison revendique toujours
Ces gens là n'aiment point les vers ni les idées
Leurs âmes par l'esprit ne sont point obsédées
Il leur faut Rocambole et les airs d'Offenbach
Des femmes, des chevaux de l'or et du tabac
J'écris pour les penseurs n'en fut-il plus au monde
Qui goutent sagement au fruit d'Eve la blonde

Et qui de Mnémosyne ouvrant les autels
On peut-être le droit de le croire immortels
Si mes vers sont gardés et peuvent me survivre
Si pour quelques amis on en fait un bon livre
Ma muse leur dédie un salut fraternel
Avec l'heureux souhait d'un sourire éternel
A la gloire, à l'oubli sans peur je me résigne
Aimant parfois les pleurs, surtout ceux de la vigne
Je me laisse juger comme un ecce homo :
Donc, à mes chers lecteurs vel duo vel nemo

Éliphas Lévi
Novembre 1871

CPSIA information can be obtained
at www.ICGtesting.com
Printed in the USA
BVHW010045200123
656708BV00023B/178